D1175742

Contesting
TEXTS

Jews and Christians
in Conversation about the Bible

Edited by

Melody D. Knowles, Esther Menn,
John Pawlikowski, O.S.M., and Timothy J. Sandoval

FORTRESS PRESS
Minneapolis

CONTESTING TEXTS
Jews and Christians in Conversation about the Bible

Scripture quotations are from the New Revised Standard Version Bible, copyright © 1989 by the Division of Christian Education of the National Council of the Churches of Christ in the USA; from the New King James Version, copyright © 1979, 1980, 1982 Thomas Nelson, Inc.; from *The TANAKH: The New Jewish Publication Society Translation according to the Traditional Hebrew Text*, copyright © 1985 by the Jewish Publication Society; all are used by permission.

Cover image: Japanese paper, photo by Isabelle Rozenbaum
Cover and book design: Ann Delgehausen, Trio Bookworks

Library of Congress Cataloging-in-Publication Data
Contesting texts : Jews and Christians in conversation about the Bible / edited by Melody D. Knowles . . . [et al.].
    p. cm.
    Includes bibliographical references and index.
    ISBN-13: 978-0-8006-3842-9 (alk. paper)
    ISBN-10: 0-8006-3842-5 (alk. paper)
    1. Bible—Criticism, interpretation, etc. 2. Bible—Criticism, interpretation, etc., Jewish. 3. Christianity and other religions—Judaism. 4. Judaism—Relations—Christianity. I. Knowles, Melody D.
    BS511.3.C655 2007
    220.6—dc22

                                    2006026177

The paper used in this publication meets the minimum requirements of American National Standard for Information Sciences—Permanence of Paper for Printed Library Materials, ANSI Z329.48-1984.

Manufactured in the U.S.A.

11   10   09   08   07   1   2   3   4   5   6   7   8   9   10

Contents

Contents

Acknowledgments

The conference on which this book is based was made possible by funding from Catholic Theological Union, the annual Shapiro Foundation lecture fund at Catholic Theological Union, Chicago Theological Seminary, the Lutheran School of Theology at Chicago, and McCormick Theological Seminary.

The authors in this volume make use of various translations of the Bible, including the New Revised Standard Version and the Jewish Publication Society's Tanakh translation.

Included in this volume is the full text of *Dabru Emet*. It is used with permission.

Subsequent to the Contesting Texts conference in which they were originally given, two of the presentations were published in other places: "Apocalyptic Violence and Politics: End-Times Fiction for Jews and Christians" by Barbara R. Rossing (*Reflections* 92, no. 1 [Spring 2005]); and "Can We Hope? Can Hope Be Divided?" by Walter Brueggemann (*A Mandate to Be Different: Textual Invitations in the Contemporary Church*, forthcoming). The essays have been republished here with permission.

About the Contributors

BARBARA BOWE is Professor of Biblical Studies and Director of the Biblical Spirituality Program at the Catholic Theological Union at Chicago.

WALTER BRUEGGEMANN is the William Marcellus McPheeters Professor Emeritus of Old Testament at Columbia Theological Seminary, Decatur, Georgia.

LAURENCE L. EDWARDS received his Ph.D. from Chicago Theological Seminary and is an adjunct faculty member at the Catholic Theological Union at Chicago. He also serves as Rabbi of Congregation Or Chadash in Chicago.

RALPH W. KLEIN is Christ Seminary-Seminex Professor of Old Testament at the Lutheran School of Theology at Chicago.

MELODY D. KNOWLES is Associate Professor of Hebrew Scripture at McCormick Theological Seminary, Chicago.

ESTHER MENN is Professor of Old Testament at the Lutheran School of Theology at Chicago.

DAVID NOVAK holds the J. Richard and Dorothy Shiff Chair of Jewish Studies as Professor of the Study of Religion, Professor of Philosophy, and Director of the Jewish Studies Programme at the University of Toronto.

JOHN PAWLIKOWSKI, O.S.M., is Professor of Christian Ethics and Director of the Catholic-Jewish Studies Program at the Catholic Theological Union at Chicago.

BARBARA R. ROSSING is Professor of New Testament at the Lutheran School of Theology at Chicago.

DAVID FOX SANDMEL is the Crown-Ryan Chair of Jewish Studies at the Catholic Theological Union at Chicago and Rabbi of Congregation KAM Isaiah Israel in Chicago.

TIMOTHY J. SANDOVAL is Assistant Professor of Hebrew Bible at Chicago Theological Seminary.

SARAH J. TANZER is Professor of New Testament and Early Judaism at McCormick Theological Seminary, Chicago.

SUSAN BROOKS THISTLETHWAITE is Professor of Theology and President of Chicago Theological Seminary.

STEVEN WEITZMAN holds the Irving M. Glazer Chair in Jewish Studies and is Professor of Religious Studies and Director of the Jewish Studies Program at Indiana University at Bloomington.

PART 1

Jews, Christians, and the Bible

Dabru Emet,
Jewish-Christian Dialogue, and the Bible

AN INTRODUCTION TO *CONTESTING TEXTS*

TIMOTHY J. SANDOVAL WITH MELODY D. KNOWLES,
ESTHER MENN, AND JOHN PAWLIKOWSKI

Contesting Texts and Jewish–Christian Dialogue

The essays in *Contesting Texts: Jews and Christians in Conversation about the Bible* emerge from a conference bearing the same name that took place February 28–March 1, 2005, in Chicago. The Contesting Texts conference was sponsored by four Christian seminaries: the Catholic Theological Union at Chicago, the Lutheran School of Theology at Chicago, McCormick Theological Seminary, and Chicago Theological Seminary. The editors for this volume hold academic posts at these institutions and are Christians. We hope, of course, that both Jews and Christians will find valuable insights in *Contesting Texts*. However, the institutional sponsorship of the Contesting Texts conference and the editorial direction of the *Contesting Texts* book (as well as the fact that it is being published by a Christian press) make it almost inevitable that the volume will be oriented primarily toward Christians. This Christian orientation is not inappropriate, however, given the long and often troubled history of interactions between Jews and Christians—a history that has regularly found the former suffering (at times massively) at the hands of the latter. The moral obligation to continue to seek ways to address this history and improve Jewish-Christian relations hence falls fundamentally to Christians.

Contesting Texts, the book, like Contesting Texts, the conference, however, includes contributions by both Jews and Christians, including two essays by Jewish scholars of the New Testament (Edwards and Tanzer). The volume, again like the conference, represents one particular effort to promote and further Jewish-Christian dialogue by focusing a conversation around those texts from which each faith community in some sense seeks "authority." Yet as David Novak reminds us in his essay in *Contesting Texts*, "Jews, Christians, and Biblical Authority," the notion of biblical "authority" itself is a hotly contested issue among both Jews and Christians. Indeed, what it means for any Jew or Christian to seek authority or "guidance" from the Bible (again, see Novak's essay) is not an uncomplicated question. On this matter Jews will disagree with Christians as Jews will disagree with other Jews and Christians among themselves.

Perhaps the most unique aspect of *Contesting Texts*, however, is not any particular insight regarding how Jews and Christians view the authority of the Bible. Rather, it is the fact that the majority of the editors and contributors to the volume are not theologians or ethicists who are, or have been, professionally concerned with Jewish-Christian dialogue in the sense of regularly contributing to the discussion through publications or participation in interfaith organizations devoted to Jewish-Christian relations. John Pawlikowski and David Novak are perhaps the two most obvious exceptions in this regard, for both have published significant contributions in the field of Jewish-Christian dialogue.[1] Most of the other contributors to *Contesting Texts*, by contrast, are professional biblical scholars, university and seminary professors, whose academic achievements and publications in the field of biblical studies are extensive and impressive.

Although each contributor to *Contesting Texts* has her or his own particular reasons for collaborating in the project, a number of the contributors who work in primarily Christian environments have been motivated in part by a concern for the astonishing lack of knowledge of Judaism on the part of their Christian students. Colleagues who are more familiar with contexts that are primarily Jewish likewise have occasionally alluded to the lack of knowledge of Christianity that they encounter among some Jews. In any case, all of the contributors, we believe, share the conviction that the professional interpretation of the Bible entails particular ethical or moral dimensions to which we need to attend, including an obligation to engage faithfully and critically those religious communities who claim the Bible as scripture. One of the many important ways this obligation might be embodied is by tending to the manner in which biblical interpretation might serve the project of Jewish-Christian dialogue.

A Jewish-Christian dialogue around the Bible, of course, can and ought to proceed in different ways. Professionally, Jewish and Christian biblical scholars can share and challenge one another's work, each from her or his own expertise and perspectives that have been formed, at least in part, by participating to some degree—positively or negatively, as devotees and as critics—in our different traditions. Often, for instance (though certainly not always), Christian scholars will be more conversant with the history of Christian biblical interpretation or the manner in which scripture functions in Christian liturgy. Jewish scholars, by contrast, will regularly be more familiar with the use of the Bible in Jewish liturgy and the history of Jewish interpretation of scripture. The possibility thus exists for each to bring this expertise to bear on the practice of professional biblical interpretation, as indeed regularly occurs.[2]

Jewish and Christian biblical scholars can also contribute to Jewish-Christian dialogue by focusing common critical attention on biblical passages that have historically been "sticking points" or points of concordance (or both) between Jews and Christians. In reclaiming or challenging older interpretations, Jewish and Christian biblical scholars can offer new readings of biblical texts for a new day. Likewise, the work of biblical scholars can serve as a "jumping-off point" for Jewish-Christian dialogue around other issues. Any number of discussions in biblical studies might, for example, be brought to bear upon questions that regularly arise in the context of Jewish-Christian dialogue, whether this be the problem of enduring Christian anti-Semitism, the question of Jewish concern for the land of Israel and the Israeli-Palestinian conflict, or our shared concern as Jews and Christians to seek justice in the societies and contexts in which we live and work.

Contesting Texts contains essays that contribute in different ways to each of these avenues by which biblical scholars might engage the task of Jewish-Christian dialogue. Nevertheless, the final words of reflection in the book go not to biblical scholars but to two theologians. Susan Brooks Thistlethwaite is president of Chicago Theological Seminary and has been active in a variety of national interfaith organizations, including the Interfaith Alliance and especially Faith in Public Life, as board member and spokesperson. David Fox Sandmel is rabbi of congregation KAM Isaiah Israel in Chicago and has worked closely with the authors of *Dabru Emet* (see below) while on staff at the Institute for Christian and Jewish Studies in Baltimore. In two "afterwords," Thistlethwaite and Sandmel each reflect briefly on the different contributions to *Contesting Texts*, the volume as a whole, and the ongoing task of Jewish-Christian and interfaith dialogue.

Dabru Emet and Renewed Jewish–Christian Dialogue

The Reformed theologian Jürgen Moltmann notes in his book *God for a Secular Society: The Public Relevance of Theology* a familiar pattern in Christian attempts to dialogue with persons of other faiths. He speaks of the dialogues "we all know," which "run according to the following pattern: a Christian theologian puts questions—a rabbi, a mullah or a swami readily replies. But they ask nothing on their own account, because they aren't interested in Christianity."

Moltmann's words suggest that it is regularly Christians who initiate interfaith conversations, Christians who invite representatives from other faiths to dialogue, and Christians who eagerly listen in an attempt to learn from and state conclusions about the other they are attempting to engage—with the other usually offering explanations obligingly. Moltmann intimates as well that these same Christians are sometimes surprised, and a little disheartened, by the fact that their "interlocutors" often do not share the same sort of passion for "dialogue," or hearing from their Christian counterparts, as the Christians themselves.[3]

Any number of reasons might explain (at least in part) why this state of affairs in Christian interfaith dialogue exists. Christianity's strong missionary impulse (absent or not as vital in other faiths), for instance, demands that Christians engage and, in some shape or fashion, come to theological terms with other religions. Christians who are interested in engaging in serious interreligious dialogue, moreover, are also often citizens of North American and European countries. Hence, unlike some (certainly not all) of their potential interlocutors, they usually already accept the "specifically modern, originally Western" preconditions for the possibility of interreligious dialogue (versus other possible forms of encounters between religions), namely, "the separation between religion and state power" and a commitment to "individual religious liberty."[4] These same North Atlantic Christians also regularly occupy or participate in hegemonic political, social, and economic positions vis-à-vis their dialogue partners. This sort of inequality between interlocutors likewise cannot help but affect the process and practice of, indeed the very possibility of and desire for, genuine dialogue.

The document entitled *Dabru Emet* (Hebrew for "Speak the Truth") is especially noteworthy in that it represents a shift in the usual practice of Christian dialogue with other faiths described by Moltmann, where Christians are the primary initiators, learners, and subsequently (usually) *pronouncers* as well. First published in the *New York Times* in September 2000, *Dabru Emet* is remarkable in that it is not a "Christian Statement on Jews and Judaism," but rather a "Jewish statement on Christians and Christianity." This is significant even though, as David Novak (one of the authors of the document) reminds us, the framers of *Dabru Emet* took up the task of penning a Jewish statement on Christianity "primarily because various Christians" had "asked us for it."

Nonetheless, the authors of *Dabru Emet*, four prominent Jewish scholars who speak only for themselves and not for all of Judaism, of course, note that in the years since the Holocaust or Shoah (Hebrew for "Destruction"), "Christianity has changed dramatically."[5] They, and presumably the more than 150 rabbis and Jewish scholars from the United States, Canada, the United Kingdom, and Israel who signed the statement, believe as well that "it is time for Jews to learn about the efforts of Christians to honor Judaism" and that it is time for Jews to "reflect on *what Judaism may now say about Christianity*" (italics added).[6] Whereas in the past, as Novak again puts it, "Jews were forced to justify our differences *from* others, especially our differences *from* Christians to Christians" (italics original), today Jews are experiencing challenges from Christians more dialogically.

Thus, in what the authors call a "first step" in this Jewish effort to speak of Christianity, *Dabru Emet* offers eight concise statements about "how Jews and Christians may relate to one another," with the document subsequently briefly elaborating each statement. The eight propositions are as follows:

1. Jews and Christians worship the same God.
2. Jews and Christians seek authority from the same book—the Bible (what Jews call "Tanakh" and what Christians call the "Old Testament").
3. Christians can respect the claim of the Jewish people upon the land of Israel.
4. Jews and Christians accept the moral principles of Torah.
5. Nazism was not a Christian phenomenon.
6. The humanly irreconcilable difference between Jews and Christians will not be settled until God redeems the entire world as promised in Scripture.
7. A new relationship between Jews and Christians will not weaken Jewish practice.
8. Jews and Christians must work together for justice and peace.[7]

Dabru Emet, the Bible, and Contesting Texts

Dabru Emet was not the explicit focus of the Contesting Texts conference, nor is it addressed explicitly by the majority of the essays in the Contesting Texts book (Novak's contribution is the major exception). Nonetheless, this document can prove helpful in framing many of the issues addressed in Contesting Texts as well as many of the issues involved in contemporary Jewish-Christian relations more generally.

The authors of Dabru Emet, for instance, allude to several developments in Christianity over the last half century that have made the appearance of this sort of Jewish document on Christianity possible. The most important of these advances are the public statements of remorse, repentance, and hope for reconciliation offered by official Christian bodies in response to a long and varied history of Christian anti-Judaism, anti-Semitism, and enmity and violence toward Jews. Such statements are fundamental prerequisites for Jewish-Christian dialogue, for without the public expression of remorse and repentance for past wrongs, there can be no way forward into a new future.[8]

No less important as a condition of possibility for the emergence of a new Jewish-Christian dialogue like that represented by *Dabru Emet* have been certain developments in Christian theology and biblical studies. Most fundamental in this regard has been the recognition by Christian theologians of the abiding validity of God's covenant with the people of Israel, the Jews. Many Christian theologians recognize that this claim, primarily grounded biblically in Paul's words in Romans 9, also entails "consequences for Christian understanding of salvation," as the Christian Scholars Group on Christian-Jewish Relations has put it in a document entitled "A Sacred Obligation: Rethinking Christian Faith in Relation to Judaism and the Jewish People."[9] God does not break God's promises! Indeed, if the first covenant to the Jews has been annulled, as supersessionist ideologies have claimed, the Christian confidence in a new covenant with the same God is necessarily called into question.[10] Thus, according to the Christian Scholars Group, "If Jews, who do not share our faith in Christ, are in a saving covenant with God, then Christians need new ways of understanding the universal significance of Christ."

The recognition by scholars, both Jewish and Christian, of the indebtedness of Christian liturgy to Jewish practices and the acknowledgment of the thoroughly Jewish nature of Jesus of Nazareth, members of the Jesus movement, and the earliest church also constitute important developments that have opened up new space for Jewish-Christian relations. Along with Christian writers, Jewish scholars of the New Testament such as Daniel Boyarin have been key voices in demonstrating that New Testament polemics against "the Pharisees" and "the Jews" ought to be viewed largely as internal Jewish polemic and that the so-called parting of the ways of Judaism and Christianity likely took much longer than is usually recognized. Laurence L. Edwards points this out in his contribution to *Contesting Texts*, "Luke's Pharisees: Emerging Communities." Edwards's essay itself demonstrates how the Pharisees in Luke-Acts function as a trope, something like mediating figures between what will become Christianity and rabbinic Judaism.[11]

Equally important in paving the way for renewed possibilities for Jewish-Christian dialogue has been the Christian recognition that a Jewish reading of the Hebrew scriptures is possible.[12] At first blush, such a statement seems absurd since a long and rich history of Jewish biblical interpretation, beginning in the pages of the Bible itself, has always existed![13] The claim, however, seeks to repudiate the supersessionist notion that denied not the simple existence of a Jewish reading of the Old Testament, but its legitimacy and integrity theoretically and theologically.

In his essay in *Contesting Texts* on the common vocation to hope that he believes Jews and Christians share, "Can We Hope? Can Hope Be Divided?" Walter Brueggemann, for instance, alludes to the prominence that historical-critical biblical scholarship enjoyed among many Christians during the last century and a half. As Brueggemann elaborated in his address at the Contesting Texts conference, with its emphasis on situating a single meaning of a text exclusively in relation to the text's historical context, historical-critical scholarship refused to import, in overt or traditional ways anyway, patently Christianizing or Christological readings of the Hebrew scriptures that de-legitimize Jewish readings. Brueggemann's essay also highlights the more recent recognition by Bible scholars of the multivalency of texts—the fact that a piece of literature can legitimately be said to possess more than one, single meaning. This theoretical position, along with the theological corollary that the One who speaks through the biblical text is always free to speak afresh to whomever this One chooses, has likewise facilitated a Christian recognition of the coherency and legitimacy of a Jewish reading of the Bible.

The second statement of *Dabru Emet*, of course, highlights that issue that *Contesting Texts* also explicitly recognizes and attempts to engage: Jews and Christians share those scriptures that "Jews call 'Tanakh' and Christians call the 'Old Testament'" and that, we might add, many professional biblical scholars, in an effort not to unduly claim hegemony for either Christian or Jewish interpretation, call the Hebrew Bible (or Hebrew and Aramaic scriptures).[14] However, even the shared Jewish and Christian scriptures are, of course, not completely coterminous with one another. Besides the traditional Jewish practice of reading the Tanakh together with Rashi's commentary, the most obvious difference between the two canons is the different order in which the biblical books appear in the Tanakh and the Old Testament.[15] In addition, Roman

Catholic and Christian Orthodox traditions include a number of books in their Old Testaments, the so-called apocryphal or deuterocanonical texts, that are absent in the Tanakh and the Protestant Old Testament.[16] Moreover, although the term *Hebrew Bible* seeks, valuably, to construct a kind of neutral space for the academic study of the Bible, this academic discipline itself was largely constructed by Christians, especially Protestant Germans, and the shape of the field continues to bear the marks of this history.[17]

Though not always as explicitly as the document's second proposition that Jews and Christians share scripture, each of *Dabru Emet*'s seven remaining statements likewise concerns the Bible in fundamental ways. That "Jews and Christians worship the same God," as the first proposition of *Dabru Emet* states, is affirmed by Jewish and Christian individuals and communities not simply in the abstract, but specifically in light of an encounter with the witness of scripture. Indeed, as Ralph Klein notes in his essay in *Contesting Texts*, "Promise and Fulfillment," both the Tanakh and the New Testament bear testimony to the one God who makes promises and who is faithful to fulfill those promises, though Christians and Jews will not always agree on how and when such promises are fulfilled.

Dabru Emet's fifth proposition, one of the most controversial, that "Nazism was not a Christian phenomenon," and the document's seventh proposition, that "a new relationship between Jews and Christians will not weaken Jewish practice," do not, on an initial, superficial reading anyway, have much to do with the Bible and biblical interpretation. However, with a moment's reflection, one can remember that Jewish practice has profound roots in the Bible and in the biblical interpretive traditions of Judaism. Similarly, the murderous crimes of Nazism, as the longer text of *Dabru Emet* points out, could not have occurred without a long history of Christian enmity and violence toward Jews. This violence was not only a result of a Christian failure to embody the gospel to which their Bible bears witness. It was also sanctioned by a supersessionist ideology wherein the New Testament was thought to have supplanted the Old, and by New Testament passages—received within an anti-Jewish interpretive tradition—that demonize Jewish figures. Again, Edwards's essay in *Contesting Texts* is relevant in this regard as are especially the contributions of Barbara Bowe and Sarah Tanzer. Bowe's essay, "The New Testament, Religious Identity, and the Other," draws especially on the work of, among others, Emmanuel Levinas and theorizes the complex process of "othering" in social relations that is relevant to New Testament studies. Tanzer's contribution subsequently focuses on the "othering" of Jews in the Gospel of John and highlights the pedagogical challenges this sort of text poses today both in the classroom and in Christian congregations.

The fourth proposition offered by *Dabru Emet*, that "Jews and Christians accept the moral principles of Torah," is surely correct in large measure. However, though the ethical vision of the Bible's first five books is something around which Jews and Christians can find common ground, the proposition simultaneously gestures toward differences between the two communities. As Novak in his essay on biblical authority notes, the question of the status of certain commandments in the Torah is one that divides Christians and Jews. If the heart of Jewish readings of the Bible has been directed toward the Torah and the practices of embodying its principles personally and institutionally, Christian interpretation of the Bible has historically been oriented toward the New Testament and has, in fact, found little place for the *halachic* material of the Torah.[18] Indeed, when Christian attention has focused on the Old Testament, the Prophets (particularly the "Latter Prophets" or classical, writing prophets) have been placed front and center, not the books of Moses.[19] Christians have often viewed the prophetic religion of Amos or Isaiah, with its emphasis on social justice and its occasional critique of certain Israelite cultic practices (though never the rejection of the cult itself), to be superior to the religion of the Torah, which in the past has been (and unfortunately still is) too often regarded as representative of a debased legalism. The classic historical-critical formulation of the history of pentateuchal literature, devised by, among others, K. H. Graf and especially Julius Wellhausen, Christians both, enshrined and offered a kind of "scientific" legitimization to this view.[20]

Wellhausen was a product of the intellectual movement known as Romanticism and understood Israelite religion to have reached its zenith with the free, natural religion of especially the eighth-century prophets.[21] According to Wellhausen's theory of the literary-historical development of the Pentateuch, or the first five books of the Bible (Genesis through Deuteronomy), the earliest strata of these texts, the J (Yahwist) and E (Elohist) sources (ninth–eighth century BCE) were followed by those sources that represented a subsequent devolution in the history of Israelite religion: the D (Deuteronomist) source (late seventh–sixth-century BCE) and finally the postexilic (post-539 BCE), "legalistic" P (Priestly) source. For Wellhausen, Jewish religion continued to devolve into the debased form it was to embody at the time of the advent of Christ, an event that restored true worship of the Divine. To be fair, Wellhausen's romantic view of history led him to see the same sort of devolution in the history of Christianity, which declined from the true religion propagated by Christ, through the increasing legalism of Roman Catholicism, reaching its nadir at the time of the Reformation, the movement inaugurated by Martin Luther and others that served to once again re-birth genuine religion.

Wellhausen's contempt for all institutional religion, of course, does not mitigate the disastrous view of Judaism that these "historical-critical" conclusions embodied and promulgated. Yet even the Wellhausian consensus, which dominated biblical studies for a hundred years, did not and, to the extent that it is still propagated, does not go uncontested by many, especially Jewish scholars. The work of someone like Yehezkel Kaufmann, who was active especially in the first half of the twentieth century, confirms this, as do more recent pentateuchal studies that argue the P source predates the D source.[22]

Dabru Emet, Contesting Texts, and Contemporary Issues in Jewish–Christian Dialogue

Perhaps no other issue energizes and problematizes Jewish-Christian dialogue today as much as *Dabru Emet*'s third claim that "Christians can respect the claim of the Jewish people upon the land of Israel." Although this recognition of the claim upon the land can be, and regularly is, forthcoming from Christians of various stripes, Christians regularly fail to comprehend the grounds for, and the depth of, Jewish commitment to *Eretz Israel*. Moreover, Christians, at least those who are most interested in a serious encounter with Jews and Judaism, are often nonplussed at the intensity of Jewish hope that dialogue presuppose, or at least give birth to, a recognition of the Jewish claim to the land.

Although *Dabru Emet* is correct that Christians, as members of a biblically based religion, "appreciate that Israel was promised—and given—to Jews as the physical center of the covenant," there are broader contexts in which persons will relate to or "hear" statements such as this. One important factor is that Christians who are serious about engaging in a dialogue with Jews are rarely conservative-minded, traditional, biblical literalists. Rather, they are mainline liberal Protestants and Catholics. Schooled as these Christians and their clergy are in the way facile readings of the Bible can mask and legitimate contemporary unjust power relationships and ideologies, these Christian often shrink from claims that anything the Bible mandates or presents can or ought to be literally realized today.

With their justified suspicion of biblical literalism, what nonliterally-minded Christians, however, do not usually fully appreciate is that Jewish claims to the land are generally cast in terms of the security of the Jewish people and are only rarely made with strong appeals to the biblical promise of the land, or to one or another biblical description of the extent of the land. Indeed, the halting reaction to Jewish attachment to the land by some Christians sometimes seems to be more a reaction to the interpretive practices of fellow Christians as it is a response to a claim to the land. That is, liberal Catholic and Protestant Christians can hear the claim to the land, rooted as it is in the biblical narrative, as akin to an objectionable form of biblical literalism that they associate with the conservative theology and politics of certain fellow Christians. Jews, however, can hear any Christian ambivalence regarding the Jewish right to *Eretz Israel* as an astonishing lack of regard for the security and well-being of the people with whom these same Christians claim a desire to be in dialogue—indeed, the same people whose security and well-being other Christians have so often in the past denied and threatened, most massively not much more than a mere half century ago!

Barbara R. Rossing's essay in *Contesting Texts*, "Apocalyptic Violence and Politics: End-Times Fiction for Jews and Christians," is pertinent to the biblical-theological (and political) questions regarding why and how Christians can respect the Jewish claim to the land. As she points out, those Christians who support Jewish claims to the land and the state of Israel more fully on the basis of a literal reading of the Bible often do so in light of a dispensationalist theology and hermeneutic. Though in the short term this theology acknowledges a place for Jews and Judaism, in the long run it has no place for either. Such a theological position hardly seems the basis for an enduring or serious Jewish-Christian dialogue.

A further issue related to the question of Jewish commitment to the land that can emerge in contemporary Jewish-Christian discussions is the enduring tragedy of the Israeli-Palestinian conflict. The views of individual Jews and Israelis, like those of individual Palestinians and Muslims and Christians, in relation to this remarkably complex problem are diverse. In discussions of this issue, however, Christians, on the one hand, may fear that their Jewish partners will regard any criticism of the policies of the state of Israel (or acts of solidarity with Palestinians) as expressions of anti-Semitism. Christians might likewise hear as disingenuous Jewish claims that criticisms of the state of Israel are *not* equated with anti-Semitism, if no criticism of that body is actually brooked. Jews, on the other hand, can rightly be suspicious that Christian criticisms of the state of Israel may mask unrecognized, or worse, deliberately concealed, anti-Semitic sentiments.

Similarly, many Christians focus their critiques on Israeli policy (rather than Palestinian aggression) because of the violence and imbalance of power obviously apparent in the Israeli military occupation, and because of a not-always-articulated belief that violence in resistance to such an occupation is justified. Jews, however, may regard Christian criticism of Israeli aggression in the occupation with suspicion if the same sort of renunciation of Palestinian violence toward Israelis (especially nonmilitary citizens) is not forthcoming. Indeed, any Christian condemnation of Palestinian violence against Israelis that is not presented in the strongest of forms can be viewed as woefully inadequate by some Jews as something that again reveals Christian indifference to Jewish well-being and security. In a similar manner, of course, Palestinians can be suspicious that Christian, especially European and North American, alliances with Jews serve the political status quo and unduly neglect Palestinian claims to justice.

Besides recognizing how Christians and Jews may or may not "hear" one another when an issue like Palestinian and Israeli aggression and violence is "on the table," what is perhaps most important to remember, as David Rosen reminds us in his September 2005 Templeton Lecture, is that the Israeli-Palestinian conflict is not, at root, a religious conflict.[23] It is a political dispute over territory. Nonetheless, in this conflict religion is regularly exploited by interests on all sides. Both faithful Jews and Christians (and Muslims as well) thus can and ought to speak to the situation, drawing on the resources of their faith traditions. Those Christians and Jews (and Muslims) interested in interfaith dialogue, moreover, will also be open to the concerns and critiques one community might offer another, viewing these perhaps as opportunities to refine their own particular deliberations on the most vexing issues of our day. Indeed, as Novak suggests in this volume, "challenges" from our dialogue partners "make claims" upon us, and the experience of dialogue "frames the way we now talk with our own" in our *intra*-faith conversations.

Brueggemann, as we noted, claims in his contribution to *Contesting Texts* that Jews and Christians share a common vocation to "hope." He challenges both Christians and Jews to foster an imagination that is able to envision, that is, *hope for*, a future that transcends current arrangements, not simply as regards Jewish-Christian relations generally, but even as regards something as intractable as the Israeli-Palestinian drama. When it comes to the Bible, moreover, he exhorts us to foster a hopeful interpretive imagination as well, one that is able to read our shared sacred texts in a way that speaks to the situations in which our communities find themselves today.

Steven Weitzman's contribution to *Contesting Texts*, "Unbinding Isaac: Martyrdom and Its Exegetical Alternatives," is perhaps just one sort of example of the kind of broad, interpretive enterprise Brueggemann has in mind. Weitzman's essay is a reading of the Jewish historian Josephus's understanding of martyrdom and sketches how different Hellenistic Jewish texts that deal with martyrdom invoke the *Akedah*, the story of the binding of Isaac.[24] Weitzman explicates the motives for offering one's life as a testimony to faith as these motives emerge in the works of Josephus and discovers in the historian's pages a critique of religious martyrdom. Rather than unequivocally condoning or condemning the practice of martyrdom, Josephus opts, according to Weitzman, for a third way—"virtual martyrdom." The ongoing Israeli-Palestinian conflict and the broader global context, where the litany of those willing to die and kill for God includes not merely Muslims but Jews and Christians as well, are also not lost on Weitzman, who encourages Jews, Christians, and Muslims alike to engage our sacred texts anew and avoid a failure of interpretive imagination, especially when and where the stakes involve life and death.

Dabru Emet's final proposition that "Jews and Christians must work together for justice and peace" is one that we imagine all Jews and Christians, in all our diversity, will want to affirm together. The repairing or healing of God's world, what Jews call *tikkun olam*, is our shared vocation. Yet even a claim such as this, which commands widespread assent in both communities, is one that may lead to conflict between Jews and Christians when the way of embodying its impulse in particular contexts, such as the Israeli-Palestinian dispute, is not particularly clear, or when it comes to particular theological efforts to articulate its meaning, as in the case of Christian liberation theology.

As we noted above, Jewish attachment to the land and the Palestinian-Israeli conflict are topics that can breed misunderstanding and suspicion (sometimes justified) between Jews and Christians. Similarly, certain forms of Christian liberationist theological thinking can prove deeply objectionable to Jewish readers, as the Jewish New Testament scholar A. J. Levine pointed out forcefully in her plenary address at the 2005 meeting of the International Council of Christians and Jews. Without claiming to address all of the variety of matters involved with this issue, the concerns might be said, generally speaking, to be of two related sorts: the macro-level issue regarding the analogical pattern of thinking regularly employed in liberation theology and the issue of the exegesis of individual biblical texts.[25]

Among the basic tenets of most liberation theology is the claim of God's preferential option for the poor, outcast, and oppressed. Although the varieties of liberation theology are complex, regularly an analogy is drawn between the poor and marginalized for whom, according to the biblical witnesses, the God of Israel, or Jesus of Nazareth, expresses a profound concern, and the poor and oppressed of different times and places.[26] Just as God demonstrates special concern for the oppressed and impoverished in the Bible, so God opts for, or especially favors, those who suffer discrimination, poverty, and social-political repression today.

It is sometimes claimed that this mode of biblical-theological analogical thinking is illegitimate. It seems, however, that the problem is less that the mode of thinking is invalid and more that it is sometimes carried out in inadequate or incomplete ways. An important matter here has to do with the fact that in the Hebrew Bible and the New Testament, God or Jesus is often opting for certain oppressed Israelites or Jews over and against other Israelites or Jews. Subsequently, once the oppressed biblical Israelite or Jewish figures are firmly identified with the poor and oppressed generally, or with those of a particular time and place, their particularity as Israelites and Jews is sometimes forgotten, while the Jewishness and Judaism of their wicked oppressors are not! It is thus not difficult to see how such a situation can lead Christian readers to anti-Jewish and anti-Semitic conclusions.

However, it is, of course, not always the case in the biblical material appropriated by liberation theologians that the oppressors are Israelites or Jews. The exodus narrative, so important to much, especially early liberation theology, which sees in God's liberation of oppressed slaves from Egypt a model of God's liberating will for all, is a good example. The oppressors in the biblical exodus narrative—both in its original context and pattern in the book of Exodus and in its theological reappropriation as a symbol for the Jewish return from exile in other parts of the Hebrew Bible—are not Israelite regimes. They are rather the potentates of Egypt and Babylon respectively.

The problematic aspect of some, certainly not all, liberationist appropriations of the Exodus model (and other biblical texts)—and here we are moving into the realm of inadequate or incomplete exegesis alluded to above—thus seems *not* to be the claim that God desires freedom and an alternative mode of existence for poor, oppressed slaves in Egypt, or that God forcefully wills that deported citizens return to their homeland. The problem, or inadequacy, of the appropriation is that the particularity of these slaves and exiles as, on the one hand, descendants of Abraham out of whom God promised to build a great people and, on the other hand, exiled citizens of a place called Judah, is sometimes forgotten or erased. That is, the analogical identification of the poor and oppressed with those who are especially favored by God can end up ignoring that strand of the biblical witness that emphasizes God's promises and attachment specifically to Abraham, Isaac, Jacob, and their descendants. Thus "Israel" is essentially replaced by the poor and oppressed. It is thus again not difficult to imagine how this sort of erasure of Israelite or Jewish particularity can lead to devastating conclusions by Christians regarding the ongoing viability of Judaism. When such erasure is avoided, however, the analogical mode of appropriation is not illegitimate. As Jewish scholar Jon D. Levenson (himself wary of some liberationist thought) has noted, Martin Luther King Jr.'s analogical appropriation of the Exodus motif to construct theological and ethical meaning for the descendants of African slaves during the civil rights struggle in the United States was, for example, entirely appropriate.[27]

Tending closely to the manner in which Christian biblical exegesis proceeds and to the way analogies from the Hebrew Bible serve Christian theological discourse (liberationist or not) is obviously a vitally important task for Christians concerned with Jewish-Christian dialogue. In the context of liberation theology's appropriation of the Exodus narrative, for instance, such careful attention will have the merit not merely of recognizing in scripture the divine preferential option for the oppressed, or what Levenson calls the immense concern the Hebrew Bible reveals for the poor and vulnerable. It will also have the merit of recognizing a further vital theological motif in the pages of scripture, namely, the chosenness of Israel.

None of this important work, however, eliminates the need for Christians to reconsider as well other aspects of their theological traditions that might prove an impediment to promoting positive Jewish-Christian relations. Certain theological claims in the New Testament and in the Christian theological tradition that, for example, speak of Israel "according to the flesh" or the church as a "new Israel" can also lead to negative theological judgments regarding the ongoing validity of Judaism. Such theological formulations hence likewise deserve the attention of Christians concerned with Jewish-Christian relations. The point, however, is not to insist uncritically that any particular theological language or tradition be eliminated or rejected. It is simply to suggest that Christians who are committed to thinking about their religion's relationship to Judaism likely will need to consider a range of theological constructs afresh in light of their commitment to the inter-religious dialogue.

In moving from the study of the Hebrew Bible to the study of the New Testament, one can also identify certain sorts of exegetical and theological difficulties and inadequacies vis-à-vis these uniquely Christian scriptures that can hinder the development of positive relations between Jews and Christians. Like those problematic aspects of the interpretation of the Hebrew scriptures, these inadequacies can sometimes be associated with liberationist perspectives and likewise need to be remedied for the sake of constructive Jewish-Christian dialogue.

For example, in the Gospels, opposition to Jesus, and indeed responsibility for his death, is at points associated with other Jewish personalities. This fact has provided the rationale for countless acts of violence perpetrated against Jews by Christians. It is thus vitally important for exegetes (liberationist or not, Christian or not) who consider these sorts of texts to parse out precisely who the Jewish opponents of Jesus are and to explicate the dynamics of the opposition. As noted above, on the one hand, advances in New Testament studies understand these conflicts in the Gospels to be reflecting first-century intra-Jewish debates. On the other hand, biblical scholarship also recognizes that the Jewish figures in the New Testament with whom Jesus comes into contact cannot facilely be identified with "all Jews" (compare again Edwards's and Tanzer's essays in this volume). Similarly, the role of other textual figures in the Gospel narratives, whether explicitly mentioned or merely implied, particularly that of the Roman imperial authorities, needs to be fully considered by exegetes. Finally, all these sorts of New Testament passages, and especially those that do in fact more broadly condemn Jews collectively, need to be scrutinized theologically, for as we noted earlier, Christian theologians are increasingly recognizing the moral and theological inadequacy of any position that implies divine rejection of the Jews.

That Jews and Christians differ regarding the status and significance of Jesus of Nazareth is, of course, obvious. Christians regularly accord some sort of divine status to Jesus and recognize him as the expected messiah of Israel through whose life, death, and resurrection God has acted decisively to save humanity, indeed all of creation. As again Klein's essay in *Contesting Texts* underscores, Jews do not recognize Jesus' divinity or his status as messiah, nor do Jews share the Christian view that God's promises to Israel and the world have been decidedly realized or fulfilled in Jesus. These are differences between Jews and Christians that, as *Dabru Emet* claims, may not be resolved "until God redeems the entire world as promised in scripture." However, in the interim it is important that especially Christian exegetes, including liberationist thinkers, tend to the manner in which other sorts of claims regarding the uniqueness of Jesus are articulated.

One may, for example, recall that one of the advances in New Testament studies in recent decades alluded to above is the recognition of the thoroughly Jewish nature of Jesus, the Jesus movement, and the earliest church. Christian claims regarding the uniqueness of Jesus (or Paul or any other New Testament Jewish-Christian figure or text) thus need to be thought through carefully, taking seriously the reality of Jesus' and the New Testament's Jewishness. Many Christians, perhaps especially those of a liberationist bent, will for example often highlight the positive role women played in Jesus' inner circle or his posture of acceptance toward the poor and outcast of society. However, if Jesus and the New Testament are thoroughly products of their Jewish milieu from which they emerge, it is important to remember that the uniqueness of Jesus in regard to such matters ought not be overstated. If the claims to distinctiveness are overstated, they not only become suspect on historical grounds, but also can be heard by Jews as a not-so-subtle moral and theological indictment of first-century Judaism, and implicitly, any manifestation of Judaism.

Careful exegetes, of course, will continue to tend to the distinctive theological and ethical contributions of Jesus and the New Testament and the way the New Testament texts reveal how significant differences were beginning to develop between the emerging Christian community and (other) Jews in the first-century Mediterranean world—for instance, regarding such vital matters as Torah observance. However, when it comes to cherished and powerful social values, Christians concerned with liberation lose nothing in recognizing that the Jew Jesus and other Jewish-Christian figures of the New Testament shared their liberating values and teachings with authentic strands of Judaism, both in antiquity and today. To the contrary, in recognizing the continuity between Jesus and his teachings and the Judaism that formed him, Christians concerned with liberation are reminded of the great ally in the struggle for social justice they have in the past often found in their Jewish neighbors—most notably perhaps in the civil rights movement in the United States—and the ally they still regularly encounter today. They are reminded that the noblest social sentiments of Christianity are deeply rooted in Judaism. And indeed, with such recognition both Jews and Christians can be reminded of their shared heritage as sibling faiths, whose common vocation, as again *Dabru Emet* puts it, is to work for justice and peace—to construct a world, as the psalmist once imagined, where "justice and peace shall kiss" (Ps 85:10).

For Christian theologians and teachers and preachers in North America and Europe, who live and work in cultural and intellectual contexts side by side with Jews or where the pernicious effects of Christian supersessionism and the lamentable history of Christian enmity and violence toward Jews are, or ought to be, well known, there can be no excuse for reproducing the kinds of exegetical and theological distortions sketched above. Nor is there an excuse for permitting them to pass unchallenged in the classroom or parish. However, it is sometimes the case that the kinds of anti-Jewish biases discussed above appear in the works of Christian writers, including liberationist thinkers, from outside of North America and Europe. Christian scholars and institutions in North America and Europe hence ought to consider the nature of their responsibility to engage their sisters and brothers in Latin America, Asia, Africa, and elsewhere who produce writings (whether liberationist or not) that reproduce older problematic views of Jews and Judaism. This situation, however, like Jewish-Christian relations itself, is terribly complex.

It is complex not least of all because that North Atlantic Christians who are interested in Jewish-Christian dialogue—because of a long history of European and North American imperialism and exploitation of the globe—generally occupy a hegemonic position economically, socially, politically, and ecclesially vis-à-vis Christians in other parts of the world. It is thus not a simple matter for so-called first-world Christian communities and institutions to insist on, or to dictate, the manner in which theologians and exegetes from other parts of the world carry out their theological work. Indeed, such an effort, legitimate as it might be in the eyes of some North Atlantic Christians and Jews, could easily be regarded by others outside of this context as a new sort of colonial endeavor.

The situation is complex, moreover, because of the institutional arrangements (again largely a product of Western colonialism) that likely have contributed to a situation in which Christians from non–North Atlantic contexts can produce texts that contain anti-Jewish formulations. These arrangements in fact perhaps more fully indict European and North American Christendom than those Christians from the so-called developing world who author the sometimes problematic texts. This is because the materials and advanced training that some Christian writers from the developing world have received have not infrequently been from European and North American universities and theological schools. Without denying that aspects of the rhetoric of the New Testament itself might easily lead some Christian readers to anti-Jewish conclusions, it is likely that these institutions too often have preserved and passed on the subtle and not-so-subtle anti-Jewish biases of the first world to others from other contexts.

The complexity of the situation in which the anti-Jewish biases of first-world Christians can be passed on to others outside of the first world is revealed by one further fact. In non-first-world contexts, where in comparison with the North Atlantic communities there has historically been no, or a comparatively small, Jewish presence and where there has not been the same experience of a long and tragic history of destructive Christian encounters with Jews, these biases do not always carry the same valence. Hence they are not always recognized to be as harmful as they are in first-world contexts.

The situation, of course, is different in the context of Palestine and the conflict between Israelis and Palestinians. In this context there exists a distinct risk that clear negative reflexes to very real Jewish social identities might emerge in some Christian theological discourse. This risk has become particularly evident with the emergence of a

Palestinian liberation theology when the legitimate theological analogies of that particular theological discourse have not been articulated precisely. Some, especially politically progressive Christians, have and will continue to contest with some Jews whether, or to what extent, the writings of someone like Palestinian liberation theologian Naim Ateek is anti-Semitic.[28] Christians and Jews will disagree as well as to the best and necessary ways to engage this work. In the same way, Christians have and will continue to disagree with one another, and Jews have and will continue to disagree with one another over these very same issues.

However one determines the vices or virtues of the work of someone like Ateek or of other Palestinian liberation theologies, the complexity of the Israeli-Palestinian dispute will remain. Hence, because of the intensity of the sentiments of all parties involved and the lack of clarity and consensus as to the right or best ways to intercede and proceed, Christians who desire to honor both the Palestinian and Israeli sides in the conflict (again, whether liberationists or not) will have to be prepared to live with and engage constructively the passionate disagreement that will inevitably arise both from some Israelis and Jews on the one hand and from some Muslims and Palestinians on the other hand. They will also have to be prepared to acknowledge missteps in this endeavor, to change courses, and to beg the pardon of those wronged by their missteps.[29]

What then ought to be the primary response of Christians in North America and Europe to aspects of liberationist and other Christian writings from non–North Atlantic contexts that may reproduce the anti-Jewish biases of their Western sisters and brothers? The question is difficult, but perhaps one response is for first-world Christians to ensure that the educational and theological resources they produce and often pass on to other Christians are free of, and actively challenge, anti-Semitic notions. First-world Christians concerned with constructing and preserving positive Jewish-Christian relations will also need to consider the precise manner in which they might want to engage their sisters and brothers around this issue. Any appropriate engagement, however, will take into account, but not reproduce, the imperialistic and colonial encounters of the past while seeking to honor voices from the developing world in all their particularity. Finally, of course, Christian teachers, priests, and pastors, whose students and parishioners engage liberationist (or any) texts or voices in which anti-Jewish prejudices are evident, ought to challenge such views and attempt to move their communities toward more constructive positions and practices.

"Christians," "Jews," and the Multiplicity of Our Relations

Throughout this introduction we have occasionally spoken of "Jews" and "Christians" without specifying more specifically *which* Christians or Jews we have in mind, as in fact do some of the essays included in *Contesting Texts*. There is, of course, some broad agreement around basic tenets that, on the one hand, all or most Christians will share (for example, the centrality of the life, death, and resurrection of Jesus of Nazareth) and that, on the other hand, all Jews will share (such as the primacy of the Torah in Jewish liturgy and practice). Neither Judaism nor Christianity, however, is a monolithic tradition. Each faith is remarkably diverse. There are evangelical and mainline Protestants as well as Roman Catholics of different stripes; there are Christians who are politically conservative and others who are politically progressive. Similarly, there are Conservative and Orthodox, Reformed and Reconstructionist Jews, some of whom are politically liberal, others of whom are more conservative.

It is thus important to remember that all Jews and all Christians will not think alike on all issues. When it comes to any number of important matters (from the Israeli-Palestinian crisis to the manner in which Jewish-Christian relations itself ought to proceed), it is very possible, for instance, that traditional or liberal Jews may disagree not only with Christians, but with other Jews, just as more progressive or conservative Christians will contest with one another. Indeed, on a variety of issues, the lines of agreement and disagreement between some Jews and Christians often do not appear to be drawn primarily in religious categories but in terms of political and social orientation. More politically liberal Jews regularly find affinity in the views of more politically and theologically progressive Christians. Politically and theologically conservative Christians and more religiously traditional Jews, who would not be

25

able to find much common ground in religious matters, not infrequently share perspectives on social and political questions. Such a situation thus underscores the need not merely for Jewish-Christian dialogue, but for continued and vigorous Jewish and Christian *intra*-faith dialogue.

For a number of reasons, including the more recent Christian public gestures of remorse and repentance for past wrongs alluded to above, the Jewish-Christian relationship is one that more and more Jews and Christians are able to engage. Many are attracted to the task because of the profound theological, ethical, and historical heritage that the two faiths share. Others are moved by a concern for the likewise weighty contemporary ramifications that are potentially at stake in a revitalized Jewish-Christian relationship, or in its deterioration. Yet no one should understand our concern to engage in Jewish-Christian dialogue as a lack of concern for, or as an effort to minimize, the need for both Jews and Christians, collectively or separately, to attend to other relationships. This is true whether this engagement is with movements within our faith traditions or with those that transcend our traditions—be it Jewish or Christian dialogue with Muslims (or other religions), Christian or Jewish relations to ethnic minorities inside or outside of our communities, or some other sort of relation. Indeed, in his essay on hope in *Contesting Texts*, Brueggemann alludes to the Christian theologian Karl Barth's view on intra-Christian dialogue and suggests that Jews and Christians need to engage "totally unexpected voices" in order to continue in our shared vocation of offering hope to the world. It may be, as Brueggemann intimates, that only by tending to the variety of our relations, even the peripheral or most difficult ones, will we be able to hear such enabling "unexpected voices."

The Pontifical Biblical Commission offered its statement "The Jewish People and Their Sacred Scriptures in the Christian Bible" with the hope that the document would "advance the dialogue between Christians and Jews," and in a spirit of mutual "esteem and affection." On an initial, cursory reading, the phrase "esteem and affection" may sound like so much rhetoric from a discourse of "official pronouncements," and indeed such language is not foreign to this sort of discourse. However, the terms *esteem* and *affection* are worth dwelling on for a moment. The word *esteem*, for instance, not only signifies a disposition of respect or admiration, but includes also the sense of valuing or honoring another. Likewise, *affection* can connote not merely a "fondness" or "kind feeling" for another, but "a zealous attachment" as well. We believe the scholars who produced "The Jewish People and Their Sacred Scriptures in the Christian Bible" understood and intended the phrase "esteem and affection" to carry just this sort of full sense. Hence, while recognizing that Jews and Christians not only share much, but also can, will, and ought to contest with one another not only around matters of theology and biblical interpretation, but also at the level of faith-informed politics and social policy, we present *Contesting Texts: Jews and Christians in Conversation about the Bible*. And like the Pontifical Biblical Commission, we do so with a similar hope of promoting in some small way Jewish-Christian relations and in the same spirit of esteem and affection.

Jews, Christians, and Biblical Authority

David Novak

The Theological Challenge of the Dialogue

I am proud to be one of the four authors of *Dabru Emet* ("Speak the Truth"), a "Jewish Statement on Christians and Christianity," first published in the *New York Times* in September 2000. It could not have been presented to the general public if the type of theologically serious Jewish-Christian dialogue taking place at conferences such as Contesting Texts in 2005 in Chicago had not already been taking place for at least one-third of a century beforehand. I call Jewish-Christian dialogue "*the* dialogue," since for those of us who have been participating in it, it is like no other dialogue, and there does not seem to be any other dialogue like it in intensity and duration taking place between any other two communities in the world today.

Assuming a certain familiarity on the part of the reader with the Jewish-Christian dialogue, I would like to focus on a specific point in the dialogue, part of *what* comprises the content of the dialogue. Yet we need to be mindful that no basic content of the dialogue emerges *from* the dialogue itself. The dialogue does not create its own content; it only develops its own contexts. Everything in the dialogue is brought to it by its Jewish and Christian participants. The dialogue is not revelation. Hence the point I wish to discuss, biblical authority, is something brought *to* the dialogue *by* its Jewish and Christians participants respectively. The dialogue itself then helps its Jewish and Christian participants discover *how* they can, respectively, deal with a specific point in the dialogue like that of biblical authority once they return home to discuss it in the context of intrareligious dialogue. The theological dialogue that takes place—or should take place—in our own religious communities results when Jews again talk of Jewish theology with fellow Jews and Christians again talk of Christian theology with fellow Christians. One great result of the dialogue is that a new horizon to theological discussion is brought back home from it. (But if we cannot bring any new perspectives back home from the dialogue, then does it not seem to be a way for Jews and Christians to, in effect, run away from home.)

In what might be called the "post-dialogical" experience in our own communities, the Jewish or Christian *other* stands on the horizon of that experience. We do not return home unchanged inasmuch as our subsequent experience now has a new horizon. We have brought home a new guest, a guest who seems to become a permanent resident of sorts, one who stands between us and a stranger external world. (This guest is like the *ger toshav*, literally the "resident sojourner," in rabbinic theology, one who is farther from us than our Jewish brothers and sisters, yet closer to us than the *nokhri*, literally "the stranger.") This guest is our horizon. This guest is, therefore, present in our intracommunal conversations, even if by then he or she is only listening in. We Jews can even assume that we too function as similar guests on the horizon of our Christian partners in the dialogue. In fact, several Christian interlocutors have told me so, in so many words, over the years.

That dialogical horizon is not only taken *from* the dialogical experience; it is also present in our respective preparations *for* the dialogical experience. Hence it is not only post-dialogical; it is just as much pre-dialogical. In other words, our very anticipation of the dialogue with the other frames the way we now talk with our own, especially when we talk of what we plan to talk of with the other later. In fact, as my friend Menachem Kellner of the University of Haifa (himself a signatory to *Dabru Emet*) has shown in his magisterial book, *Dogma in Medieval Jewish Thought*, much of Jewish dogma—that is, what Jews have thought they must necessarily affirm theologically with the force of law—has been formulated in response to external challenges to Judaism.[1] Challenges are both positive and negative. These challenges make claims on us before we can make our own counterclaims on those who first challenged us. In fact, Jewish claims on the Catholic

Church to rethink its view of Jews and Judaism were a major motivation leading to the positive rethinking of the question of Jews and Judaism formulated in the Vatican II statement *Nostra Aetate* (1965). Like *Nostra Aetate*, our own little document, *Dabru Emet*, is motivated by similar Christian claims on Jews to rethink our view of Christians and Christianity.

Until the not-so-distant past, Jews experienced these challenges in disputations, wherein Jews were forced to justify our differences *from* others, especially our differences *from* Christians *to* Christians. In the context of a disputation, challenges are essentially negative. But in the context of dialogue, challenges are essentially positive. Today, happily, Jews are experiencing these challenges dialogically; that is, we are being asked to show what we have in common *with* Christians just as we have asked Christians to show what they have in common *with* us and, of course, that being done without any minimization of what greatly divides us from each other. Nonetheless, whether negative or positive, these challenges are unavoidable demands made upon us, demands that require serious rethinking of our own views on our part. We cannot escape these challenges by hiding in obscurantist obsession with the past, a historicist obsession that would defame Judaism by making it appear to be dead rather than alive. To be alive is to be in the world both responsively and responsibly, however uncomfortably. Challenges come from those others with whom we live in the world.

These challenges have forced Jews to more explicitly articulate points of Jewish theology that have heretofore been most often left implicit and imprecise. But let it be emphasized again: these theological points are Jewish before they become dialogical. The fact, though, that it is only because of the dialogue that some Jews now have to deal with these points at all only shows how shallow their education in Jewish thelogy has been heretofore. Hence the late Rabbi Joseph B. Soloveitchik was not altogether wrong in his misgivings about the dialogue due to the theological naïveté of many Jews. Nevertheless, if the unavoidable challenge of the dialogue has forced some Jews to play theological "catch-up," that might well be a good, even if unintended, consequence of the dialogical experience as challenge. (Thus I think Rabbi Soloveitchik—to paraphrase T. S. Eliot—was right about the dangers of the dialogue, but for the wrong reason.) Preparing for the dialogue, we Jews must not only anticipate the Christian standing on the horizon in front of us, but take into immediate consideration beforehand the Jews with whom we already not only talk regularly, but also worship regularly. As such, anything we *would* say to the Christians on the horizon in front of us should be something we *could* already say to our fellow *religious* Jews in good faith. There is no double standard of truth, where we say one thing to others while either winking at our own or telling them something else when out of earshot of the others.

During the sessions when we were working toward a final version of *Dabru Emet*, I used to emphasize to my fellow authors that I would not agree to any proposition that could not be justified to the traditional Jews with whom I regularly talk Torah and with whom I worship regularly. So, for example, my friend Isaac, a learned and pious Jew with whom I regularly talk Torah and with whom I worship regularly in the same synagogue, is someone with whom I have discussed every one of the eight propositions of *Dabru Emet*. Isaac himself has no interest in Jewish-Christian dialogue.[2] Yet I would not have continued in the whole *Dabru Emet* project if I had not been able to convince Isaac that in so doing I was, minimally, not in violation of Jewish law and that there is, maximally, some positive support for what I have been doing from classical, authoritative Jewish sources, plus some precedent from earlier Jewish thinkers, themselves both pious and learned in these classical, authoritative sources.

Isaac's positive acceptance of *Dabru Emet*, first the project and then the final document, would have been a desideratum. That I did not get from him or from anyone like him. Nevertheless, the fact that a Jew like Isaac did not reject *Dabru Emet* on a legal or dogmatic basis was for me enough of a sine qua non that I was able to continue with *Dabru Emet* until its final formulation and publication.

The Authority of the Bible

What we see so far is that *Dabru Emet* involves three levels of discourse: one, the discourse with Christians for whom *Dabru Emet* is intended; two, the discourse with the Jews in the internal Jewish community whence one comes; and three, the discourse with one's fellow authors in the course of writing the document itself. Interestingly enough, the question of the authority of the Bible for Jews and for Christians was the issue that excited the most controversy, not among the Christians for whom *Dabru Emet* is intended, and not among the traditional Jews with whom I live, but among the authors of *Dabru Emet* itself. The controversy among ourselves was a controversy over one word: *authority*. What the controversy over this one loaded word indicates is that an inner Jewish division, one that is rarely explicit in ordinary Jewish discourse today, was uncovered by the fact that we *Dabru Emet* authors (and cosigners) are a group of Jews who had taken it upon ourselves to make a statement of Jewish theology to Christians about Christianity primarily because various Christians had asked us for it. Just as one has to resolve certain ambiguous meanings in his or her own language when having to translate some of its basic concepts into another language, so making a Jewish statement to Christians about themselves in a language understandable to them forced us to try to overcome certain ambiguous meanings in modern Jewish theology. (That we failed to overcome completely one such ambiguous meaning is revealed by the ambiguous language of the proposition of biblical authority—which I'll address later in this chapter.) Indeed, unlike any other issue dealt with in the composition of *Dabru Emet*, the issue of authority, specifically the authority of the Bible, exposed divisions among us so deep that they almost threatened to sink the ship before it could ever be launched.

The question of the authority of the Bible is the question of the authority of God's revelation. Whether there is any relationship with God outside of revelation is a perennial question in Jewish theology. Nonetheless, even if there is such a relationship outside of revelation for Jews, that relationship could not be a singularly Jewish relationship like a Jewish relationship with God constituted by the revealed Torah. For those Jewish thinkers who accept the authority of revelation, there is still the question of how that authority is to operate today. That requires more than simply repeating an ancient dogma; it requires radical rethinking even by those of us who are most orthodox. (As the great Catholic theologian Bernard Lonergan is reported to have said: "Some ideas are passed from book to book to book without any evidence of ever having gone through a mind.") For those Jewish thinkers who either deny revelation altogether or deny that revelation has any communicable content or deny that the content of revelation has authority, there is still the question of where religious authority is to be found. Even these more liberal Jewish thinkers have to admit that not everything can be permitted and that not everything can be affirmed and a coherent religion remain nonetheless. The question of authority cannot be avoided without religious chaos ensuing. An antinomian religion, much less an antinomian Judaism, is a contradiction in terms, an oxymoron.

We now need to look at the proposition of biblical authority, which is the second of the eight propositions of *Dabru Emet*:

> **Jews and Christians seek authority from the same book—the Bible (what Jews call "Tanakh" and Christians call the "Old Testament").** Turning to it for religious orientation, spiritual enrichment, and communal education, we each take away similar lessons: God created and sustains the universe; God established a covenant with the people Israel; God's revealed word guides Israel to a life of righteousness; and God will ultimately redeem Israel and the whole world. Yet, Jews and Christians interpret the Bible differently on many points. Such differences must always be respected.

Despite the seemingly straightforward language in this text, there is an inherent ambiguity here. This ambiguity bespeaks the ambiguity in modern Jewish theology on the problem of revelation. I read enough Christian theology and talk with enough Christian theologians to be assured that there is a similar problem in modern Christian theology. Could we then say that at least this proposition should be taken as a statement of Jewish ambivalence to similarly ambivalent Christians? (Ambivalence is predicated of subjects; ambiguity is predicated of the objects with which they are concerned.) Or am I permitted to personally emend this proposition—deconstruct it, if you will—and thus attempt to replace its inherent ambiguity with greater theological clarity? But when I do emend this proposition, which I ask you to consider today, I do so in my own name alone. I do not presume to speak for the three other authors of *Dabru Emet*, let alone for the almost two hundred Jewish leaders who cosigned the document when it was first published in 2000, and let alone for those who after 2000 have adopted the document as expressing their views of Christians and Christianity. Furthermore, I seriously doubt whether there will ever be a revised version of *Dabru Emet*, and that is as it should be. So we the authors can now speak only as individual theologians.

So I need first to locate the ambiguity within the statement of biblical authority, then attempt to restate it with less ambiguity. (Restating it with no ambiguity is, as postmodernism has taught us, beyond any fallible author or authors.) But first I must relate to you the initial context in which this proposition was first proposed, subsequently compromised, and finally formulated.

A Dispute for the Sake of God

Dabru Emet is very much the work of the four authors whose names appear on it: Tikva Frymer-Kensky, Peter Ochs, Michael Signer, and myself. However, although Michael Signer originally convened the group (through the offices of the Institute of Jewish and Christian Studies in Baltimore), I wrote the original working paper, whose substantial rewriting became the document *Dabru Emet*. In terms of rewriting, though, almost all of the changes made to the original working paper were more stylistic than substantial. That seems to be due to the fact that the four members of the group already knew each other and each other's work long before we actually got together to work on *Dabru Emet*. As such, I was as much influenced by my three friends as I was trying to influence them. The largely positive personal and intellectual chemistry of the group enabled us to engage in sustained work over several years, bringing our work to a concrete conclusion. Also, even though we all have theological interests unrelated to Jewish-Christian dialogue, we all had enough experience in and commitment to the dialogue to give each of us the constant motivation needed to bring our joint project to fruition. We all were able to agree and to hope throughout the whole arduous process of our work together that *Dabru Emet* could advance the overall Jewish-Christian relationship, whose most basic activity has indeed been the dialogue itself. That kept us going, and we all think the subsequent interest in *Dabru Emet* throughout the world has justified our common hope for its being taken seriously.

The proposition of the *authority* of the Bible, nevertheless, was the one major sticking point in our deliberations, so much so that another one of the other authors and I threatened to disband the group itself unless we—and the two others with us—could reach an agreement on the proposition pertaining to the Bible. Our dispute, specifically the dispute between one of the other authors and myself, was "a dispute for the sake of God," to use an important rabbinic term. Literally, the term is "a dispute for the sake of heaven"—*le-shem shamayim*—"heaven" being a rabbinic synonym for the Transcendent, who is "beyond," who *transcends*, this world—"being-there," *sham*—in the sense of not being reducible to any this-worldly agenda. Hence a dispute "for the sake of heaven" is a dispute that cannot be explained away as a mere difference of private opinions. Our dispute was truly over the principle of religious authority itself, notwithstanding whatever prejudices made such a dispute especially significant for each of us.

The other author objected to my use of the word "authority" altogether. The argument this colleague made, as I recall, was that invoking authority is inevitably "authoritarian," that it stems from the worship of power itself, with which God is thereby identified. And since we inevitably respond to any manifestation of power fearfully, invoking powerful authority is advocating a religion whose essential mode of action is fear. How does one respond to this kind of intra-Jewish challenge?

The best way to argue against this theological rejection of the concept of authority, it seemed to me then and now, is to note that in the Bible (and in subsequent rabbinic tradition), God is not only the supreme Power evoking fearful response; God is just as much the supreme Benefactor evoking a loving response. Thus in one talmudic passage, the fear of God (*yir'at ha-shem*) is seen to be the motivation for keeping the negative commandments of the Torah (the "thou shalt nots"), and the love of God (*ahavat ha-shem*) is seen to be the motivation for keeping the positive commandments of the Torah (the "thou shalts"). As such, there is a correlation between the fear of God and the love of God. There is also a dialectic between love of God and fear of God: love of God prevents fear of God from becoming dissociative hatred of God; fear of God prevents love of God from becoming unrestrained identification with God. Moreover, the two most prominent names of God in the Bible reflect this dialectic of love and fear in our relationship with God. For the Rabbis, the tetragrammaton (YHWH)—often translated into English as "the Lord" (following the Masoretic pronunciation: *adonai*)—bespeaks God's quality of compassion (*middat rahamim*), whereas *Elohim*—often translated as "God" (following the Septuagint's translation: *theos*) bespeaks God's quality of judgment (*middat ha-din*).

Since both love and fear characterize correct responses to the commandments of God, whether to act or to refrain from acting, God as both Power and Benefactor is acting *authoritatively* whenever God commands either negatively (*mitsvat lo-ta 'aseh*) or positively (*mitsvat 'aseh*). Perhaps one could say that in the fear of God we respond more obediently, and in the love of God we respond more cooperatively. In the fear of God we stand away; in the love of God we draw near. Either way, though, there is simply no way of avoiding the concept of authority in Judaism without a total slide into antinomianism. Indeed, doesn't the denial of authority become the rabbinic definition of "the benighted one says in his heart: there is no divine Judge [*ein elohim*]" (Ps 53:2) namely, the one who says "there is no law and there is no Judge [*lei din ve-leit dayyan*]" (author's translations)? Can there be an anarchic religion that is still recognizably Jewish or Christian (or Islamic)?

Unlike God's rightful authority, which is revealed in scripture, *authoritarianism* (which we all have good reason to detest) is the exercise of absolute authority by those who are less than divine. It is authority that speaks in its own name, not basing its claims on sinaitic revelation nor intending the ends of that revelation we infer from the text of scripture or which scripture presupposes. As such, authoritarianism does not let itself be limited by the authority of the One who ever transcends and judges all such creaturely pretension. Wrongful authoritarianism is morally and religiously detestable precisely because it deprives rightful authority of its absolute status. The true antidote to the wrongful authority exercised by authoritarians is not no authority at all. That would be a religio-political impossibility in and for any covenanted community, which is what the Jewish people and the Christian church claim to be. Instead, the true antidote to tyrannical authoritarianism is the exercise of the wholly rightful authority of God and then the partially rightful authority of those who subordinate their own political power to that highest authority.

Dabru Emet speaks of biblical authority as "God's revealed word" for both Judaism *and* Christianity. To avoid mention of biblical authority when speaking of Christianity is to defame Christianity as being antinomian, even if only by omission. Surely, Jewish and Christian commonality, which the dialogue is meant to uncover, should not be located in a common antinomianism. The fact is, though, that Judaism and Christianity do not dispute that there are authoritative commandments of God and that these commandments are revealed in the Hebrew Bible/Tanakh/Old Testament. Even Rabbi Joseph Albo, a famous fifteenth-century Spanish Jewish disputant against Christianity, conceded that Christians live under a divinely given law (*dat elohit*), thus concluding that Jews are mistaken when some of us say Christianity has totally rejected God's Torah. (From the Christian side, only a Marcionite would say this; and let it be remembered that Marcionism was the first heresy denounced by the early church.) Our differences, however, concern *which* of these authoritative commandments are perpetually binding and which were meant only for a certain period in history, and *how* some of these perpetual commandments are to be practically interpreted. As *Dabru Emet* puts it: "Yet, Jews and Christians interpret the Bible differently on many points. Such differences must always be respected." By "interpretation," we are certainly talking about interpretation of the biblical text that always, in one way or another, commands us to do something involving someone other than the text itself. Such normative interpretation is not the type of self-referential hermeneutics from which no active claims are ever made upon the reader other than reading itself.

Needless to say, we did not resolve our dispute in Jewish theology among ourselves before concluding the writing of *Dabru Emet* for publication. Instead, like most such groups, we worked out a compromise. What was this compromise? Why did we compromise? Can that compromise ever be overcome? Ought it be overcome? If so, how can it be overcome? Here again, let me reiterate that I can do this only in my own name.

A compromise only covers up an ambiguity; it does not resolve it. Any such compromise can last only as long as the next dispute over the matter that has been merely covered up. The ambiguity or paradox here is as follows: The fundamental proposition itself (the first sentence presented in boldface type) speaks of the *authority* of the Bible for Jews and for Christians. But the brief elaboration of that fundamental proposition thereafter speaks of biblical *guidance*: "God's revealed word guides Israel to a life of righteousness." Now in my original working paper, the assertion of authority was not explained as being guidance. Authority does not *guide*; authority *governs*. Saying that "authority guides" is inaccurate predication. It is as inaccurate as saying "guidance authorizes." (Both assertions involve the category errors that analytic-linguistic philosophers are so fond of pointing out to nonphilosophers, especially to theologians.) Rather, *counsel guides* while *authority governs*. "Counsel" is another name for "guidance." What is the essential difference between guidance and governance, between counsel and authority?

To say that the Bible has authority is to say that God has revealed commandments in the words recorded in scripture. ("Sacred Scriptures"—*kitvei ha-qodesh*—especially when having prima facie prescriptive meaning—*gezerat ha-katuv*—are authoritative ipso facto.) The authority of the Bible is because it is revealed by God (however much transmitted by humans). Actually, *Dabru Emet* speaks of Jews and Christians "seek[ing] authority from the same book." But is not seeking authority our willing subjugation to whatever we determine God has commanded—that is, *authorized*—us to do or not do? "Seeking" is English for the Hebrew *midrash*, which comes from the verb *darosh*: "to inquire," that is, to primarily inquire of God's Torah what it is that God wants us to do—even if that "doing" is only affirming a dogma. Only secondarily is midrash an enquiry into what God informs us about in the Torah. Thus normative (*halachic*) midrash has theological priority over narrative or speculative (*aggadic*) midrash.

Humans themselves, when speaking primarily in our own name, can offer only counsel or guidance. We should listen to human counsel for two reasons: one, because of *who* gives it, who should be a person or persons of known wisdom and virtue; two, because of *what* is being counseled, which should be something that makes sense (something I wish I could have been wise enough and good enough to counsel myself directly, without external consultation). But the rejection of good counsel is not a sin, unlike the rejection of rightful governance. Also, the acceptance of good counsel only gets one general approval from the very group he or she is likely to consult in the first place. Counsel can only suggest; it cannot command obedience or even beckon devotion.

To separate carefully between authority and counsel, between governance and guidance, does not mean that counsel or guidance is unimportant in Jewish religious life (and, presumably, in Christian religious life as well). Rather, it only means that guidance presupposes governance in a way that governance does not presuppose guidance. Thus rightful authority can operate without good counsel, but counsel cannot operate without rightful authority in the background. Nevertheless, authority without what the Rabbis called "good counsel" (*etsah tovah*) would not operate well. Let me explain by briefly analyzing how the Rabbis used the biblical word for "commandment"—*mitsvah*—in two different but nonetheless related senses.

The prima facie meaning of *mitsvah* is "commandment"—an authoritative or governing order. So, for example, we read: "The entire commandment [*mitsvah*] which I command you today, you shall keep" (Deut 8:1, author's translation). But there is a secondary meaning of *mitsvah* in rabbinic literature. It is something an exalted, perhaps even an inspired, human being *suggests one ought to do*, but which, nonetheless, is something one still may not do and not do it with impunity. The most such omission can entail is general disapproval from the very humans advocating it in the first place. Thus such counsel advocates what might be termed "good deeds" (*ma'asim tovim*). Good deeds are distinct from "right deeds" in the sense of "right [*tsaddiqim*] statutes and ordinances" (Deut 4:8). Not doing these right deeds means one has thereby done wrong just as not doing a wrong deed means one has thereby done what is right.

When it comes to doing what is merely a good deed, however, one is doing what the law has not commanded but what still *seems* to be what ought to be done. So, for example, the Rabbis say that "it is preferable [*mitsvah*] for one to seek arbitration" in a dispute rather than seek strictly legal adjudication, even though one may reject this counsel or guidance with legal impunity. Clearly such counsel, even when it is inspired counsel, is secondary to what has been explicitly commanded. Thus in a criminal case, unlike a civil suit, one is commanded to seek strictly legal adjudication. As such, arbitration here is out of the question. Furthermore, counsel is ultimately for the sake of keeping a commandment, even if that commandment is a general one. So the Talmud sees arbitration, where there will be no "winner" and no "loser," to be in the interest of seeking a "peaceful settlement" (*mishpat shalom*—Zech 8:16). Here we see how counsel or guidance supplements the Torah as a system of commandments and thus enhances peace as a commanded end greater than strict justice in many areas of interpersonal interaction. Such counsel is sometimes called a "preferred deed" (*mitsvah min ha-muvhar*). Thus revelation, as it were, authorizes inspired or even only reasonable counsel, yet that same counsel is ultimately meant to enhance the law that has been revealed.

Along these lines, even more theologically, doesn't even God himself agree to an arbitrated settlement of his case against us by accepting our repentance (*teshuvah*) in lieu of full payment for our sins? Like any arbitration, repentance requires that one waive his or her right to be fully vindicated just as God waives his right to be fully vindicated when he forgives us of our sins. Nonetheless, God does not waive his prior right to command us in the first place, the very right that our sins have violated. Without the priority of commandment, we could not cogently affirm God either as Lawgiver (*noten ha-torah*) or as Judge (*dayyan ha'emet*) or as the Forgiving One (*soleah*).

The Question of Revelation

I do not think that traditional Jews or traditional Christians should have any trouble affirming the authoritative governance of the Hebrew Bible. Our differences here—and they have been significant enough to keep each of us in our separate communities—are not over law versus no law, understanding law to be essentially commandment (*mitsvah*). Instead, our differences have been, and will be for the foreseeable future, over which commandments are to be kept perpetually and which commandments are no longer to be kept, having had authority only in the irretrievable past. Nevertheless, turning governance into guidance, or turning authority into counsel, could be seen as a liberal attempt to overcome the great divide between Judaism and Christianity over the Law, in effect making that divide even greater than it really is. It has been liberal Jews who, in the name of morality, have accused Christianity of being antinomian, of permitting everything. And it has been liberal Christians primarily, also in the name of morality, who have accused Judaism of being legalistic, of turning the livelier spontaneity of virtue into the deadening habit of behavior controlled by rules.

In this liberal view, it seems to me, guidance functions somewhere in between the authority of law on the one hand and the antiauthority of anarchy on the other hand. So in the words of the proposition on the Bible, the Bible is recognized as being, for both Jews and Christians, a source for "religious orientation, spiritual enrichment, and communal education," and it is called a source of "similar lessons." I might add that all of these terms were put forth by my colleague who so objected to the use of the term "authority." The definition of authority's function as that of guidance was accepted by my colleague and myself as a life-saving compromise to prevent *Dabru Emet* from becoming either aborted or a stillbirth. So I finally agreed to this compromise so that all of my work would not be nullified by my refusal to sign the final document. My colleague seemed to feel the same way.

In accepting this eleventh-hour compromise, I figured that as long as the word *authority* appeared in connection with the Bible, however it was predicated, I could afterward interpret it differently than its prima facie meaning in the text of *Dabru Emet*. That is what I did in my article "Mitsvah" in the companion volume to *Dabru Emet*, entitled *Christianity in Jewish Terms*.[3] Significantly enough, in that volume there were two responses to my article "Mitsvah," one by the more liberal Jewish theologian Elliot Dorff, the other by the more traditional Christian theologian Stanley Hauerwas. Would you be surprised to learn that Hauerwas was more in agreement with my view of *mitsvah* than was Dorff?

Another key word quoted above is "lessons." It seems to go back to a major break with Jewish tradition beginning in the Enlightenment of the late eighteenth century and already promoted in the early nineteenth century by what came to be called "Reform" or "Liberal" Judaism. The break is evidenced by a change in the translation of the biblical word for revelation: *torah*. Until the Enlightenment, though, there would have been few if any Jewish theologians who would have objected to the first translation of scripture into another language, the Greek Septuagint, translating the word *torah* as *nomos*, that is, "law." Actually, this is a case in which the original Hebrew term *torah* changed the meaning of the Greek term *nomos* significantly rather than the other way around. Up until that time, it seems that *nomos* meant human-made law, in contrast to *physis* ("nature") meaning an eternal/divine order. *Torah* qua *nomos* now meant scriptural law, whether pertaining to human-divine relations or only to inter-human relations, is now to be taken as God's commanded order for the universe as a whole. And this is the cosmic order in which Israel as the recipient of the historical revelation of that Law is privileged to be an intelligent and free junior partner of God himself in God's lawful governance of the universe. No other people is so privileged. Thus the election of Israel is for the sake of bringing at least some of the cosmic Torah down to earth.

The Enlightenment, specifically the Jewish Enlightenment (closely paralleling the more radical Protestant Reformation) and the Liberal Judaism it paved the way for, radically changed the meaning of Torah. Instead of Torah as *nomos*, Torah was now translated as *Lehre* from the German: "teaching" (as in the word "lesson" we have seen in the text of *Dabru Emet*). That would not be so radical if *Lehre* was meant to be a translation of the verbal source of the noun *torah*, which is *yarah*, meaning "to direct" as an archer *directs* his arrow to a designated target. Clearly, the archer *commands* the arrow where to go; it would be incorrect to say the archer merely *guides* the arrow to that designated target. Unlike merely guiding the arrow, the archer would be extremely disappointed if the arrow did not reach its designated target, the target the archer "commanded" it to reach. Indeed, if this happened, a good archer would probably mend the arrow or mend the bow, removing the very flaws that had prevented the arrow from reaching the target the archer intended. The archer, then, has "taught" the bow and arrow where to go in the sense that a teacher *assigns* a lesson to his or her students to learn and then put into practice. But the choice of *Lehre*, or "teaching," for *torah*, conversely, does not seem to partake of the normative meaning of *torah* as a verb and then as a noun.

Lehre no longer meant the enunciation of God's right to command specific commandments. Rather, its liberal Jewish use clearly showed the term "teaching" was meant to have a more advisory meaning. It was meant to be *guidance*. This, of course, reflected the Enlightenment's emphasis on greater voluntariness, especially in the type of religious life one wanted for oneself. Here again, there is a role for counsel in Judaism (and in Christianity too), but that role is secondary, not primary. Counsel is desirable but not strictly necessary for the covenant. Unlike counsel, the covenantal system of commandments (*mitsvot*) is called the Torah, and it has a necessarily legal structure called *halacha*.

Some have seen giving counsel and seeking counsel to be rooted in the Torah itself, even if its specifics cannot themselves be mandated. So if counsel is to be for the sake of peace (*shalom*), then its giving and its receiving are mandated by the general admonition "Seek peace and pursue it" (Ps 34:15). Nevertheless, the voluntariness of counsel, which at the prima facie level one may take or leave, does not extend to one's relation to the authority of revelation itself. It might be added that in earlier Liberal Judaism, Jewish morality, unlike Jewish "ritual," was still left at the level of law, not just teaching. But in some more current Liberal Judaisms, even Jewish morality is removed from the authoritativeness that characterizes *halacha*. Here, it would seem, everything had become mere counsel: only *a* voice, but never a veto—anywhere.

In conclusion, *Dabru Emet*, which is by now a key item on the dialogical agenda, requires considerable reinterpretation from both sides of the great divide in modern Jewish theology that I have been discussing with you today. So just as I want biblical authority to govern before its interpreters can offer authentic Jewish guidance, I suspect that my colleague, with whom I so passionately argued during the writing of *Dabru Emet*, would want guidance without predicating it of authority at all. Which of us provides a more coherent and more adequate Jewish theology should be left to the judgment of those in the Jewish community interested in this sort of theological question. And which of us provides a more sustained theological bridge to our Christian dialogue partners should be left to the judgment of those in the Christian community interested in this sort of question. In either case, the question of authority in general, and biblical authority more specifically, will surely appear again and again both in intrareligious dialogue and interreligious dialogue—both at home and abroad, as used to be said. As with any good conversation, we in the present enter it neither at its beginning nor at its end.

Promise and Fulfillment

Ralph W. Klein

Promise and fulfillment are characteristic activities of the God of the Bible and are richly in evidence in both testaments of the Christian biblical canon.[1] Promise and fulfillment are ways of talking about God's faithfulness and reliability, demonstrated in words and saving actions in the past and hoped for and trusted both in the present and in the future. Christians see fulfillment of God's promises in the life, death, and resurrection of Jesus and in the existence and preservation of the Christian church. Many aspects of promise and fulfillment are ideas about God held in common by Christians and Jews, but they have also often been a source of division and offense when Christian claims for fulfillment give the impression that God's faithfulness and presence are not experienced in their fullness among Jews and in Judaism. This chapter will explore the theme of promise and fulfillment within the Old Testament[2] and the way that the theme plays out in the relationship of the two testaments in order to clarify the limits and the legitimacy of the New Testament claims. Such a clarification is critical for Jewish-Christian understanding.

Promise and Fulfillment in Genesis

Two promises dominate in the stories of Israel's ancestors, Sarah and Abraham: land and descendants. The Lord's first statement to Abram is "Go from your country and your kindred and your ancestral home to the *land* that I will show you. I will make of you a great *nation*" (Gen 12:1-2).[3] Before Abraham and Sarah could become parents of a great

47

nation, they had to start with one child of their own, but this first promise was delayed for a long time and even doubted by them. Abraham and Sarah considered adopting their servant Eliezer in an attempt to help God out in fulfilling this promise (Gen 15:1-3), and Abraham actually engendered a child by the Egyptian maid Hagar in a dubious attempt to bring about the promise's fulfillment (16:1-16). But Abram believed the promise when God promised him as many children as the stars (15:5-6).[4] Sarah finally conceived and bore Isaac when both she and Abram were very old, beyond reproductive age. Through this birth the Lord did for Sarah as he had promised (21:1-2).

The promise of land is also delayed; in fact, its fulfillment lies on the other side of four centuries of servitude in Egypt (Gen 15:13-16).[5] The only land that the ancestors themselves owned was a burial plot, the Cave of Machpelah, where Sarah and Abraham, Rebekah and Isaac, and Leah and Jacob were buried.[6] The burial of each ancestor in the Cave of Machpelah was a kind of small fulfillment of the land promise and at the same time a reaffirmation of the land promise itself. Only after the conquest under Joshua and the distribution of the land (Joshua 1–21) can the narrator proclaim "Thus the LORD gave to Israel all the land that he swore to their ancestors. . . . Not one of all the good promises that the LORD had made to the house of Israel had failed; all came to pass" (Josh 21:43, 45).

The Promise of a Line of Prophets
. . . and a Future Prophet

The book of Deuteronomy hails Moses as a prophet and accompanies that affirmation with a distinctive understanding of his prophetic role. At Horeb, Deuteronomy's name for Sinai, Israel found the divine voice that spoke the Ten Commandments to be unbearably frightening and begged Moses in the future to listen to the Lord himself and then hand on, or mediate, that word of God to the people (Deut 5:23-31; cf. Exod 20:18-19). The prophet, therefore, in Deuteronomy's view is a person who hears the word of God and announces it to the people This understanding of prophecy is put in the form of a promise in Deut 18:15, 18: "The LORD your God will raise up for you [again and again][7] a prophet like me from among your own people; you shall listen to such a prophet.

. . . I shall put my words in the mouth of the prophet, who shall speak to them everything that I command." The Deuteronomic theologians in the seventh century no doubt thought that prophets like Moses could be seen in people such as Elijah, Amos, Hosea, Isaiah, Micah, and Jeremiah. These and other similar prophets were fulfillments of the promise made to Moses.

But a later writer recognized a disjuncture: however good Elijah, Isaiah, and the rest had been, they were not quite up to the standards of Moses.[8] This writer recorded his misgivings in Deut 34:10-11: "Never since has there arisen a prophet in Israel like Moses, whom the LORD knew face to face. Moses was unequaled for all the signs and wonders that the LORD sent him to perform in the land of Egypt, against Pharaoh and all his servants." This verse recognizes that the line of prophets was at best a partial fulfillment of the prophet like Moses, and therefore this verse gives the promise of Deuteronomy 18 a new, far more eschatological significance. If the Lord had promised to raise a prophet like Moses and had not yet fully done so, the ultimate fulfillment of Deuteronomy 18 still lay in the future.

Postbiblical Judaism expected such an eschatological prophet.[9] When Judas the Maccabee restored the temple after its desecration by Antiochus, the people tore down the polluted altar and stored the stones in a convenient place until "a prophet" should come and tell them what to do with them (1 Macc 4:46). When Simon the Maccabee was installed as high priest, they decided that his term should last forever, or at least until "a trustworthy prophet" should arise (1 Macc 14:41). The people who wrote the Dead Sea Scrolls expected two messiahs *and* an eschatological prophet. "They shall govern themselves using the original precepts by which the men of the *Yahad* (community) began to be instructed, doing so until there come the Prophet and the Messiahs of Aaron and Israel" (Rule of the Community 9:10-11).

Early Christians capitalized on this promise of an eschatological prophet and saw in Jesus a fulfillment of the prophet like Moses. When Jesus fed five thousand, the people said, "This is indeed the prophet who is to come into the world" (John 6:14).[10] Jesus' feeding of the five thousand resembled Moses' feeding Israel with manna in the wilderness. In a sermon in the book of Acts, Peter proclaimed that God had raised Jesus from the dead and added, "Moses said, 'The Lord your God will raise[11] up for you from your own people a prophet like me. You must listen to whatever he tells you. . . .' When God raised up his servant, he sent him first to you, to bless you by turning each of you from your wicked ways" (Acts 3:22, 26). Early Christians tried to live out another prophetic word from the book of Deuteronomy when they held all things in common (Acts 4:32). After all, had not Moses said that there should be no poor among the people (Deut 15:4)?[12]

Prophecies That "Failed"

What if God promises something and it does not happen? Deuteronomy proposes this as one criterion for distinguishing between true and false prophets. "You may say to yourself, 'How can we recognize a word that the LORD has not spoken?' If a prophet speaks in the name of the LORD but the thing does not take place or prove true, it is a word that the LORD has not spoken" (Deut 18:21-22).[13] Many of the prophets whose words of judgment are now contained in the biblical canon were proved true by the Assyrian and Babylonian invasions of 722/721 and 587/586 BCE. Even in the best circumstances, however, this is not the most useful criterion for distinguishing between true and false prophecy, since a person may need to decide what to do in the very near future and cannot wait to find out whether history will vindicate or falsify the word of the prophet.

When God or a prophet makes a promise, however, it is always a risky business, because trying to tell how history will turn out is like aiming at a moving target. In 587 BCE the prophet Ezekiel announced that Nebuchadrezzar would bring judgment on the island city of Tyre (Ezek 26:7-21). Some sixteen years later Ezekiel revised that prophecy. Despite a lengthy, thirteen-year siege, Nebuchadrezzar had little to show for his attack on Tyre. Now Ezekiel announced that God would instead give Nebuchadrezzar a victory over Egypt since Nebuchadrezzar had "worked" for God in bringing judgment against Judah and Jerusalem (Ezek 29:17-20). Walther Zimmerli described this as the faithfulness and freedom of the LORD: faithful to his word of reward to Nebuchadnezzar, but free to adapt it to the changed circumstances of history after Tyre's stubborn defense.[14]

At other times prophecies may have a partial fulfillment that leaves an expectation that God will someday carry out the still-outstanding details of his promise. The promise of a new exodus from Babylon in Second Isaiah may be a case in point. Second Isaiah opens with a divine address to the heavenly council, telling them to give comfort to Jerusalem, which had already received twice as much punishment as it had coming (Isa 40:1-2). A second voice from the divine council gives orders to other angelic beings to build a superhighway from Babylon to Jerusalem, leveling the mountains, filling in the valleys, and taking out the S curves. God would make an appearance during that new exodus as a witness to all the nations (Isa 40:3-5). A related passage in Isaiah 35 announces a concomitant renewal of human beings with disabilities and almost a new creation: the blind will see, the deaf will hear, the lame will leap, the tongue of the speechless will sing, and water will break out in the desert.

In the years following the Persian takeover of Babylon, some Jews did return from Babylon, with Cyrus's permission and encouragement, and they even rebuilt the temple. But their numbers were relatively small,[15] the new temple was disappointing to many who had known Solomon's temple (Ezra 3:12-13), and the community was faced with inner divisions (see Isaiah 56–66). There surely was no "interstate" from Babylon to Jerusalem, no revitalized desert, and no wholesale healing of people within Israel.

The people who wrote the Dead Sea Scrolls saw a fulfillment of this prophecy of Second Isaiah in the establishment of their community. In the Rule of the Community, we read: "They shall separate themselves from the session of perverse men to go to the wilderness, there to prepare the way of truth, as it is written [Isa 40:3]: 'In the wilderness prepare the way of the LORD, make straight in the desert a highway for our God'" (1 QS 8:13-14). Their refuge by the shore of the Dead Sea was seen as a way of preparing a way in the wilderness.

In the New Testament Matthew used similar exegesis in an attempt to understand the ministry of John the Baptist: "This is the one of whom the prophet Isaiah spoke when he said, 'The voice of one crying out in the wilderness: "Prepare the way of the Lord, make his paths straight"'" (Matt 3:3).[16] Preparing the way is now interpreted as moral regeneration and not as building a highway through the desert. When John was later thrown in prison, he sent some of his disciples to Jesus and asked, "Are you the one who is to come, or are we to wait for another?" Jesus answered, "Go and tell John what you hear and see: the blind receive their sight, the lame walk, the lepers are cleansed, the deaf hear, the dead are raised, and the poor have good news brought to them" (Matt 11:3-5). Jesus' answer to John is "Yes, I am the one who is to come," but it is couched in words that see, in his miracles of healing and in his identification with the poor, a fulfillment of the promises in Isaiah 35 and 40.[17] Thus both some Jews and early Christians identified additional fulfillments of Isaiah's words in the things they had experienced, beyond those experienced in the immediate decades after the ministry of Second Isaiah.

In considering Old Testament promises, one must also consider the possibility that some promises from the beginning were meant metaphorically and not literally. Ezekiel's vision of the new temple in 40:1—44:3 seems to assign symbolic meanings to the various measurements of the temple and the sacred area of the land, with the sealed East gate indicating that the Lord would never again leave the temple. Similarly, his description of the new boundaries of the land and the tribal portions in 47:13—48:29 stresses a separation from the territory of Transjordan that was always more vulnerable to apostasy. This metaphorical description of the land assigned equality of size and power to each of the twelve tribes, with some advantage to those tribes descended from the wives instead of the concubines of Jacob, and with the whole land centered on the temple and the regions of the priests and Levites. The stream that comes from the temple and renews the Judean wilderness and brings a multitude of the fish to the Dead Sea in 47:1-12 is designed to show that when the Lord is present with his people, nothing is impervious to change. Such promises are open to multiple fulfillments. In the Gospel of John, the body of Jesus is identified with the temple (2:19-21), and the stream of water flowing from his side at the crucifixion (19:34) could be seen as analogous to the stream of water Ezekiel saw.

The Promised Messiah

Many Christians who undertake critical biblical studies are surprised at the relative infrequency of the messianic hope in the Old Testament[18] and how the initial significance of these passages in their Old Testament contexts is quite different from their interpretation in the New Testament and subsequent Christian theology. Study of the messianic motif in the Old Testament discloses a transition from an expectation of a new or better king of the Davidic line in the very near future to the development of a more eschatological expectation of a messianic figure and finally to further transformation of this hope in subsequent Jewish and Christian theologies.

At the base of all messianic expectations in the Old Testament is the oracle of Nathan in 2 Samuel 7. There the Lord turned aside on principle David's offer to build a house (temple) for the Lord, stating that he had been content to move about in a tent or tabernacle, only to authorize David's son (Solomon) to build the temple.[19] The Lord also promised to make David's house and kingdom sure and to establish his throne forever. In its final form the oracle of Nathan gives a ringing endorsement to the Davidic dynastic house. Even if individuals in that line would commit iniquity and require punishment, the Lord promised not to take his steadfast love from this dynasty as he had taken it away from Saul.

The theological and political power of this oracle played a major role in the preservation of the Davidic dynasty over a four-century period. But the surety of this promise also played a role in the dynasty's weakest moments, and especially when it ceased to rule, for prophets concluded that this promise was still valid and would lead either to a replacement king or eventually to a figure who might be called an eschatological messiah. While the noun מָשִׁיחַ "messiah" (anointed one) is used some thirty-nine times in the Hebrew text, it is never used as a technical term in the Old Testament "messianic" passages as a designation for the future king.

Space permits us to look at only a few of the Old Testament passages dealing with the messiah.[20] Passages dealing with a future king in First Isaiah are of uncertain meaning or of uncertain date—or both. In Isaiah 7 the prophet Isaiah attempted to get King Ahaz to trust in the Lord for deliverance from the invading Syrian and Ephraimite forces, but as we learn from the narrative history of Ahaz, the king eventually ignored this advice and sent a bribe to Tiglath-pileser III, the king of Assyria, to persuade him to attack Damascus and force the withdrawal of Syria and Ephraim from their attack on Jerusalem (2 Kings 16). Isaiah offered to give Ahaz a sign, apparently to indicate God's readiness to intervene on his behalf, but Ahaz declined and said that he did not want to put God to the test. Isaiah interpreted this as a hypocritical excuse and decided to give Ahaz a sign anyway: "That young woman (over there) is with child and shall bear a son, and shall name him Immanuel" (Isa 7:14). It is generally agreed today that the mother-to-be in question was not a virgin, but which woman Isaiah had in mind is unclear and casts some doubt on whether this should be considered a messianic passage at all. Although there are many proposals about this woman's identity, the two most common suggestions are that she was the wife of Isaiah or the wife of Ahaz. If the woman is Ms. Isaiah, Immanuel would be the third child she would bear with a role in Isaiah's ministry—see Shear-jashub ("the remnant will return") in Isa 7:3 and Maher-shalal-hash-baz ("the spoil speeds, the prey hastens") in Isa 8:3. Perhaps a majority of scholars believe that the woman is indeed the wife of Ahaz so that the child to be born would be of the royal line. In neither interpretation, however, is the child hailed as a future king with specific responsibilities, and the sign offered by Isaiah may be nothing other than the child's name, Immanuel, meaning "God is with us." This name itself could be good news or bad. It would be good news if God's presence meant deliverance from the invading forces, or bad news if God was coming in judgment. The positive connotation appears in Isa 7:16 and 8:10 and the negative connotation in Isa 7:17 and 8:8.

A second passage in Isaiah seems to refer to a new son born in the royal household whose birth indicates the continued effectiveness and validity of the promise to David (Isa 9:2-7). The passage speaks of this king's authority and just rule, but the most significant thing about him is his name, traditionally translated as "Wonderful Counselor, Mighty God, Everlasting Father, Prince of Peace" (Isa 9:6). The name itself is unusual for at least three reasons: Israelite kings normally do not have a series of four names, Hebrew names are usually sentences and not attributes, and it would be very unusual in the Old Testament to infer that the king had godly status.[21] I prefer to translate the name, therefore, as two sentences: "The mighty God is planning a wonder; the everlasting

Father is planning a captain of peace."[22] That is, this name, like that of Immanuel, points to God's support of the king, just as the last line of this pericope affirms: "The zeal of the LORD of hosts will see to it that this will happen." Strangely, this verse is not cited in the New Testament as a prophecy fulfilled in Jesus.[23]

A third messianic passage in Isaiah is 11:1-9 (cf. also a series of supplements to this promise in vv. 10-16). This passage seems to presuppose the end of the Davidic dynasty, or at least it predicts that end. It speaks of the stump of Jesse, meaning that the dynastic tree associated with David has been cut down. From that stump of Jesse will sprout a branch or shoot; that is, a new David will arise. This new king will be endowed with the divine spirit, as were the first two kings, Saul and David (Isa 11:2). All subsequent kings ascended the throne not by virtue of their being endowed with the divine spirit, but because they were descended from David. The new king promised in Isaiah 11 will be a righteous judge, an advocate for the poor and weak (11:3-5), and his reign will usher in an era of nonviolence, symbolized by wolves living with lambs, leopards with young goats, and the like (11:6-9).

Two passages from Jeremiah will round out this brief survey of the messianic hope of the Old Testament. I think Jer 23:5-6 is from the prophet himself, although there are many dissenters from this dating. Jeremiah speaks of the Lord's promise to raise up a "righteous branch," perhaps better translated as "legitimate heir." If the latter translation is correct, this promised new king would be an apt replacement for Zedekiah, a puppet king installed by Nebuchadnezzar after his attack on Jerusalem in 597 BCE.[24] The new king's reign, as in Isaiah 11, would be marked by justice and righteousness. Again, the king receives a new name: "The LORD is our righteousness," or perhaps better, "The LORD is the source of our vindication." Either translation shows, as in the three Isaiah passages, that divine aid is the basis for the king's real strength. The Hebrew for this name (*YHWH tsidqenu*) would seem to be a pun on Zedekiah (*Tsedeqiyah*) with the two elements in Zedekiah's name in reverse order. It seems likely to me that Jeremiah is talking about a replacement for Zedekiah in the near future and not yet about an eschatological figure.

A second messianic passage, in Jer 33:14-16, is secondary since verses

14-26 are not included in the Septuagint, the second-century BCE translation of the Bible into Greek.[25] Its secondary character is confirmed by literary critical judgments, namely, that the territory envisioned in this promise is much smaller—Judah and Jerusalem instead of Judah and Israel—and because the name is applied not to the new king himself, but to the city of Jerusalem.[26] The longer pericope in verses 14-26 presupposes that alongside the unbroken Davidic line will be an unbroken line of Levitical priests, and that God will have an unbreakable covenant with each of these lines. This passage is especially interesting because it shows the further development in some circles of Jeremiah's idea of a replacement for king Zedekiah with the notion of a an unbroken line of Davidides and an unbroken line of Levitical priests.[27] The promise continues—and changes.

Before turning to the New Testament, we need to note that some passages dealing with reigning Israelite kings came to be read in late Old Testament times with messianic significance. I am thinking especially of the royal psalms (Psalms 2, 45, 72, 89, and 110). These psalms originally dealt with issues such as coronation, the righteous rule of kings, the marriage of the king, or the theological consequences of the king's defeat. Once Israel no longer had a king, it seems likely that many believers read these psalms messianically, that is, as referring to a future king rather than a contemporaneous king.

Jesus as Christ/Messiah in the New Testament

One of the central affirmations of the New Testament is that Jesus is the fulfillment of Israel's messianic hope. The Greek word *Christ* is a translation of the Hebrew word *messiah*. Before we look at specific passages, however, I would like to rephrase what I said in the first sentence of this paragraph. One of the central affirmations of the New Testament is that Jesus is the fulfillment, and radical reinterpretation of, Israel's messianic hope. I note four changes that are significant departures from the messianic hope that began in the Old Testament and developed further in early Judaism:[28]

1. The New Testament makes the death of Jesus one of his most significant features. That death, of course, has multiple interpretations in the New Testament, but all of the New Testament writers find deep

meaning in his death (and resurrection). There is not a single Jewish text, in or out of the Old Testament canon, however, that talks about the saving significance of the death of the messiah. In fact, the only mention of the death of the messiah occurs in 2 Esd 7:29-30, where at the end of the age, we are told that all will die, including the messiah, and then the end will come. Paul was well aware of this departure from Jewish thought when he wrote, "We proclaim Christ [messiah] crucified, a stumbling block to Jews and foolishness to Gentiles, but to those who are the called, both Jews and Greeks, Christ the power of God and the wisdom of God" (1 Cor 1:23-24). Christians therefore should not be surprised if Jews have a different expectation of the character or even fate of the messiah.

2. While there are varying Christologies in the New Testament, some higher than others, Jesus is widely identified as Lord, a figure to be worshiped, and he is identified, in one sense or another, as the Son of God. Although the doctrine of the Trinity is not fully developed in the New Testament, there are clearly movements in that direction, specifically with regard to the role of Jesus as Son. Again the Old Testament totally lacks references to the divinity of the messiah, and where it has been detected by some, as in Isa 9:6, I believe this is based on a faulty translation of the passage (see the discussion above).

3. The New Testament does see the new (messianic) age breaking in with Jesus. His miracles are the signs of that age, and his resurrection is seen by Paul as the first fruits of the new age (1 Cor 15:20). And yet the New Testament also speaks of Jesus' second coming and affirms that the new age is "already and not yet." This distinction between already and not yet, between a new messianic age that is partially but not wholly present, is again a radical departure from the view of the Old Testament itself and early Judaism. This adjustment of the promise to fit the realities of history is not different in kind from adjustments we saw in interpretations of the prophecies of Ezekiel and Second Isaiah as history changed.

4. The New Testament conflates a number of expected figures from the Old Testament in its depictions of Jesus. Jesus is messiah/Christ, but he is also the prophet, the servant, the Son of Humanity, the incarnate *logos*, and even a figure like Melchizedek (Hebrews 7).

This Took Place to Fulfill . . .

Christians from the beginning have seen in Jesus the "Yea and Amen" to all of God's promises (cf. 2 Cor 1:20). Also from the beginning they had to account for a number of features about Jesus that must at first have been very surprising, even offensive to many of them. Clearly, Jesus' closest disciples had trouble at first dealing with his death and interpreting the reality and significance of his resurrection. As decades wore on, the separation from mainstream Judaism and the separate existence of the church were theological issues in need of interpretation and justification. But it is clear that the early Christians saw the gospel of Jesus as continuing the redeeming work of the God of the Old Testament. They searched the scriptures they had (the Old Testament), as Jesus had urged them (Luke 24:27, 32), with the expectation that these scriptures would confirm the message of Jesus and help them to understand who he was and who they now were. Their search was undertaken as first-century people, using exegetical methods at home in the world of Judaism. Their search was also undertaken in contentious, even polemical times as the conflict with Judaism increased. Their speaking of fulfillment was usually an attempt to affirm continuity with the Old Testament past and full acceptance of its authority. The last thing they thought they were doing was starting a new religion. We need to keep this in mind as we discuss fulfillment in the New Testament, realizing that modern Christians might draw lines of continuity with the Old Testament in different ways and with more current methods of interpretation. This is not to say that the exegetical methods of the New Testament writers were wrong, but only that their methods were part of antiquity and need to be understood both sympathetically and critically by readers of the New Testament today. But it also means that Christians should not be surprised that Jews see the promises of their Bible, the Tanakh, fulfilled in different ways, or as still waiting to be fulfilled.

Some New Testament Fulfillments

We have noted that early Christians sought to understand the significance of the life and ministry of Jesus by interpreting the scriptures of their time (what we would call the Old Testament). Thus they often started with a tenet of their faith and moved backward, attempting to find a promise in the Old Testament of what they had experienced and to interpret what they had experienced as fulfillment of that promise. Christians came to believe, for example, that Jesus was born of the virgin Mary and that the child conceived in her was through the power of the Holy Spirit (Matt 1:20). They sought to explain this miracle by referring to the scriptures. Matthew concludes, "All this took place to fulfill what had been spoken by the Lord through the prophet: 'Look, the virgin shall conceive and bear a son, and they shall name him Emmanuel,' which means, 'God is with us'" (Matt 1:22-23). The biblical allusion is to Isa 7:14.

This type of interpretation resembles in many ways that used in the seventeen or eighteen Pesharim (biblical commentaries) among the Dead Sea Scrolls. The Pesher on Hab 2:2 reads: "When it says, 'so that with ease someone can read it,' this refers to the Teacher of Righteousness to whom God made known all the mysterious revelations of his servants the prophets." Thus Habakkuk, who lived in the late seventh century, is understood as prophesying about the Teacher of Righteousness, who was a leader in the community responsible for the Dead Sea Scrolls in the second century BCE. The interpreters who wrote these commentaries assumed that prophetic proclamation dealt with the end-times and that they themselves were living in the end-times. Hence prophetic proclamation dealt directly with them and their situation. Matthew was apparently schooled in this type of exegesis. A passage written by Isaiah in the heart of the controversies of the eighth century BCE was assumed to have significance about the end-times, that is, the era of Jesus. It helped in this case that Matthew was reading the scriptures in their Greek translation, where the word translated "young woman" by the NRSV was rendered by *parthenos*, the standard Greek word for "virgin." Matthew also would have been pleased that the child's name from Isa 7:14, Emmanuel ("God is with us"), fit so well with his understanding of the significance of the birth of Jesus. The virgin birth of Jesus therefore was seen in continuity with the message of Isaiah and hailed as "fulfillment." Thanks to the comparison with the Pesharim of the Dead Sea Scrolls, we can now understand better how and why Matthew wrote this way. But just as the Pesher on Habakkuk cited above does not determine the meaning of Habakkuk in the seventh century

BCE, so Matthew's understanding of Isa 7:14 does not determine what the prophet was trying to say in his eighth-century BCE context.

When King Herod's mad policies threatened the infant Jesus, Joseph was warned in a dream to take Mary and Jesus and flee to Egypt and to stay there until the death of Herod. Matthew observes, "This was to fulfill what had been spoken by the Lord through the prophet, 'Out of Egypt I have called my son'" (Matt 2:15).

Matthew refers here to Hos 11:1, but modern readers of Hosea soon learn that Matthew's understanding of this verse was not that of the eighth-century prophet. In Hosea, "Out of Egypt I called my son"[29] referred to the exodus of Israel from Egypt, which was taken as evidence of God's election of Israel as his child and his support of Israel right from the beginning. The next verse in Hosea confirms this understanding, because the prophet claims that despite this early benefaction, Israel had proven to be disobedient and had pursued Baals and idols throughout its history. The original context in Hosea, therefore, takes the exodus as a starting point for a history of disobedience, surely the last thing that Matthew would want to say about Jesus! Modern readers of the Bible assume that context and original setting determine a text's meaning; that is not an assumption shared by Matthew or by the persons who wrote the Pesharim at Qumran. For Matthew the successful flight of the infant Jesus was evidence of the faithfulness of God to his promises, which led him to read Hos 11:1 in an eschatological context. In Matthew in general, the life of Jesus often recapitulates the history of Israel. The Sermon on the Mount presents analogies to the revelations Moses received from God on Mount Sinai.

Christians today can share Matthew's conviction that the rescue of Jesus provides evidence of the faithfulness of God, and Christians today can affirm that the faith of the Old Testament has continuities with the faith of Christians. If we were today trying to demonstrate this faithfulness or these continuities by allusions to the Old Testament, we would express them with exegetical methods appropriate to our time. A historical-critical understanding of Hosea 11 offers a possible resource for Christian theologians. As that chapter proceeds, the disobedience of Israel leads to divine exasperation. Despite lavish divine parental care, Israel seems locked in behavior designed to lead to judgment. But

God in Hosea 11 wrestles with conflicted feelings. Disappointment in Israel's behavior comes into conflict with divine parental loyalty:"How can I give you up, Ephraim? How can I hand you over, O Israel. . . . I will not execute my fierce anger; I will not again destroy Ephraim; for I am God and no mortal" (Hos 11:8-9). The doctrine of retribution insists that sin must be followed by punishment, but the God of Hosea 11 states that he is not bound by the rules of retribution. The happy contradiction between God's anger and God's love, in which the latter wins out—so central to the Christian understanding of the faith—is also a central conviction of the prophet Hosea. A modern Matthew could hail this as promise and fulfillment or at least as a significant theological continuity.

Promise and Fulfillment
as the Bond between the Testaments

The earliest Christians had only what is now called the Old Testament as their scriptures. Later the New Testament books came to have similar canonical authority for the church. Lines of continuity with the God and the faith of the Old Testament could be expressed in a number of ways, including promise and fulfillment. The coupling of promise and fulfillment is a time-tested and widely held understanding of the relationship between the testaments. Luke's description of Jesus in conversation with two disciples on the way to Emmaus is a typical example of this approach. After Jesus had reproached them for their failure to believe what the prophets had declared, Luke continues the story as follows:"Then beginning with Moses and all the prophets, he interpreted to them the things about himself in all the scriptures" (Luke 24:27).

Some Christians, even in modern times, have denied that continuity. The prominent New Testament scholar Rudolf Bultmann thought the Old Testament was a shattering failure and wrote, "How far, then, does Old Testament Jewish history represent prophecy fulfilled in the history of the New Testament community? It is fulfilled in its inner contradiction, its miscarriage. . . . Faith requires the backward glance into Old Testament history as a history of failure, *and so of promise*, in order to know that the situation of the justified man arises only on the basis of this miscarriage."[30] In the same context Bultmann also referred to "the false way of salvation which we find in the law." Despite his many illuminating comments on the New Testament, Bultmann had a blind spot in his understanding of the Old Testament and did not adequately recognize the strong lines of continuity in the theological affirmations of both testaments.

The pairing of promise and fulfillment is a welcome way to express that continuity. But this assertion too is capable of misunderstandings. We have seen that prophecies in the Old Testament can have multiple fulfillments. Second Isaiah's word about the end of the exile had an immediate, partial fulfillment in the Jews who returned to Jerusalem in the early Persian period. But there were still aspects of that prophecy that cried out for more ultimate fulfillment, as seen, for example, in the Dead Sea Scrolls and in the New Testament's interpretation of John the Baptist. Christians need to recognize that Jewish sisters and brothers see evidence for the faithfulness of God, and therefore for fulfillment of his ancient promises, in the oral revelation recorded in the Talmud, in the creation of a new state in the land of Israel, and in the ongoing presence of God in the lives of Jews and Judaism. What Christians and Jews hail as fulfillments refer back to the promises of the same God.

The New Testament is not only fulfillment. It also contains promises and prophecies that still cry out for fulfillment. From the beginning Christians have prayed "Maranatha," "Our Lord, come" (1 Cor 16:22), looking forward to additional fulfillments of God's promises in the return of Jesus in triumph. Paul's wonderful statement in Gal 3:28 is still in many ways more promise than fulfillment: "There is no longer Jew or Greek, there is no longer slave or free, there is no longer male and female; for all of you are one in Christ Jesus." And what might be the fulfillment of this prophecy of Paul, "And so all Israel will be saved" (Rom 11:26)? The second petition of the Lord's Prayer reads, "Thy kingdom come!" putting future expectation or fulfillment at the heart of the New Testament message.

Contemporary Judaism recognizes that many of God's promises were fulfilled in the life of ancient Israel and in the subsequent history of Judaism. Some of the promises that Christians have seen fulfilled in the life of Jesus, such as the dawning of the messianic age, are seen by them as continuing *and as yet unfulfilled* eschatological expectations.

Promise and fulfillment are indeed important talking points between Jews and Christians. We need to honor our different understandings of this theological slogan and learn to wait together for God's future.

PART 2

Texts of Violence: Early Jewish and Christian Interpretations

Apocalyptic Violence and Politics

END-TIMES FICTION FOR JEWS AND CHRISTIANS

Barbara R. Rossing

The question of religious violence generates great debate in popular culture, Christianity, and political commentary today, from Mel Gibson's film *The Passion of the Christ* to Left Behind, the all-time best-selling Christian thriller series. In their Left Behind novels, Tim LaHaye and Jerry Jenkins take biblical violence and bloodshed to a new level, building on the model of Hal Lindsey's *The Late Great Planet Earth* (1970), which interpreted Revelation's weaponry in terms of helicopter gunships and thermonuclear war. The soon-to-be-released Left Behind video game, *Left Behind: Eternal Forces*, encourages Christians to kill nonbelievers. Even *New York Times* columnist Nicholas Kristof, normally reticent about criticizing religion, raises concern about the Left Behind phenomenon: "This portrayal of a bloody Second Coming reflects a shift in American portrayals of Jesus, from a gentle Mister Rogers figure to a martial messiah presiding over a sea of blood."[1]

Much of the debate about violence in the Christian Bible concerns the book of Revelation, specifically its portrait of Jesus. Jesus is the main character in Revelation, but the problem arises because Revelation portrays Jesus in different, even conflicting ways. Revelation 19 depicts Jesus as killing his enemies with a two-edged sword coming from his mouth—a sword first introduced in Rev 1:16, modeled on an image from the prophet Isaiah (Isa 49:2). Yet by far the most frequent image for Jesus in Revelation is a Lamb, who "conquers" not by killing but by giving his life nonviolently. The crucial question is how these images of Jesus interact in Revelation—whether the nonviolent Lamb trumps the sword-wielding Jesus, as I argue, or whether the images of Lion and Lamb are held in tension as Stephen Moyise and other scholars argue,[2] or whether the more violent martial portraits supersede the Lamb, as some critics and the Left Behind authors argue.

Closely related to the question of divine violence and the image of Jesus in Revelation is the question of ethics: Does the book of Revelation call on followers of Jesus to participate in violence? In the Left Behind scenario, Christian soldiers actively prepare to fight God's end-times war.

Politics and also foreign policy come into play, since increasing numbers of U.S. Christians believe that the book of Revelation predicts an end-times battle of Armageddon in Israel, with implications for the entire Middle East. Left Behind readers and millions of fundamentalist "Christian Zionists" argue that absolute support for Israel's sovereignty over the entire Holy Land is necessary, even including demolishing the Dome of the Rock so that the Third Jewish Temple can be rebuilt. Palestinian Muslims and Christians have no place in this fundamentalist Christian script. As Israeli scholars Gershom Gorenberg, Yehezkel Landau, and others have pointed out, it is also a very dangerous script for Jews, since all Jews who do not convert in the end-times are killed. To quote Gorenberg on *Sixty Minutes,* "If you listen to the drama they're describing, essentially it's a five-act play in which Jews disappear in the fourth act." This has not stopped some Israeli settlers and others from accepting financial and political support from such right-wing Christian groups to expand Jewish reach in the occupied West Bank.

Even Christians who do not hold such extreme positions tend to perceive Revelation as overwhelmingly violent, much more so than the rest of the Bible. In a National Public Radio interview, progressive religion scholar Karen Armstrong made the point that whereas Christianity is nonviolent in core scriptures, Revelation is problematic because it reflects Christianity's violent strand that "seeps into the scripture." She contrasts the nonviolent Jesus of the Gospels with the Jesus of Revelation who is "leading armies and destroying the enemies in battle with great gusto."[3]

Two Models of "Conquering" (*Nikan*) in Revelation:
The Nonviolent Lamb or Violent Rome

I want to explore this question of apocalyptic violence and politics in Revelation by tracing the theme of "victory" or "conquering" that runs through the book. Revelation's word for "victory" is the Greek verb *nikan*, the same word used in Roman imperial theology of *nikē*—a word that can be translated in English as "victory" or "conquering." It is precisely this word that allows both proponents of triumphalist violence and proponents of nonviolence to lay claim to Revelation.

In Revelation, both Jesus and the evil beasts claim to be "victors" who "conquer." Revelation tells the gripping story of a conflict between the forces of the Lamb and the forces of the beast, in which the Lamb wins or "conquers." Followers of the Lamb also take part in the conflict against the beast and share in the Lamb's victory or conquering. But in my view, "conquering" does not entail violence in Revelation. Rather, Revelation carefully delineates between two very different models of conquering—the beast's (Rome) violent model versus the Lamb's nonviolent model—and this difference is crucial in the unfolding nonviolent drama of the book.

Key to understanding this dual use of the theme of victory or conquering is the historical and political context of Revelation. John wrote the book during a time of tremendous Roman militarism and military conquest, toward the end of the reign of Domitian (probably circa 96 CE). Rome was still glorying in its victory over the Jewish Revolt in 67–70 CE. Rome's propaganda celebrated with victory processions in the provinces, the minting of "capta" coins depicting Judea as a captive with her hands bound behind her back, and monumental construction projects such as the Arch of Titus and the Temple of Peace in Rome.

Romans not only celebrated victory; they *worshiped* Victory, the Roman goddess of military victory named *Victoria* in Latin or *Nike* in Greek. Portrayed as a winged goddess, she is the inspiration for the wing-like "swoosh" on Nike running shoes today. In the province of Asia Minor, John and the Christians of his churches were confronted daily with images of Rome's flying Victory goddess emblazoned on monuments and altars in their cities. Provincial cities erected statues of Victory—or Nike—sometimes with her foot on the globe, symbolizing

Rome's conquest of the whole world. Coins portrayed her standing beside the emperor, a daily reminder of Rome's military success. The message was unmistakable: no one should dare to oppose Rome's divinely sanctioned dominance and victory over the whole world. Rome's military victories assured peace and prosperity.

But John, writing only one generation after Rome's crushing of the Jewish Revolt, declared a prophetic "no" to Rome's vision of victory and imperial conquest. Indeed, John lays claim to the empire's own word *nike* and redefines it in order to declare this prophetic "no." In my view, the sixteen references to *nikan* in Revelation can best be understood as John's countermessage to the Roman Empire's theology of victory, or *nike*.

The theme of "conquering" or "victory" first appears in Revelation 2 and 3, in the seven opening letters to the seven churches. These letters name followers of Jesus as "victors" (*ho nikōn*, literally "the one who conquers"), from the Greek verb *nikan*. John's labeling of readers as "victors" or "the one who conquers" right from the outset of the book, using the same politically loaded term as the name of Rome's goddess Nike, or Victory, sets up the book's program of challenging Rome's own imperial theology of Victory. "To the victor I will give to eat of the fruit of the tree of life that is in the paradise of God," the letter to Ephesus promises (Rev 2:7). Six more promises of future blessing are given to "the victor" in Revelation's opening letters to the churches—promises that will come to fulfillment in the final vision of New Jerusalem, at the end of the book, when the "victors" receive their inheritance.

The most important reference to the theme of conquering is the vision of Jesus in the divine throne room in Rev 5:5—a vision that "lay(s) the rhetorical foundation and provide(s) the key symbolic images for all that follows."[4] God holds a sealed scroll that must be opened. The voice from the throne tells John, "Do not weep. See, the Lion of the tribe of Judah, the Root of David, has conquered [*enikēsen*], so that he can open the scroll and its seven seals." But here Revelation pulls off an amazing surprise, a complete reversal of imagery. Instead of the conquering lion that readers are led to expect, Revelation introduces a Lamb. The fact that the Jesus is introduced as a slain Lamb rather than the expected lion in Revelation 5 gives the first and most important image for God's nonviolent model of conquering. The Greek word *arnion* is not just "lamb" but the diminutive form, like "little lamb," or "Fluffy" as one pastor calls it. The Lamb is slaughtered but standing—that is, crucified but risen to life. The image has no precedence in Jewish apocalyptic literature, as Loren Johns has convincingly shown.[5] Although some scholars have posited that the Lamb of Revelation builds on a militaristic lamb-redeemer figure in the traditions of early Judaism (*Test. Jos.* 19.8; *Test. Ben.* 3.8; *1 Enoch* 89–90), or on the astrological ram constellation Aries, the image of Jesus as a Lamb is the creation of the author. The goal of the image is to stress Jesus' vulnerability. At the very heart of God is a slain Lamb, Jesus. And the key to the book is that this slaughtered Lamb has somehow "conquered."

Revelation next introduces Rome's imperial model of violent conquering, a model very different from that of Jesus. This Roman model is represented in Revelation 6 by the four powerful horses of Roman power—conquest, war, famine, and death. Each of the horses reveals a different and terrifying aspect of Rome, with special attention to the economic injustice unveiled by the third horse. The first horse brings victory or "conquering" (*nikan*), a term repeated twice for emphasis: "I looked, and there was a white horse! Its rider had a bow; a crown was given to him, and he came out conquering and to conquer" (Rev 6:2). In subsequent chapters the beasts of Revelation 11 and 13 also represent Rome's violent conquering. The imperial beast that ascends from the bottomless pit, for example, "will make war [*polemos*] and conquer and kill" God's two witnesses (Rev 11:7), leaving their dead bodies to lie in the street.

The term "conquering" can thus be used both violently and nonviolently in Revelation—but that does not mean that "conquering" for God's people involves violence as the writers of the Left Behind series and others want to claim. Indeed, Rev 12:11 describes the way God's people conquer: "They have conquered him [Satan] by the blood of the Lamb / and by the word of their testimony [*martyria*], / for they did not cling to life even in the face of death."

This verse is crucial for determining the role of readers in the plot of Revelation. The first way God's people conquer in Rev 12:11 is "by the blood of the Lamb." Blood is a strong theme in Revelation, a fact that the Left Behind series and Hal Lindsey's works capitalize on with an

almost ghoulish fixation. The fourth Left Behind novel, *Soul Harvest*, for
example, closes with the image of hail turning to blood (based on Rev
8:7) and a readiness to welcome God's war: "Following God's shower of
hail, fire, and blood, remaining skeptics were few. There was no longer
any ambiguity about the war."[6]

But does the blood of the Lamb necessitate war and bloodshed, as
Lindsey and LaHaye/Jenkins want to claim? Not if the Lamb's way of
conquering is the model. If the slain Lamb is the model for Christians,
it means that the blood of Revelation is first of all the *Lamb's own blood*,
shed for the world. Even the blood staining Jesus' garments in Rev 19:13
must be presumed to be his *own* blood, not anyone else's—despite echoes
of Isa 63:1-6, the winepress of God's wrath and the staining of garments
with the juice of enemies, referenced in Rev 19:15.[7] To follow the model
of Jesus the Lamb means that God's people conquer not by attacking
anyone or shedding the blood of others, but rather by identifying with
Jesus' own blood that was shed when he was crucified by the Romans.
This point has been convincingly argued by some of the great advocates
of peace who have written on Revelation—Mennonite theologian John
Howard Yoder and most recently Lee Griffith—and it is supported by
the best New Testament scholars on Revelation.[8] Although "Revelation
has acquired the reputation of being a book of considerable blood and
terror," Griffith argues in *The War on Terrorism and the Terror of God*, this
reputation "may not be so well deserved." Revelation does not advocate
the use of violence or bloodshed. Revelation is more a book about terror
defeated than terror inflicted, "which is why worship and liturgy are such
a central feature of the book."[9]

The second way that God's people conquer Satan in Rev 12:11 is by
giving their word of testimony and being willing to give even their lives.
"Testimony" or witness (Greek: *martyria*) has amazing power both for
Jesus and for his followers in Revelation. The term comes from a court-
room context, as Elisabeth Schüssler Fiorenza, Pablo Richard, and
others have noted. The idea is that Christians conquer by putting the
unjust empire on trial and telling the truth about it. The story of the
two witnesses in Revelation 11 shows the power of testimony, as does
Jesus' own testimony (Rev 1:2). Chilean scholar Pablo Richard draws
an analogy to the power of testimony in oppressive contexts today: "In

Revelation, testimony always has a power to change history, both in heaven and on earth. . . . John believes that the faith of the holy ones is what is going to make the empire tremble."[10]

Revelation thus promotes an ethic of resistance to empire—specifically *nonviolent* resistance through the power of *martyria* or testimony, a word that also has the dual meaning of martyrdom. John identifies with his readers in Asia Minor who share both in the tribulation, inflicted by the empire, and resistance to it (Rev 1:9). (We should translate the Greek word *hypomonē* not as "patient endurance" but as "resistance," following the suggestion of Pablo Richard.) The resistance the book envisions is what Ward Ewing calls "Lamb Power."[11] Revelation aims to convince readers that Jesus' model of "Lamb Power" is a model of victory more powerful than Rome's model of *nike* or violent military conquering.

Throughout the middle chapters of Revelation, the words "conquering" (*nikan*) and "make war" (*polemeō*) continue to appear in close association, fueling the impression that the book is pro-war. There is no question that the book is full of conflict. But even in terms of the words themselves, there is a crucial difference between the words "conquer" (*nikan*) and "make war" (*polemeō*) in Revelation. Evil rulers "make war" (*polemeō*) on the Lamb one final time in Rev 17:14, but the Lamb "conquers" them—a typical use of the two words.

A nonviolent reading of Revelation thus emerges by tracing the book's careful redefinition of the word "conquer" (*nikan*) to make clear that the Lamb and God's people conquer only by their testimony and faithfulness—not by making war or killing. War is something done by evil beasts and by Rome, not by God's saints or the Lamb. The Lamb never "makes war." To be sure, two verses of Revelation do refer to Jesus as "making war" (Rev 2:16 and 19:11), but even here, the *way* he makes war is crucial. Jesus makes war not with a sword of battle but "by the sword of his mouth"—that is, his word. Jesus' word is his only weapon. This is a reversal almost as unexpected as the substitution of a lamb instead of a lion, and it undercuts violence by emphasizing Jesus' testimony and the word of God.

Moreover, in terms of ethics, there is no reason for thinking that any Christians take part in the war in Revelation 19. The authors of *Left Behind* and others who follow John Nelson Darby's nineteenth-century dispensationalist theology try to claim that "raptured" saints are part of the "army of heaven" that returns to earth with Jesus after seven years to fight in what they call the "Glorious Appearing." But there is no Rapture in Revelation or anywhere in the scriptures. The fact that the army in Rev 19:14 is said to be clothed in white linen does not make it equivalent to the "saints" or Christians, as dispensationalists try to argue on the basis of the saints' white linen in Rev 19:8.[12] The army in Rev 19:14 is clearly identified as a heavenly army, and, amazingly, no actual attack or war is ever pictured. The war is over as soon as it begins. This is because the victory has already been won in Jesus' crucifixion and is not to be fought in a final cataclysmic war.

The message of Revelation becomes thus a reframing of the whole concept of "victory," giving victory first to the Lamb by his crucifixion and resurrection, and then to us. Nowhere in Revelation do God's people "wage war." What they do is "conquer" or "become victors" (the same word in Greek)—and they do that by the Lamb's own blood and by their courageous testimony, not through Armageddon or war. In contrast to Rome's theology that defined victory as violent military conquest, Revelation develops a countertheology of the victory of Jesus, God's slain Lamb, in which "evil is overcome by suffering love," not by superior power.[13]

The narrative of Revelation "turns the popular American understanding of the Apocalypse on its head," as David Barr argues convincingly. Revelation transforms and subverts violent stories, as in chapter 5 when the expected lion is replaced by the Lamb:

> It is poor reading to overlook this inversion and to read as if the Lamb has not replaced the Lion in this story. Similar inversions occur at every point in the story—even in the climactic scene in which the heaven Warrior kills all his enemies, for his conquest is by means of a sword that comes from his mouth, not by the power of his arm.[14]

Because the central image of Revelation is the slain Lamb, not the Lion, "John's story stands firmly against violence and domination."[15] For all its holy war imagery, Revelation does not promote war.

Hijacking the Lamb

What does this discussion of apocalyptic violence have to do with Jews and Christian contesting texts? First of all there is the question of how the divine warrior in Revelation both draws on and changes the portrait of the divine warrior in the Hebrew scriptures. The argument I am trying to make—that the blood of the Lamb is the Lamb's own blood—becomes more difficult if this image draws on Isaiah 63, where the blood on the warrior's garments is that of Edom, the enemy of God. I believe that Revelation deliberately transforms Isaiah 63 and other imagery of the Hebrew Bible in a more nonviolent direction—but of course, that argument can be problematic if Christians set up the Hebrew Bible as a kind of violent "foil" over against which the New Testament is made to look nonviolent. This kind of characterizing of the Hebrew Bible as more violent than the New Testament is prevalent among some Christians, and we need to speak against any such tendency. We must also recall the many ways Revelation builds on nonviolent and even healing imagery in the Hebrew Bible—such as the healing tree of life of Ezekiel 47.

Equally important is the interpretive question of how Revelation, especially the warrior Jesus in Revelation 19, gets used by American fundamentalist Christians to justify war, whether in Iraq or Lebanon, because they view end-times war and Israeli sovereignty as God's plan for the Middle East. In my view, today's Christian fundamentalists have hijacked the nonviolent Lamb of Revelation as the predominant image of Jesus and replaced him with the fierce Lion, a move that has terrifying and violent consequences for both Jews and Christians, especially when they seek to use the Bible in U.S. foreign policy. Drawing on the interpretation invented by British preacher John Nelson Darby in the 1830s, they split the traditional second coming of Jesus into two parts—first a so-called Rapture, when born-again Christians get to escape up to heaven, then seven years of tribulation, followed by the so-called Glorious Appearing seven years later, when Jesus returns for what ends up being a third time. They claim that this scenario is laid out in Dan 9:25-27 and that the world is now counting down for a series of ever-worsening disasters leading up to the end. It is an inaccurate and even dangerous notion. In the near-term, however, it promotes a very pro-Israel foreign policy, and it is for that reason that some right-wing Israelis have been willing to accept support from such Christians.

Dispensationalists are to be commended for giving an important corrective to supersessionist views of Christianity. God's covenant with Jews has not been superseded by the church, as some Christians have wrongly argued. Yet dispensationalist fundamentalists operate with an almost apartheid-like separation between Christians and Jews, a mentality that also blinds them to seeing Palestinian Christians in the Middle East as God's people. They also operate with an extremely deterministic view of prophecy and even of God that we must repudiate.

I am grateful for the emphasis on the importance of the state of Israel as a prerequisite for any Jewish-Christian dialogue. I emphatically support Israel's existence within pre-1967 borders, and I believe we must condemn suicide bombings, rocket attacks, and all violence in the region. I also believe that we must constantly be working to repudiate anti-Semitism as my own Evangelical Lutheran Church in America did with Martin Luther's writings. Christian scholars and communities must also counteract anti-Judaism in our New Testament interpretation and that of our students.

This whole question of support for Israel is one of the most difficult in Jewish-Christian dialogue. Does support for Israel mean that Christians can never critique Israel's actions? As a Lutheran Christian I have a responsibility not only to Jews but also to Lutheran Palestinians longing for an end to Israeli occupation, who suffer as a result of Israel's construction of the separation barrier. While I support Israel's right to exist and condemn all violence against Israel, I cannot remain silent in the face of expansion of Israeli settlements and settler roads in the West Bank, demolition of Palestinian homes in East Jerusalem, and construction of the separation barrier deep within the West Bank rather than on the internationally recognized "Green Line" border. I am concerned for Palestinian refugees, for example, who are no longer able to get to the Augusta Victoria Hospital on the Mount of Olives for medical care because of the separation barrier. I draw on Jewish voices who eloquently argue that the only way Israel can truly find security is through fostering the establishment of a viable, contiguous Palestinian state alongside a secure Israel. Given the precarious existence of

Palestinian Christians today and their precipitously dwindling numbers especially in Jerusalem, I hope that Jews as well as Christians can agree to support the continued presence of Palestinian Christians in Jerusalem and can work for a vision of a shared Jerusalem as a capital for both states. Such support for a Palestinian state would run counter to the program of right-wing, Left Behind Christian fundamentalists who want Jerusalem to become an exclusively Israeli city. Tim LaHaye and others invoke the biblical vision of Revelation and other texts to support their position, but theirs is a misreading of both the biblical text and the current situation.

Where can we find biblical resources for such a shared vision? The book of Revelation ends not with Armageddon but with the image of New Jerusalem (Revelation 21–22), a multiethnic city with open gates. Through the center of this beautiful city flows a river of life, watering the tree of life. The leaves of the tree of life are "for the healing of the nations" (Rev 22:2). Could such a world-healing tree of life, drawing on the prophet Ezekiel's vision (Ezekiel 47), offer an image of healing for the Middle East? The tree of life is holy also in Islamic tradition and offers an image of ecological healing that our world urgently needs. In contrast to fundamentalist visions of end-times violence and triumphalism, the heart of the Bible's apocalyptic vision for our world is not violence and death but rather the renewal and healing of the nations—beginning with Jerusalem.

Unbinding Isaac

MARTYRDOM AND ITS EXEGETICAL ALTERNATIVES

STEVEN WEITZMAN

If Abraham did not do at all what the story tells, if perhaps because of the local conditions of that day it was something entirely different, then let us forget him, for what is the value of going to the trouble of remembering that past which cannot become a present?

—SØREN KIERKEGAARD, *Fear and Trembling*

Among many still-reverberating cultural effects, the events of September 11, 2001, have changed the guild of biblical studies. Seeking to distance religion from the terrible violence of that day, politicians and pundits argued in the immediate aftermath of 9/11 that those responsible for this catastrophe had hijacked an otherwise peaceful religious tradition, twisting it to legitimize an aberrant ideology outside normative Islam. Recent biblical scholars have challenged that view, arguing that violence is at the core of all three major Western religions. In his 2003 presidential address to the Society of Biblical Literature, John Collins observed that the justification of violence "is not limited to Islam, but can also be found in the attitudes and assumptions that are deeply embedded in the Jewish and Christian scriptures."[1] In a still more recent article, Yvette Sherwood draws a direct line between Genesis 22, where Abraham is ready to slay his son Isaac, and the 9/11 hijackers who believed their slaughter of the innocent to be as justified as the patriarch's would-be sacrifice.[2] These scholars come to this issue from very different perspectives, but in the end, they reach the same conclusion: 9/11 imposes a new interpretive responsibility on critical biblical scholarship—to expose the Bible's dark side, its sanction of violence.

I take the ethical challenge posed by these scholars seriously but also believe that implicating the Bible in the history of violence is not the only task of biblical scholarship. Collins sometimes speaks as if the Bible is a moral agent, as if it can be held accountable for how it is construed by later interpreters. In fact, without interpretation, the Bible is inert, the components of a bomb, perhaps, but not the bomber. It is the reader who detonates its interpretive potential and is therefore accountable for any consequences. My own view is that it is the responsibility of the biblical scholar to expose *all* of the ethical options latent in the Bible's lines, or perched between them.

To illustrate this point I want to focus on a particular reading of biblical violence developed in Jewish antiquity, one that aims to reinterpret narratives often used to justify the act of martyrdom. Martyrdom has come to be associated with Islam, but of course it has deep roots in Christian tradition, which was initiated through an act of voluntary death and ultimately derives from Jewish culture as it developed in the Greco-Roman period (though some recent scholars of Jewish antiquity, noting that the term "martyrdom" to describe voluntary death only arises in later Christian discourse, balk at using this language to describe earlier Jewish practice). Although sharply curtailed in later Jewish interpretive tradition, martyrdom remains a possibility to this day within Jewish culture, as documented by the tombstone of Baruch Goldstein, slain after he killed twenty-nine Palestinians in the Tomb of the Patriarchs in Hebron:

> Here lies the saint, Dr. Baruch Kappel Goldstein, blessed be the memory of the righteous and holy man, may the Lord avenge his blood, who devoted his soul to the Jews, Jewish religion and Jewish land for His hands are innocent and his heart is pure. He was killed as a martyr of God on the 14th of Adar, Purim, in the year 5754.

The Hebrew Bible certainly has been read as licensing this kind of behavior, but the history of biblical interpretation demonstrates that there has long been more than one way to respond to it, some readers finding in the very texts that seem to justify martyrdom a life-affirming alternative.

Before I examine one of these responses, I need to make it make clear from the outset that there is a profound difference between ancient Jewish martyrdom and that associated with contemporary suicide bombings or attacks like that of Baruch Goldstein. The perpetrators of the latter kind of martyrdom use their deaths to take others with them—they are murderers as well as martyrs. Ancient martyrs sacrificed their own lives alone. Having made this distinction, however, we also must acknowledge that the difference is not always as sharp as one would like it to be. In fact, some ancient sources cast Jewish martyrdom as an aggressive act committed in the midst of a violent struggle, expressly undertaken by its perpetrators so as to bring harm to the enemy, if only indirectly. This is the implication of one of the earliest accounts we have of Jewish martyrdom, the account in 2 Maccabees of the mother and her seven sons put to death by Antiochus IV during his efforts to suppress Jewish religious tradition. Each of the brothers says something before dying, anticipating resurrection as a reward for their fidelity to the law and venturing to predict that God will exact revenge against the enemy. The last of these speeches is of particular interest:

> [The seventh son] said, "What are you waiting for? I will not obey the king's command, but I obey the command of the law that was given to our ancestors through Moses. But you, who have contrived all sorts of evil against the Hebrews, will certainly not escape the hands of God. For we are suffering because of our own sins. And if our living Lord is angry for a little while, to rebuke and discipline us, he will again be reconciled with his own servants. . . . I, like my brothers, give up body and life for the laws of our ancestors, appealing to God to show mercy soon to our nation and by trials and plagues to make you confess that he alone is God, and through me and my brothers to bring to an end the wrath of the Almighty that has justly fallen on our whole nation." (2 Macc 7:30-33, 37-38)

In the son's choice to accept death rather than betray the laws, this speech suggests that the Maccabean martyrs were not merely being pious but seeking to launch an indirect attack against the enemy. Seeing the suffering of his people, an outraged God would intervene to exact vengeance against the enemy. Early Jewish martyrs lacked the weaponry to harm their enemy, but if Maccabean literature is any indication, they did not lack the will, believing that their willing sacrifice paved the way for the enemy's defeat.

The practice of martyrdom, as Marc Brettler has argued, is not to be found in the Hebrew Bible itself, except in its latest composition, Daniel, in sections composed in the Hellenistic period.[3] As read by Jews in the Greco-Roman period, however, the Bible was thought to exemplify the practice. The story of the binding of Isaac in Genesis 22 was particularly influential—that is, Genesis 22 as interpreted by early Jews who imagined Isaac willingly accepting his sacrifice.[4] Another account of the Maccabean martyrs from the first or second century CE, in 4 Maccabees, explicitly evokes the Isaac of this tradition, the brothers citing him as a model: "While one said, 'Courage, brother,' another said, 'Bear up nobly,' and another reminded them, 'Remember whence you came, and the father by whose hand Isaac would have submitted to being slain for the sake of religion'" (4 Macc 13:10-11). In the *Biblical Antiquities* (*Liber antiquitatum biblicarum* [*L.A.B.*]), a first-century paraphrase of biblical narrative falsely attributed to Philo, Jephtha's daughter also recalls Isaac's example as she exhorts her father to make good on his vow to sacrifice her:

> Who is there who would be sad in death, seeing the people freed? Or do you not remember what happened in the days of our fathers when the father placed the son as a holocaust, and he did not refuse him but gladly gave consent to him, and the one being offered was ready and the one who was offering was rejoicing? And now do not annul everything you have vowed but carry it out. (*L.A.B.* 40.2)

When this reading of the Isaac story first arose is not clear, but it seems roughly contemporaneous with Jewish martyrdom itself, going back at least to the first century BCE judging from an apparent allusion to the tradition in a biblical paraphrase recovered from Qumran, 4Q225.[5] The image of Isaac willingly embracing his sacrifice would continue in later rabbinic literature, one sage going so far as to imagine Isaac binding himself upon the altar (*Sifre Deuteronomy* 32).[6]

My focus, however, is on another way of reading the Hebrew Bible, one developed in an effort to discredit or at least qualify the heroics of martyrdom. The interpretation in question was one developed by the first-century Jewish historian Josephus. A major source of information about Jewish history in the Greco-Roman period, Josephus's writings also preserve important and complex examples of early Jewish biblical exegesis. In what follows I explore how Josephus used biblical interpretation to develop a subtle critique of martyrdom and even perhaps to develop an alternative to it.

At first glance, Josephus would seem to admire the act of dying for one's religion as a noble way of preserving one's autonomy, dignity, and tradition.[7] A recent survey of his literary corpus finds sixty-two accounts of voluntary death there, and in many of these scenes, the act of voluntary death is motivated by the pious wish to defend the law or by an uncompromising commitment to God. Indeed, Josephus reports in the *Jewish War* that he himself had been "prepared to die" to save Jerusalem from destruction (*J.W.* 5.419). In other passages, however, Josephus expresses deep reservations about taking one's own life, discrediting it as a rash and even impious act. He is most explicit in his opposition when explaining his own refusal to commit suicide during the Jewish Revolt. In 67 CE Josephus and his men found themselves pinned down by the Romans in a cave at Yodefat (also known as Jotapata) with no avenue of escape. Many of their comrades had already taken their lives by that point (*J.W.* 3.331), and the remainder now resolved to do so as well. Given what he says elsewhere about Jews cheerfully dying for the law, one might think that Josephus gladly would have joined them, but in fact he reports that he did everything he could to talk them out of it, appealing to philosophical and theological arguments against suicide in a lengthy speech. He points out that nature itself opposes suicide; among animals, after all, there is not one that deliberately seeks to kill itself (369–70). God rejects it too, Josephus argues later in the speech, condemning suicides to hell (375–77). Josephus's men were unmoved by his appeal and forced Josephus into a suicide pact, but he somehow managed to be among the last two soldiers standing and persuaded his fellow that it was best to surrender to the Romans after all (387–91). The Josephus of this scene is an ardent dissenter from the ethic of martyrdom.

Josephus's reservations surface in subtler ways in his descriptions of past acts of voluntary death. Let us consider Josephus's famous account of the mass suicide at Masada as a case study. His account certainly contains a number of elements that would have resonated as heroic for both Jewish and Romans readers: the rebel commander Eleazar gives two lengthy speeches that make suicide appear to be a reasoned and pious act undertaken to preserve freedom and nobility (*J.W.* 7.323–88). Reinforcing the nobility of the act is the response of Roman spectators within the narrative, the soldiers who discover the bodies of the slain: "Instead of exulting as over enemies, they admired the nobility of their resolve and their contempt of death" (7.406). Even as it sends out these positive signals, however, the narrative calls the rationality of the act into question. Thus, while Eleazar's speech creates a first impression of reasoned and calm deliberation, that impression quickly breaks down as his followers, "overpowered by some uncontrollable impulse," cut him off and rush about "like men possessed" (7.389).[8]

It is tempting to see something self-serving about Josephus's opposition to voluntary death. Since he himself faced the choice of whether to take his own life or surrender to the Romans when trapped, Josephus's negative portrait of voluntary death can be seen as a retroactive effort to justify his decision not to kill himself, using Jewish history to expose the act's folly and impiety. The historian may have had other reasons for opposing voluntary death as well. As I have argued elsewhere, Josephus's reservations about voluntary death were in fact reflective of the time and place in which he wrote.[9] The Romans had their own tradition of heroic voluntary death embodied by figures like Seneca, but as classicist Donald McGuire has shown, in the period in which Josephus was writing, the Flavian age, many Roman writers were deeply ambivalent about the act, undercutting apparently laudatory accounts of suicide by associating the act with irrationality, recklessness, and criminality.[10] Flavian authors had good reason to avoid appearing to endorse voluntary death, for to do so was to risk censorship or even death by an imperial rule deeply suspicious of suicide as the one act it could not control. McGuire argues that the negative strain in Flavian suicide accounts, their effort to undercut the heroism of voluntary death, reflects an effort to evade the peril of extolling this practice. This same explanation can be applied to Josephus, who, as a Flavian author, took the same risks as his contemporaries in writing about suicide.

Whatever the reasons for Josephus's reservations about suicide, in expressing those reservations, he faced a challenge: his opposition to voluntary death was at odds with Jewish tradition as understood by many Jews in this period, a tradition that sanctioned martyrdom in defense of religious tradition. As Josephus acknowledges in his account of the Masada suicides, there were many arguments in favor of voluntary death, including the idea that Jewish law itself requires Jews to die rather than surrender their freedom (*J.W.* 7.387). Even moderates seem ready to embrace the act when they feel Jewish tradition is threatened, such as the high priest Ananus, who despite his moderation declares a readiness to sacrifice himself for God and the Temple: "It were a noble end to die at the sacred portals, and to sacrifice our lives, if not for our wives and children, yet for God and for the sanctuary" (*J.W.* 4.191). Reflected in such passages is an acknowledgment of voluntary death as an admirable course for Jews who saw no other way to defend their tradition. How then did Josephus reconcile his own opposition to martyrdom with the practice's heroic luster for Jews?

Often, it would seem, Josephus does *not* attempt to reconcile the two strains; many of his suicide accounts simply seem conflicted or equivocal, as we have seen in the Masada narrative. In a few episodes, however, the historian takes a different approach, compromising between martyrdom and its rejection by developing a kind of middle ground between them, what I would refer to as the act of would-be martyrdom, an act that emulates martyrdom without committing actual self-violence. One place where Josephus hints at this option is in his retelling of the Maccabean Revolt. Drawing on 1 Maccabees, Josephus recounts the speech delivered to the Maccabees by their dying father Mattathias, who urges them

> to remain constant as such and to be superior to all force and compulsion, being so prepared in spirit as to die for the laws, if need be, and bearing this in mind, that when the Deity sees you so disposed, He will not forget you, but in admiration of your

heroism will give them back to you again, and will restore to you your liberty. (*Ant.* 12.281)

Josephus is here paraphrasing a preexisting source, Mattathias's death-bed speech in 1 Maccabees 2:49-64—"Now, my children, show zeal for the law, and give your lives for the covenant" (v. 50)—but he has subtly altered his source to allow for the possibility that the Maccabees do not actually have to die to achieve salvation. Merely being "prepared in spirit as to die" can ensure God's protection. The ensuing history of the Maccabean Revolt as Josephus tells it bears this out, for when the enemy sees that the Maccabees are *"prepared to die* if they could not live as free men," he retreats in fear, thus making it possible for the Maccabees to reclaim the Temple.[11] In Josephus's version of the Maccabean Revolt, it is possible to achieve what the martyr does, to save the law, without actually dying for it: a mere willingness to die, *the exhibition of intent*, can have the same effect.

Josephus introduces a similar revision in his account of how Jews saved their religious traditions under Roman rule. When the procurator Pilate attempted to install imperial images in Jerusalem, the Jews were able to stop him through a dramatic performance:

> [The Jews,] casting themselves prostrate and baring their throats, declared that they had gladly welcomed death rather than make bold to transgress the wise provisions of the laws. Pilate, astonished at the strength of their devotion to the laws, straightaway removed the images from Jerusalem. (*Ant.* 18.58)

By means of a similar performance, this time before the governor Petronius, the Jews stalled Caligula's order to install a statue in the Temple (*J.W.* 2.196–98). Philo, who preceeds Josephus, tells similar stories, but in his version it is not the Jews' readiness to die that saves the law, but other factors.[12] In Philo's account of the Pilate incident, the Jews write a letter to the emperor Tiberius that prompts him to intervene. In Philo's version of the Petronius incident, the Jews do offer themselves as a sacrifice, but also essential is Petronius's innate sympathy for the Jews. Josephus modifies both of these stories so that they reflect the same idea that he inscribed into his account of the Maccabean Revolt: the Jews' willingness to die allows them to save the law without actually sacrificing themselves.

Josephus's reading of the Bible subtly legitimizes the kind of balance he was trying to strike. Josephus uses some biblical stories of proto-martyrdom to advance his criticism of voluntary death. As we have noted from Pseudo-Philo's *Biblical Antiquities*, Jephtha's daughter was transformed by early interpreters into a proto-martyr, recalling Isaac as she urges her father to carry through with her sacrifice. Josephus's retelling of Judges 11 reflects this tradition, noting that she accepted death at her father's hand "without displeasure." Whatever admiration her selflessness elicits is undercut, however, when Josephus later observes that her sacrifice was "neither sanctioned by the law nor well-pleasing to God" (*Ant.* 5.263–66). Here is that note of criticism that is characteristic of Josephus's portrait of voluntary death, the suggestion that however courageous and admirable the impulse to die, actually doing so is at odds with Jewish tradition.

When recounting another biblical episode—the binding of Isaac—Josephus seems to use biblical interpretation to model the ideal of *virtual* martyrdom reflected in the Pilate and Petronius episodes. Following earlier interpretive tradition in its treatment of Isaac as a prototypical martyr, Josephus turns Isaac into a willing accomplice in his own sacrifice:

The son of such a father could not but be brave-hearted. . . . He exclaimed that he deserved never to have been born at all were he to reject the decision of God and of his father and not readily resign himself to what was the will of both . . . and with that he rushed to the altar and his doom. (*Ant.* 1.232)

What is missing in this episode are the negative elements that surface so consistently in Josephus's other accounts of voluntary death, the intimations of irrationality and recklessness. What distinguishes Isaac from someone like Jephtha's daughter, of course, is that Isaac does not actually die in the end but, as Josephus goes on to recount in *Ant.* 1.234, would live on to attain "extreme old age." In Josephus's hands, Isaac becomes the prototype not of martyrdom but of virtual martyrdom, showing the resolve to die in obedience to God, coming to the point of death, but then being spared through the intervention of a sympathetic authority and going on to a long and happy life. As read by Josephus, Genesis 22 establishes the possibility of successfully balancing between the martyrological impulse and survival.

Josephus's efforts both to endorse and to distance himself from voluntary death remind me of a contemporary figure famous, or infamous, for his ability to vacillate between survival and martyrdom: Yassir Arafat. In the days leading up to his death, when Arafat's health was astonishingly ambiguous, a Palestinian spokesperson made a statement that remains with me to this day as a fitting epitaph: "Arafat is in a critical state between life and death." It strikes me that this is an excellent description of Arafat's entire career: When the Israeli tanks trapped him in his compound in Ramallah, Arafat declared himself ready to die, telling CNN, "I hope I will be a martyr in the Holy Land" (March 29, 2002), a message repeated often on Palestinian Authority television. And yet somehow, as happened so often in his life, Arafat managed to survive even as he embraced death. Josephus was a similar kind of figure. In his personal conduct, he was certainly Arafat-like: besieged by the Romans at Yodefat, he too declared himself ready to die, and yet after allowing his comrades-in-arms to take their lives, he changed his mind and made his escape to the Romans. His narrative reflects a similar kind of vacillation, sometimes embracing martyrdom, sometimes rejecting it, often hovering somewhere in between.

One of the risks of this kind of equivocation is that it tends to inspire distrust and contempt. This is what happened to Josephus. He was reviled by fellow Jews who, thinking he had killed himself heroically, were disgusted when they discovered he was still alive. Although Josephus hardly offers an example worth emulating, his interpretive maneuvers nonetheless merit some reflection as one wonders whether there is an antidote to the celebration of martyrdom in our own day. Josephus found a way to remain true to martyrological tradition, extolling the courage of would-be martyrs like Isaac even while rejecting martyrdom's self-defeating irrationality.

"Is there anyone in Palestine who does not dream of martyrdom?" Arafat once asked (September 19, 2003). In a culture that embraces martyrdom as a glorious form of heroism, outsiders or moderate insiders who reject it as immoral or self-defeating risk discrediting themselves. Is there any way to reach the martyrological mind-set and convince it not to sacrifice itself? Perhaps not, but Josephus does model one possible approach, to continue to valorize the intent to die while discrediting those who actually act on this intention. In fact, rabbinic Judaism arguably embraced this approach in order to survive. To be sure, it has never fully abandoned martyrdom as an option; indeed, some Jews embraced it during the Crusades and the expulsion from Spain in response to persecution. Still, rabbinic exegetes, seeking to balance sanctification of God's name (the rabbinic term for martyrdom) with the sanctity of life, did find ways to curtail martyrdom and even developed forms of virtual martyrdom—nonlethal acts reckoned as equivalent to martyrdom, such as killing one's evil desire by reciting the Shema with devotion, for instance, or visualizing one's death.[13]

There are implications here not just for Judaism but for other religious traditions as well. From what little I know of Islam, for example, it too has developed various forms of virtual martyrdom. In one tradition, for instance, Islam promises the one who calls others to prayer the reward of forty thousand martyrs.[14] Whether such traditions can counteract more lethal exegesis remains to be seen, but the Qur'an holds out interpretive options as surely as the Jewish scriptures do. None of this is to acquit the Hebrew Bible of its historical role in legitimizing violence, but it does aim to mitigate this charge by taking note of the many interpretive options latent within the Bible—the embrace of death, the embrace of life, and, as Josephus seems to have discovered, the embrace of a posture somewhere in between. The failure to recognize the interpretive possibilities is a measure not of the text's moral limits but of the poverty of one's own literary and ethical imagination.

PART 3

Religious Identity and the Other in the New Testament

The New Testament, Religious Identity, and the Other

BARBARA BOWE

In addressing the New Testament, religious identity, and the other, I will begin by drawing together some important theoretical perspectives on what we mean by "the other." Then I review some of the more recent reflections on the process of religious self-definition, the notions of boundary maintenance, and the role of conflict in this self-defining process. And, finally, I want to reflect briefly on the rhetoric of difference (both ancient and modern) and specifically on the rhetorical use of vilification as a tool of self-definition and its deleterious effects. In chapter 7 in this volume, Sarah J. Tanzer addresses more specifically some concrete examples from the Gospel of John and its corresponding communal situation on this same topic.

Who Is the Other?

Let me begin with the question, who is the other? Philosophers teach us that the human condition engages us in "three interrelated and overlapping spheres, each of which is a necessary condition of the other two: the inter-human, the social, and individual agents."[1] The interhuman sphere refers to that ordinary human experience of continuous encounter with other human beings outside of ourselves. This encounter—whether benign, engaging, or confrontational—has three aspects often referred to as the awareness of alterity, inter-subjectivity, and the interpersonal encounter. The notion of alterity points to the fact that we become aware, first of all, that there is a great chasm separating us from those outside ourselves, making it impossible for my subjectivity to know or experience truly that of another. In some respects, this statement is a truism that needs no demonstration or proof. But to quote Edward Farley in *Good and Evil: Interpreting a Human Condition*, "That which makes the other genuinely other is not a temporary obstacle which a cognitive strategy will remove. Gathering more information, changing perspective, adopting different methods of inquiry, or developing a better technological instrument will not give me the other's experiencing as my experiencing."[2] At the same time, this experience I have of the other's otherness is also an awareness that in the eyes of that person, "I" too am also other: seen, experienced, interpreted by someone else outside myself. Thus my own autonomy and its claims are called into question.

Second, to speak of intersubjectivity is to acknowledge that even as I am aware of my own solitary existence and separation from all those outside myself, as I encounter the other I am somehow drawn into the mystery of the other. This unconscious movement toward the other (whether for good or ill) presupposes the existence of intersubjectivity as a prior condition. Or as Farley again contends, "We can try to jump the gulf to the other only if the gulf is in some way already bridged by intersubjectivity."[3]

Third, there is the interpersonal realm, and this is the aspect that concerns our topic most directly. The interpersonal is the arena of conscious and intentional turning toward the other. Here, two great Jewish philosophers, Martin Buber and Emmanuel Levinas, have especially led the way. They build on earlier writings of Johann Fichte, Georg Hegel, Edmund Husserl, and especially Max Scheler, who saw in the very structure of human emotions such as empathy, sympathy, and the sense of communal fellowship, the engagement of an interpersonal dynamic that affirms "a genuine emotional participation in what makes the other."[4] But Buber and Levinas go further and want to look more closely both at conscious dialogue and at the mystery of personal encounter as the key to our true humanness. For Buber, to be human is to stand in the presence of an other and to be in the midst of the I–Thou relation, with its potential for separateness and for dialogue. It is this encounter that touches the core of what it means to be human. It is a moment fraught with both terror and possibility.

For Levinas, the metaphor of the face—*le visage*—embodies the fullness of what it means to be "other." "Every face says, 'I am other to you.' Every face says, 'I am not you.' Every face says, 'Don't kill me, don't absorb me into your world, don't obliterate me by making me the same as you. I am other. I am different. I am not you.'"[5] But there is always a danger lurking in that otherness. "Our everyday world negotiations show us that the other is like ourselves: needy, unpredictable, self-oriented, and dangerous. Thus, relations between others are negotiations of self-interest about power, status, and use."[6] Levinas teaches that the face of the other ought to wrest from us compassion and obligation. One thinks here especially of the Lukan parable of the good Samaritan (Luke 10:30-37), where the stereotypical other and outsider, the Samaritan, embodies the compassion lacking in the other characters. By means of the parable, Jesus completely recasts the lawyer's question about "neighbors" and the necessary boundaries reinforced to maintain the ingroup and outgroup otherness. He challenges his questioner to forgo "otherness" itself and to venture into a common world where universal compassion, not a calculus of carefully negotiated difference, reigns.[7]

While the face of the other *ought* to elicit compassion, at the same time Levinas acknowledges that one can reject the call of compassion and choose instead manipulation, cruelty, and even torture. Herein lies the tragic element of the interhuman: at its heart is "a vast set of incompatibilities that originate in the irreducible otherness of the participants."[8]

Religious Self-Definition, Conflict, Boundary Maintenance, and the Other

To speak of "otherness" in the specific world of first-century Judaism and emerging Christianity is to venture, first of all, into the complex questions of religious self-definition, conflict theory, sectarian movements, and strategies of boundary maintenance. The questions to be addressed are both social-historical as well as literary and rhetorical. From the social-historical perspective, the Jesus movement, or more properly to the social science critics, the "Jesus faction," or even better, the "Jesus-centered Jewish messianic faction," was at first a person-centered coalition of followers of Jesus. Initially, it was a structurally simple and unstable faction, which, to quote John H. Elliott, "came into existence because of rivalry and competition with controlling elites and other Jewish coalitions and factions over honour and/or resources or access to resources, honour and 'truth.'"[9] The first followers, so the Gospels claim, were women and men who saw in Jesus an other who invited them into dialogue and shared activity as friend, prophet, teacher, and fellow footwasher. This loose circle of followers, after Jesus' death and the announcement of his resurrection, began to enter into a "process of differentiation and dissociation [and] gradually began to assume the character and strategies of a Jewish sect."[10]

According to Elliott, this process was marked by several common sectarian patterns: (1) by "an increase in the quantity and intensity of social tension and ideological difference between the Jesus faction and the corporate body of Israel" (e.g., Matt 10:17-23—"Beware of them, for they will hand you over to councils and flog you in their synagogues . . ."); (2) by the recruitment to the sect of those formerly excluded (e.g., the Gentile Cornelius in Acts 10:1-11, and the Samaritans in John 4:1-42); (3) by the sect's espousal of competing claims that it now embodied the authentic identity of Israel (e.g., John, Hebrews, passim, 1 Pet 2:4-10—"You are a chosen race, a royal priesthood, a holy nation, God's own people"); (4) by the replacement of the major institutions of the parent body (e.g., John 2:18-22); (5) by the claim that the parent body is the real other (e.g., "their synagogues" in Matt 4:23; 9:35; 10:17; 13:54; "synagogue of Satan" in Rev 2:9); (6) by a move within the parent body to dissociate itself from the misguided faction (e.g., in the much challenged "expulsion theory" in John 9:22; 12:42; 16:2); (7) by the sectarians' acceptance of the new label that outsiders give to them (e.g., *Christianoi*, Acts 11:26; 26:28; 1 Pet 4:16); and finally, (8) by their adoption of modes of social conduct that violate the norms of the parent body (e.g., the Gentile and Samaritan mission, mixed table fellowship).[11] Each of these features helped to establish and strengthen the boundaries that distinguished the emerging sect of *Christianoi* from the parent body of Judaism. At this stage, "boundary maintenance" was an uppermost concern. Not dialoguing with the other but precisely keeping the other as "other" was essential. Elliott concludes:

> As a deviant movement at odds with and censured by the corporate body of Judaism, the Jesus faction gradually dissociated from

the parent body first ideologically and then socially and gradually assumed the attitudes and actions of a sect, an erstwhile Jewish movement which because of its inclusion of gentiles had deviated from Jewish norms and violated Jewish social boundaries to such an extent that it could no longer be regarded as merely another Jewish faction.[12]

The Use of Conflict Theory

Conflict at the boundaries, as well as internal conflict about what and where those boundaries should be, was a natural as well as a tragic result. However, employing the social conflict theory of Georg Simmel and Lewis Coser, John Gager suggested that we should also acknowledge the positive functions of conflict in the emergence of Christianity and post–70 CE Judaism. He emphasized especially the potentially "group-binding" function of this conflict where a polemical debate with "others" served precisely to fix and strengthen the boundaries separating one group from another.[13] This is a kind of "circle the wagons" approach where the more hostile the encounter, the more intense the effort to hold firmly to the shared common beliefs that distinguish insider from outsider. There is a dual function in this kind of polemic: it aims, on the one hand, to ward off and counter the claims of the outsider and, on the other, to reinforce the shared beliefs of the insiders who may be wavering. For example, in a similar vein but with a variation on this theme, many have suggested that the literary effect of the use of irony and double entendre in the Fourth Gospel serves exactly this function—to reinforce the common ingroup "knowing" and to highlight those who fail to "know" what they know, in the same way that insider jokes can divide a room between those who "get it" and those who don't. Keeping the other other was part of the strategy.

Another axiom Coser held was that "the closer the relationship, the more intense the conflict."[14] This is surely a truism that assumes that, in fact, when the boundaries between two groups are not yet clearly defined, the movement from one to the other is threatening to the solidarity of both. In this case hostility is greatest because the other is not yet quite wholly other but is partially friend and fellow group member. Jesus' tirade against the "scribes and Pharisees" in Matthew 23, for example, begins with an acknowledgment of the admitted status of this group as those who "sit on Moses' seat" and who therefore convey legitimate teaching that the Matthean audience should observe. The charge of hypocrisy concerns their actions, not their teaching. Moreover, implicit through this whole chapter in Matthew is an equal warning to the ingroup not to fall prey to hypocrisy themselves. Remember, earlier in Matthew we heard the warning directed at the disciples: "You hypocrite, first take the log out of your own eye" (7:5). Here, the potential boundary between the Matthean group and the others is still somewhat porous, and what can be said of one is a potential danger to the other as well. Here, as elsewhere in Matthew (e.g., Matt 5:20: "Unless your righteousness exceeds that of the scribes and Pharisees, you will never enter the kingdom of heaven"), the criterion for boundary building is righteous actions, and these righteous actions become the final and determinative element of the ingroup's entry into the kingdom, as is clear in the parable of the sheep and the goats in Matthew 25.

Vilification as a Tool for Self-Definition

This brings us to a final consideration of important theoretical perspectives in looking at the New Testament, religious identity, and the other, namely, the rhetorical tool of vilification.[15] Whether in eight-year-olds on the school playground or in adult groups vying for supremacy and legitimacy, name-calling—the use of belittling epithets directed toward the other—is a recurring phenomenon with sometimes deadly consequences. (To give a contemporary example, in watching the film *Hotel Rwanda*, I was struck at how many times in the film the Hutu warlords kept referring to their Tutsi enemies as "cockroaches.")

Working in programs for reconciliation among victims of torture all over the world, Robert Schreiter has defined a number of different ways hostile groups can perceive and relate to the other.[16] He lists the following: (1) we can *demonize* the other as persons "to be feared and eliminated if possible"; (2) we can *romanticize* the other by inflating their importance and power and thereby diminishing our own status in relation to them; (3) we can *colonize* the other by treating them as "inferior, worthy of pity or contempt"; (4) we can *generalize* the other by "treating the other as non-individual and thus bereft of personal identity"; (5)

we can *trivialize* the other by "ignoring what makes the other different" from ourselves; (6) we can *homogenize* the other by "claiming that there really is no difference"; or (7) we can *vaporize* the other by "refusing to acknowledge the presence of the other at all."[17]

Vilification, as used by ancient rhetoricians and by the New Testament writers, is a strategic tool for demonizing the other by ascribing to the other traits, mannerisms, ideas, or conduct considered heinous or unacceptable to the intended audience addressed. In their study *The Social Construction of Reality*, Peter L. Berger and Thomas Luckmann also speak of this tool, which they define as "nihilation."[18] For Berger and Luckmann, nihilation is a tool to "liquidate conceptually everything outside the universe [in question]. This procedure may also be described as a kind of negative legitimation. Legitimation maintains the reality of the socially constructed universe; nihilation *denies* the reality of whatever phenomena or interpretations of phenomena do not fit into the universe."[19]

For the student of ancient rhetoric, the use of praise and blame was a well-honed skill. There were "standard elements"—classic lists of virtues and vices—that were worthy of praise and worthy of blame. In fact, it is quite possible to draw up a list of the most stereotypical and oft-repeated accusations hurled at opponents that includes charges of (1) "hypocrisy and falseness" (seen already, for example, in the charge of hypocrisy in Matt 7:5 and 23:13, and the repeated words prefixed with *pseudo-*, as in false brother, false apostles, false prophets, false teachers, and the like); (2) the reference to obscure and shadowy characters (as in Paul's indefinite reference to "some people" who sneaked into Galatia to spy on the community, often signaled by the indefinite *tines* in Greek); (3) the charge of sorcery or magic used to belittle another (as in "You foolish Galatians! Who has bewitched you?" Gal 3:1); (4) charges of *hybris* or inflated self-esteem (Matthew 23 is again an example, as is John 9—"Because you say, 'We see,' your guilt remains"; (5) accusations of moral depravity of every kind; (6) charges that the opponents have exercised a perverse influence on others (e.g., *Bk. Barn* 20.2 refers to his opponents [among other things] "corrupters of God's creation"); (7) charges that they associate with dubious or villainous people, such as Balaam (e.g., 2 Pet 2:15; Jude 11; Rev 2:14) or, God forbid, Jezebel (e.g.,

Rev 2:20-23), or even the devil himself (e.g., John 8); and finally, (8) warnings that they stand under judgment (e.g., again Matthew 23).[20]

As Luke T. Johnson has shown, these strategies of vilification and standard modes of accusation against opponents were evident among rival Hellenistic philosophical groups and various intra-Jewish groups in the process of self-definition as well.[21] Philo, for example, can say of his strategy toward Flaccus, "I praise Flaccus, not because I have thought it right to laud an enemy, but to show his villainy in a clearer light" (*In Flaccum* 7). This seems to be a strategy very close to what Matthew employs in Matthew 23 by first praising the scribes and Pharisees as authentic teachers and then lambasting them for every manner of hypocrisy. As mentioned above, our attempts to understand and critique the language of religious self-definition reflected in the New Testament documents is a venture that engages us in both the social-historical and the rhetorical worlds both in and behind the texts.

It becomes imperative, therefore, to distinguish ever so carefully between the *encoded* adversaries with their ascribed traits in the narrative world of the text and their real-life counterparts in the real world behind the text. This is true whether we are searching for the true character of Paul's rival "super apostles" in Corinth, or of the Pharisees in Matthew 23, or of the *hoi Ioudaioi* in John's Gospel. As a general rule, the greater the ingredient of stereotypical language and cliché, the more likely the element of gross distortion is present.[22] But to claim, in an adversarial relationship, that *mutual* accusation and hostility are never present is not helpful either. (Sarah J. Tanzer, in the following chapter in this volume, addresses this question in assessing the evidence of the Fourth Gospel and the present debates about the so-called expulsion theory in Johannine studies.)

Moving beyond Adversaries and Enemies

Given the adversarial nature of much of the rhetoric in the New Testament documents, is it even possible to cross the impasse separating other from other? We have pointed toward the fierce competition for adherents, the focus on procedures for self-definition, and the drive to maintain the boundaries of separation that marked the interchange in the first century between the followers of Jesus and the community of post–70 CE Judaism. Then, the forces pressuring for separation and for keeping the other other definitely had the upper hand.

But that was then, and now is now. Surely the best way forward for us now—perhaps the *only* way—is to return to and embrace the words of Levinas and turn toward the face of the other. To quote Levinas again, "Face and discourse are tied. The face speaks. It speaks, it is in this that it renders possible and begins all discourse."[23] So then, let us earnestly continue the discourse.

The Problematic Portrayal of "the Jews" and Judaism in the Gospel of John

IMPLICATIONS FOR JEWISH-CHRISTIAN RELATIONS

SARAH J. TANZER

A Gospel of Love and Hate

Kaufmann Kohler, writing in 1905, named the dilemma posed by the Gospel of John by calling it a Gospel of Christian love and Jew hatred.[1] This refers to the tension—felt not only by scholars but even more so by ordinary, thinking Christians and Jews—with a Gospel that, on the one hand, lays out the love command as the core of discipleship. This love command calls for a deep mutuality of love and service to be lived out by those who believe, including even a willingness to lay down one's life for other members of the community (John 10:13, 15). The love command has been modeled already in Jesus' action and in God, who "so loved the world that he gave his only Son, so that everyone who believes in him may not perish but may have eternal life" (John 3:16). On the other hand, this is also a Gospel in which the very presence of the Son in the world and the way one responds to him provoke judgment: "Those who believe in him are not condemned; but those who do not believe are condemned already, because they have not believed in the name of the only Son of God" (John 3:18).[2] Lack of belief speaks volumes about who you are and who your father is (which is of the greatest importance in this Gospel) and aligns us not only against Jesus, but against God and against the very witness of Abraham and Moses.

Judgment is not held back for some future moment but happens now as a result of the encounter with Jesus.[3] On the receiving end of judgment in the Gospel of John are "the Jews" and "the world." The problem is that this picture does not disappear with the first century.

Reference to "the Jews" throughout this Gospel calls to mind a people and a religion very much alive today, and yet the way "the Jews" are spoken of is overwhelmingly polemical.[4] In one of the darkest moments of the Gospel, Jesus says to "the Jews":

> "If God were your Father, you would love me, for I came from God and now I am here. I did not come of my own, but he sent me. Why do you not understand what I say? It is because you cannot accept my word. You are from your father the devil, and you choose to do your father's desires. He was a murderer. . . . Whoever is from God hears the words of God. The reason you do not hear them is that you are not from God." (John 8:42-47)

What are we to do with such a Gospel? The dilemma is very much as Kohler so aptly posed it: the Gospel of John preaches the love command as the way that believers are to treat each other while at the same time promoting anti-Judaism. It is an intractable problem that will not go away for a number of reasons. First and foremost is the reality that this Gospel is Christian scripture—it is not about to be deleted from the canon. Further, it is not some obscure, little-heard piece of scripture, but very much a foundation text for Christian belief, especially revered for its Christology (e.g., the incarnation, a very divine Jesus, the Father/Son relationship, etc.) and its love command. There are, of course, many other riches that this Gospel potentially offers. For example, the various exemplary roles that individual women play in the Gospel—the mother of Jesus, the Samaritan woman, Mary and Martha, and Mary Magdalene—offer strong biblical images of women as believers and leaders for the church to build upon; the portrayal of the community of disciples as mutually ministering to each other offers an image of the church as a cohesive egalitarian community built up by mutual love and service; and finally, the community out of which this Gospel came seems to have felt itself alienated and misunderstood by the world around it, so this Gospel might offer reassurance to other communities that find themselves in similar situations. Especially reassuring is the sense that members of the community are of God, in relationship with Jesus, and guided by the Spirit of Truth. For Christians, then, the issue becomes how to claim what can be so foundational and positive for Christianity from this Gospel, while also grappling with those aspects of the Gospel that are very problematic, especially the polemic aimed at "the Jews."

Exacerbating this issue is the authority given to scripture.[5] In the Reformed Christian tradition, it is read in churches as the "Word of God." This may work well when it is preaching love, but labeling as "the Word of God" a text that understands the world as the place of unbelief and the Jews as children of the devil is troubling. Put another way, if it is "good news," then for whom is it good news?

Christians are not the only folks whose scripture is problematic and who may need to struggle with the issue of how it is heard and understood as authoritative in the community. In Jewish scripture (the Tanakh—the Torah, Prophets, and Writings), there are many ugly references to our ancient archenemies, the Amalekites. In 1 Sam 15:3 we are commanded to kill all Amalekites: "Now go and attack Amalek, and utterly destroy all that they have; do not spare them, but kill both man and woman, child and infant. . . ." Now, I have not run into any Amalekites lately, but the Gospel of John causes problems precisely because Jews *are* still around (as is the world), and because the Gospel is understood and often publicly read as "good news" and the "Word of God."

Jews and Judaism without Judgment

Not all texts in the Gospel of John treat the Jews or Judaism with the same level of contempt. There are a relatively small number of texts in the Gospel in which Jews are portrayed without judgment, or even in a positive light. The most compelling of these occurs in the story of the raising of Lazarus (John 11), where Mary and Martha are pictured as being surrounded by Jews who have come to console them following Lazarus's death (11:19, 33, 36, 45). Although this is a very positive view of the Jewish community gathering around the bereaved sisters of Lazarus in the days immediately following the burial,[6] there are hints even in this passage of a split in how the Jews respond to Jesus. Some ironically cast aspersions by saying, "Could not he who opened the eyes of the blind man have kept this man from dying?" (11:37). A little later in the narrative, we are told that many Jews "believed in him." But others went and reported Jesus to the Jewish authorities (John 11:46). So even in those scenes within the Gospel that seem to portray Jews without judgment, there may be hints that the Jewish response to Jesus is not altogether harmless.

Inferiority and Distance

There is a second group of texts in the Gospel that subtly and not so subtly promotes distance from the Jews and suggests the compara-tive inferiority of Jews or Jewish symbols and customs. One phrase that promotes this distance is "the Passover of the Jews" (John 2:13; 11:55) or "Passover, the festival of the Jews" (6:4). The language of the phrase suggests that its author and even the community for whom the Gospel was written did not think of Passover as *their* festival. It is especially striking because, historically, the disciples, Jesus, and most of the major figures in the Gospel narrative were Jewish. Despite these phrases, Jesus is portrayed throughout the Gospel as observing the Passover by making pilgrimages to Jerusalem (2:13; 12:12). However, Passover in this Gospel is also linked clearly with Jewish culpability for Jesus' death.

Another phrase used rhetorically to emphasize that what Jesus offers (and, presumably, what the community aligned with Jesus has to offer) is superior to what Judaism offers is the repeated language of "greater than"[7] and the comparison of Jesus with heroic figures in Juda-ism. The Samaritan woman asks Jesus, "Are you greater than our ances-tor Jacob, who gave us the well, and with his sons and his flocks drank from it?" (John 4:12). Jacob was a patriarch not only of the Samaritans but also of the Jewish people, and clearly the implied answer to this question is "Yes!" The water Jesus offers is "living water"—an offer of eternal life—whereas those who drink water from the well of the Jew-ish patriarch will "be thirsty again" (John 4:13). In John 6, there are hints in the feeding of the five thousand that Jesus is being portrayed as being like Moses (Jesus' going up the mountain in 6:3; the statement that "the Passover ... was near" in 6:4; the reference to "the prophet who is to come into the world" in 6:14). But later in the chapter (6:27-50), what Jesus offers (the bread of life) is compared to what Moses offered (manna in the wilderness) and is clearly superior. The bread of life "comes down from heaven and gives life to the world" (6:33), whereas Moses gave the Jewish ancestors "the manna in the wilderness, and they died" (6:49). A little later, in a particularly polemical confrontation with the Jews, the Jews ask Jesus, "Are you greater than our father Abraham, who died? The prophets also died" (8:53). Once again the emphatic, implied answer is "Yes!" Jesus is associated with eternal life; Abraham and the prophets are associated with death. Making an even bolder claim, Jesus asserts that he has preexisted Abraham: "Very truly, I tell you, before Abraham was, I am" (8:58).

The supersessionism of the Gospel of John also extends to the Temple in Jerusalem. The Temple Cult was at the center of ancient Judaism, so much so that its destruction in 70 CE was a trauma of massive proportions.[8] In the ancient world, the Temple was understood as the locus of the divine in the world. In the Gospel, Jesus portrays himself as a replacement for the Temple (John 2:13-22).[9] In Jesus' encounter with the Samaritan woman, he makes it clear that the Temple in Jerusalem (and, for the Samaritans, the temple on Mount Gerizim) is superseded: "The hour is coming when you will worship the Father neither on this mountain nor in Jerusalem" (4:21). He goes on to speak about worshiping the Father in spirit and truth; where one worships will no longer matter. The presence of Jesus in the world has shifted the focus to *how* one worships. The role of the Temple has been rendered obsolete.

Explicit Condemnation

Finally, there are those phrases and texts in the Gospel that are fully explicit in their negative conclusions about "the Jews." These include several references to "fear of the Jews," in which the text portrays the Jews as a menacing threat (John 7:13; 9:22; 19:38; 20:19).[10] Also, in the dualistic worldview of this Gospel, the Jews are lined up with the negative pole. They are unbelieving; they love the darkness (rather than the light); they are not "of God" but are from below, of this world; they prefer the glory of men to the glory of God; and they are aligned with falsehood (and against the truth).[11] In the symbolic language of chapter 10, in which Jesus is portrayed as the Good Shepherd, Jesus makes it clear that the Jews do not belong in the flock that God has given him: "You do not believe, because you do not belong to my sheep. My sheep hear my voice. I know them, and they follow me. I give them eternal life, and they will never perish" (10:26-28). The Jews are unable to believe because they are not Jesus' own. Further, the Jews are charged with not believing the testimony of Moses concerning Jesus (5:45-47) and with not being the descendants of Abraham because, unlike Abraham, they do not rejoice at the coming of Jesus (8:56) and instead seek to kill him (8:39-40). Certainly, the most damning charge is that the father of "the Jews" is the devil and that they choose to carry out his will (8:44).[12]

This alignment of the Jews with the murdering devil is one of the ways in which the Gospel of John heightens Jewish responsibility for the death of Jesus, but it is by no means the only one. Jewish responsibility for the death of Jesus is articulated early in the Gospel. It begins with Jesus' innuendo in the cleansing of the Temple in chapter 2. As a theme, it shows up briefly in several scenes throughout the Gospel (see, for example, John 7:1 and 11:45-53) and culminates in chapters 18 and 19 with the betrayal and arrest of Jesus and his appearances before the high priest and Pilate, the Roman governor of Judea. The Jews are indicted in a variety of ways in these later scenes: the Jewish police are involved in the arrest of Jesus (18:3, 12); there is a reminder of Caiaphas's prediction "that it was better to have one person die for the people" (8:14); and the portrayal of Pilate shifts responsibility to the Jews. Pilate, who was known for his brutality, in the Gospel of John is portrayed as a "powerless" pawn of the Jews.[13] Repeatedly, he tells the Jews that he finds no case against Jesus (18:38; 19:4, 6) and seeks to release him (18:39; 19:10, 12). The Jews, however, are determined that Jesus should be crucified: they force Pilate's hand. The scene before Pilate ends with the Jews calling down judgment upon themselves by aligning themselves once again with the powers of this world and in effect denying the sovereignty of God. When Pilate asks, "Shall I crucify your King?" the chief priests answer, "We have no king but the emperor." Then Pilate hands Jesus over to them to be crucified (19:15-16). In a subtler implication of the Jews for Jesus' death, Jesus is portrayed as the Passover lamb, whose crucifixion happens at the time when Jews would be slaughtering their Passover lamb in preparation for the Passover.[14]

The Jews as "Other"

If we consider the various theoretical perspectives that Barbara Bowe has drawn together (see chapter 6), we can see how they might apply to "the Jews" in John. Those few texts that portray Jews in a nonjudgmental or even positive way would not suggest that the Jews be categorized as "other" in the Gospel. However, the examples of texts that promote distance from "the Jews" and depict the inferiority of Jews or Jewish heroic figures and customs, and those phrases or texts that are quite explicit in their negative assertions about the Jews, mark out the otherness of the Jews in this Gospel. The Jews are other than those who believe; they are other than those aligned with Jesus and hence God; they are other than the Johannine community out of which and for whom this Gospel was written. Further, if this Gospel has a missionary purpose (which I believe it does), the Jews are other than those whom the Gospel hopes to reach. They are so strongly marked out as "other," and spoken of in such insulting language, that the Gospel does not hold out any hope of bringing them into belief.[15]

Bowe discusses John Elliott's characterization of the process by which early Jesus followers, in the period after Jesus' death, gradually differentiated and dissociated themselves from Judaism.[16] Many of these sectarian patterns of boundary establishment and maintenance (e.g., increasing the quantity and intensity of social tension and ideological difference, espousing competing claims, and replacing the major institutions of the parent body) can be seen in passages about the Jews in the Gospel. Further, the use of conflict theory may well help us to understand the polemical rhetoric about the Jews in John: conflict keeps the Jews in their place as "other," countering any claims the Jewish community might have made, while bolstering the beliefs and confidence of the Johannine community who are "in the know" and in a privileged relationship with Jesus and God.

Another helpful perspective on these texts about the Jews in John observes the use of vilification by ancient rhetoricians as a means of demonizing the other. Among the stereotypical accusations often used to vilify the other are two that especially apply to the Jews in this Gospel: charges that they associate with dubious or villainous people (e.g., the devil in John 8, as well as the alignment of the Jews with those who do not believe and with the world), and warnings that they stand under judgment (found throughout the Gospel, but note especially John 12:37-50, linking the unbelief of the Jews with judgment).[17] It is also important, when we discuss how the Gospel of John may have used these various strategies in its portrayal of "the Jews" (differentiation and dissociation, the functions of conflict to establish and mark boundaries, and the polemical rhetoric of vilification) to remember that this Gospel preserves only one half of the narrative. The other half of the narrative would be the story as told from the vantage point of the Jewish community that was the counterpart to the Johannine community. If that other half had been preserved, it may well have been just as polemical in using all of these strategies to mark off the Johannine community as "Other." Unfortunately, no such narrative has been preserved.[18]

Scholarly Approaches to the Problem

The problem of "the Jews" in John has been addressed by scholars in a variety of ways that go beyond the more philosophical analyses of the "other" in antiquity. Concern about the polemical Johannine portrayal of the Jews is an important issue in Jewish and Christian interfaith dialogue and in intrareligious reflection (that is, within Christianity). It is a pragmatic problem: What shall we do with a Gospel that is so much a foundation of Christianity and yet exacerbates anti-Jewish sentiment? What is unusual is that this problem with the portrayal of "the Jews"— a problem for Christian self-definition and interfaith relations—has driven a huge amount of scholarship. The result is that scholarship seeks to resolve a seemingly intractable obstacle in Jewish and Christian interfaith relationships and in Christian self-definition.

We may sketch briefly a sampling of the types of scholarly solutions to the problematic portrayal of "the Jews" in the Gospel of John, giving an example or two of each type of solution and summarizing the merits and limits of each approach.[19] Much of the scholarship has merit as scholarship and may work in certain circumstances to mitigate the promotion of anti-Judaism. However, none of it offers a complete resolution of the problem, which, in the end, is a problem not of scholarship but of ministry.

Emphasizing One Aspect over Another

In his essay "Judaism and the Gospel of John," D. Moody Smith reminds us that in chapters 13–17 of the Gospel, there is almost no invective against the Jews, perhaps signaling that controversies with Jewish neighbors had begun to ease.[20] These chapters are closer in this respect to the Johannine epistles, in which there are no hostile references to the Jews. Smith finds this transition away from anti-Jewish polemic hopeful. So, too, he suggests that historically interpreters have focused too much on the dualism of the Gospel of John, rather than concentrating on the unity and love that the Gospel promotes. This approach calls for emphasizing certain aspects of the Gospel over others in the life of the church, while leaving aside the more problematic aspects. This sort of approach lifts up what the church finds constructive in the Gospel and turns away from its more problematic aspects. There is a kind of wonderful wishful thinking in this approach—if only the church would approach it in this way. But this approach does not treat the Gospel as a whole, and also could lead a community to deny that there is a problem by simply ignoring the more challenging aspects of the Gospel. Further, those communities that thrive on what this Gospel has to say about belief and unbelief would not be able to put this sort of approach into practice.

The Gospel Cannot Be Anti-Jewish or Anti-Semitic

This approach looks at the polemic in the Gospel as a type of "intra-Jewish" debate and concludes that by definition, therefore, the Gospel cannot be anti-Semitic or anti-Jewish. There are many variations to this sort of argument. Urban C. von Wahlde urges us to remember that the Johannine community was made up of people who were Jews by birth and who had converted to belief in Jesus.[21] He notes further that such polemic (especially in the face of persecution) was widespread in the ancient world and was also typical of polemic between different Jewish groups. For example, we hear this "intra-Jewish" polemic in the Dead Sea Scrolls. Martinus de Jonge has argued that because the polemic is intra-Jewish, "anti-Judaism" is not the right term to describe the Gospel of John: "We are not allowed to speak here of anti-Jewish tendencies unless there is clear proof that criticism came from outside, that is, from people who did not feel any bond with the persons they criticized."[22] The success of his argument depends on whether or not one judges the Jews to be "other" in the Gospel. Many others have pointed out that the particularly heated polemic is a result of intra-Jewish disagreement.[23] Another variation on this is to argue that the *intent* of the Gospel is not anti-Semitic, even though its *effect* is.[24] Although the debate about whether or not the Gospel of John is anti-Semitic or anti-Jewish does help to sort out the appropriate semantics and reminds us that conflict is most heated when it is between groups who share an identity, it does not soften the impact of the polemic on those who hear this Gospel read as the Word of God. Indeed, the problem is less related to any intent of the Gospel and more related to its effect. However, I disagree with those who insist that the Gospel represents intra-Jewish polemic. The Christological center of the polemic and various expressions such as "the Passover of the Jews" make it clear that the Johannine community and its Jewish counterpart do not share an identity, even though they may have done so in the past. Nevertheless, the intensity of the polemic may well betray a previously close relationship between the two communities.

Three other approaches ask about either the identity or the function of "the Jews," or "the Judeans" (*hoi Ioudaioi*), in the Gospel.

"The Jews" (*Hoi Ioudaioi*) Refers Only to Religious Authorities and Leaders

This approach argues that when the phrase "the Jews" is used to portray those who are consistently hostile to Jesus, it refers *only* to the Jewish leaders and *not* to the Jewish people more broadly. Von Wahlde has argued that, with the exception of John 6:41 and 52, all of the hostile uses of "the Jews" refer to the Jewish authorities and come from the second edition of the Gospel (the redaction that dominates the thought world of the Gospel). On the other hand, the more neutral use of *hoi Ioudaioi* (e.g., those who have gathered around Mary and Martha to console them following Lazarus's death) comes from the earlier edition of the Gospel (the Gospel of signs) and is used of Jewish common folk or Judeans.[25] Von Wahlde's view of the merit of this approach is that the polemic aimed at "the Jews" in the Gospel is really aimed only at the Jewish authorities and not at the broader Jewish community. Thus it cannot be said that "the Gospel is an attack on the attitudes of all Jews."[26] In other words, the anti-Jewish aura of the Gospel is a misreading; it is not the intention of the author. However, von Wahlde's approach only addresses some of the anti-Jewish rhetoric in this Gospel. It does not take up the issues raised by our second group of texts (those that promote distance from Jews and depict the comparative inferiority of Jews or Jewish symbols and customs). Nor does it address the effect of using one term (*hoi Ioudaioi*) to refer both to the hostile authorities and to the neutral Judeans—coloring at least in retrospect all occurrences of the term with the dominant hostile sense.[27]

Hoi Ioudaioi as Specific Geographical Reference to Judeans

In two different articles, Robert Fortna and Malcolm Lowe both have concluded that the term *hoi Ioudaioi* refers not to "the Jews," authorities or otherwise, but rather to "Judeans" in the strict geographical sense of the term.[28] With this conclusion Lowe advocates changing "the current mistranslations of the Gospels, since rendering *hoi Ioudaioi* as "the Jews" is not only incorrect . . . but also pernicious."[29] Fortna's and Lowe's proposals rightly nudge us forward to more carefully nuanced understandings of *hoi Ioudaioi* in the Gospel, even as they flounder in places.[30] For example, if we render this term geographically rather than in terms of a people and a religion, is it compelling to translate "the Passover of the Judeans" or "the King of the Judeans"? Or since the pivotal element in the rhetoric centers around "unbelief," can we really understand this as the unbelief of the inhabitants of the province of Judea—and does it seem likely that such intense hostility would be aimed at them? There is one other problem with translating "the Judeans": Surely most readers and hearers of the Gospel would eventually realize that most Judeans in first-century Palestine were also Jews.

Hoi Ioudaioi as the Symbol of Unbelief

Rudolf Bultmann described the symbolic function of the Jews in the Gospel of John as the representatives of unbelief and the unbelieving world in general.[31] Bultmann's symbolic interpretation is a tour de force, and it helps us make meaning of the Gospel. Many have built upon his understanding. Alan Culpepper, in *Anatomy of the Fourth Gospel*, concludes his analysis of the literary role of "the Jews" by noting, "Through the Jews, John explores the heart and soul of unbelief."[32] The merit of such interpretations is the rich way in which they help to reveal the symbolism of the Gospel and the literary functions of different characters. This interpretation on the symbolic level mitigates anti-Judaism by reducing "the Jews" to cardboard characters—representative figures—necessary to complete the symbol world of the Gospel. However, it does not correct the negative impact of the polemical presentation of "the Jews" for the average reader or hearer of the Gospel.

Historical Reconstruction of "the Jews"

Many scholars have used historical criticism to try to understand what may have been going on in the Johannine community that could incite such strong polemic toward "the Jews."[33] This approach encourages us to reconstruct, with caution, the communities behind the Gospel and offers a historical context in which to read and comprehend the anti-Jewish polemic. Any reconstruction is just that, of course, and always must be tested against the text.

J. Louis Martyn, in his description of the Gospel as a two-level drama, is perhaps the best well-known practitioner of this approach to opening up the dynamics between the local synagogue and the Johannine community.[34] Martyn analyzes the narrative of the man born blind in John 9, the three references in the Gospel to being cast out (9:22) or being put out of the synagogue (12:42 and 16:2), and a rabbinic reformulation of the "benediction against heretics" (the Birkat ha-Minim). His analysis leads him to the conclusion that toward the end of the first century, the Birkat ha-Minim was being used to exclude from the synagogue those Jews who had come to believe that Jesus was the messiah: "In the two-level drama of John 9, the man born blind plays not only the part of a Jew in Jerusalem healed by Jesus of Nazareth, but also the part of Jews known to John who have become members of the separated church because of their messianic faith and because of the awesome Benediction."[35] Although Martyn's conclusions about the use of the Birkat ha-Minim to force messianic Jews out of the synagogue toward the end of the first century have been compellingly challenged,[36] his understanding of how the text reveals the severing of relationships between the local synagogue and the Johannine community is still incredibly insightful.

The merit of using a historical-critical approach with the Gospel of John is that it can help us to locate the anti-Jewish rhetoric in a historical setting—to think in terms of real communities facing specific issues at a particular time—and therefore it does not support the conclusion that this anti-Jewish rhetoric is "truth for all time." It defuses and contextualizes one's experience of this rhetoric. Such an approach has been criticized also for leaving interpreters on the outside of the Johannine community as silent observers; for leading to a false sense of objectivity; and for leading to reconstructions that cannot be proven. For the issues of interfaith and intra-Christian dialogue, a more practical consideration is simply that we are not going to be able to make historical-critical readers of everyone, and thus the effectiveness of resolving the problem of "the Jews" through this approach has definite limits.

Regarding the Polemic as Mild by Comparison

Luke T. Johnson, observing that the "scurrilous language used about Jews in the earliest Christian writings is a hurdle neither Jew nor Christian can easily surmount," brings historical and literary approaches together in analyzing the rhetoric of slander in the ancient world.[37] This leads him to several important observations, including the conventional nature of this polemic and that by "being placed in its appropriate social and literary setting—that of polemic between ancient schools—the NT slander against Jews appears in a new light. . . . By the measure of Hellenistic conventions, and certainly by the measure of contemporary Jewish polemic, the NT's slander against fellow Jews is remarkably mild."[38] Like historical-critical approaches, this is tremendously helpful in giving a specific context to the polemic and in defusing it by locating it within that context. But again, the problem is that this is not likely to be a widely used approach with a broader audience of Jews and Christians. Thus, his hope that in the contemporary relationship of Jews and Christians it will "rob such language of its mythic force and therefore its capacity for mischief"[39] is probably unrealistic.

The Need for a Broader Approach

With these and other scholarly approaches, what we find is that scholarship does provide some helpful tools to be utilized in addressing the problem of the portrayal of "the Jews" and Judaism in the Gospel of John, but scholarship alone cannot resolve the problem. We are left with the issue of how ordinary Christians and Jews hear and respond to the polemics of this Gospel. What is needed is a broader approach that joins the results of scholarship with responses that are shaped by the specific issues of our different contemporary communities. This is not a problem that will go away, and scholarship will not be helpful on its own if it is not put to use in the contexts of our faith communities and in ministry. By *ministry* I mean thinking of a variety of contexts, not limited to—but including—Jewish-Christian dialogue, Christian education and religious formation, and Jewish reflection on the early relationships between Judaism and ancient Christianity and the legacy embedded in New Testament texts about those relationships. It is helpful to think in terms of multifaceted strategies for teaching and learning in the context of dedicated and creative ministry.

What are some of the ways this issue is being addressed in various ministry contexts? From the amount of scholarship dedicated to it, we know that the translation of *hoi Ioudaioi* ("the Jews/the Judeans") is a major issue. It has been suggested that in worship contexts we should translate it as "the Judeans" so as to avoid promoting anti-Judaism through the reading of scripture, whereas in a study session, one could translate it as "the Jews" and then discuss what is so problematic about this. Some, such as Norman Beck in *Mature Christianity*, have advocated deleting the invective aimed at the Jews or at least euphemistically replacing it.[40] Beck, for example, suggests that in the cleansing of the Temple (John 2:13-22) we replace "the Passover of the Jews" with "the Passover," and that in 2:18 we replace "the Jews said to him" with "some people in the Temple said to him."[41] In those places where "the Jews" are clearly the Jewish authorities, Beck advocates for translating "the authorities." For the dialogue between Jesus and the Jews in John 8:12-59, Beck advocates a more sensitive translation and proposes simply not repeatedly translating "the Jews" in a number of other instances where it is already clear that the Pharisees or the Jews are being addressed.[42] These proposals raise a few questions:

Do we change the translation of the Gospel for all contexts or only for certain contexts? What are the consequences of doing this?

Another suggestion has been to remove the difficult texts in the Gospel of John from the lectionary. To some extent this has already been done; you won't find John 8 in the Revised Common Lectionary. Many preachers seem reluctant to preach the more difficult texts from John. The negative portrayal of the Jews and Judaism is spread throughout most of the Gospel, so apart from removing the Gospel entirely from the lectionary, it is virtually impossible to excise the problem simply by removing a few texts from the lectionary. Besides, that approach assumes that what is read and preached in church on Sunday is *all* that matters, and it does not teach people how to deal with the difficulties of scripture—it just avoids them. Do we really want to leave these texts out there without discussing them? One preacher I know dealt with the Gospel of John creatively during Lent, having done a bit of research to make it possible to preach each week in the first person from a different character's point of view (e.g., Caiaphas, Judas, etc.) as he worked through the Gospel scenes leading up to the crucifixion of Jesus. In this way he took on the more challenging texts by bringing a different point of view to them and provoking thoughtfulness on the part of his congregants.

The Problem of Scriptural Authority

An issue that needs to be tackled more directly by each community claiming this Gospel as scripture is what authority scripture has for them. If we give scripture sole authority (*sola scriptura*), if we call it the Word of God, if we claim it is the good news[43]—then how do we deal with the invective aimed at the Jews and Judaism that is found in it? We have a text from a particular time and place, reflecting a community where tensions were at a height with its Jewish neighbors. Is this truth for all time? If not, how does a Christian community struggle with the issue of the ways in which this Gospel is authoritative for them?

This is an issue that I discuss with my Master of Divinity students. My students are much more comfortable with the Synoptic Gospels, which preach Jesus among the poor and outcast and do not portray Jesus as making himself God. Yet my students also need to recognize the centrality of Johannine Christology for the church and to reclaim the many riches of this Gospel. Besides, this Gospel is not about to be tossed out of Christian scripture, so my students must learn to struggle with the challenges that this Gospel poses.[44] I assure them that their faith will grow from struggling with the challenges and facing the issue of scripture's authority over and over again. It is important that they take up their struggles with the Gospel of John honestly in their communities of faith and not avoid the ugly and challenging parts of the text.

In the context of interfaith dialogue, the work around the issues that this Gospel raises is not for Christians alone. While Christians must try to hear these texts with "Jewish" ears and not avoid the difficult issues they raise, Jews also must try to put themselves in the shoes of Christians and empathize with the dilemma that the Gospel of John poses for them—at once a foundation text with much that is important to Christian identity and at the same time painful in the anti-Judaism that it promotes. As Jews, we have our own issues. We must examine what our own texts teach about the "other," we must reflect on the historically inward focus of the Jewish community, and we should try to avoid portraying ourselves in the position of victim in the context of dialogue. Guilt is a great silencer in dialogue. People need to take responsibility for what their sacred texts and communities teach, but guilt, when it is used to silence, does not serve either community well. In general, we must acknowledge that there is an inequity in the dialogue because of the era in which the New Testament emerged, and we must work to take full responsibility for our part in it. Most of all, we should feel that we too are invited to engage the Gospel of John seriously and to ask questions about it and to raise the issues that are difficult for us. The texts of the New Testament are Christian scripture, but they are also part of Jewish history and continue to have an impact on the Jewish community today. The task for both communities is not to back away from the challenge but to use it to enrich the dialogue.

Luke's Pharisees

EMERGING COMMUNITIES

LAURENCE L. EDWARDS

Textual interpretation always takes place within and between contest-ing ideologies and shifting historical circumstances. Today, for several important reasons, Christians are rethinking their relationship to Jews and Judaism and consequently rereading religious texts in a new light. The Shoah prompted serious consideration of ways in which traditional Christian teachings helped to sow the seeds of hatred that reached their most horrific climax in Europe in the 1940s. In North America espe-cially, Jews and Christians have increasingly come to know each other as neighbors. At the same time, a small but growing number of Jewish scholars have become interested in Christian scriptures. Joseph B. Tyson states explicitly that the pre–World War II approach of New Testament scholars to anti-Jewish motifs "was characteristically different from that of many postwar scholars"; in the post-Holocaust era, "the discussion of anti-Judaism in the NT has been vigorously debated."[1] According to John Darr, "Luke-Acts . . . has been actualized in many different ways, depending on the varying values and data that readers from diverse peri-ods and cultures have brought to it."[2] It should not be surprising, then, that "the most hotly debated issue in Lukan scholarship of the last two decades concerns the place of the Jewish people and Jewish religion in these writings."[3]

This essay consciously places itself within this newer discourse, pointing to a more complex entanglement of the origins of Christianity and rabbinic Judaism. In this effort, I align myself with the recent work of Daniel Boyarin, Judith Lieu, and others, who have argued that the so-called parting of the ways[4] between Christianity and Judaism took much longer than earlier studies have claimed. My reading will suggest that Luke's complex portrayal of "the Jews" in general, and of the Pharisees in particular, reflects a situation in which the lines between Judaism and Christianity were not yet clearly drawn.

Viewed from this perspective, Luke offers evidence for extensive overlap between emerging rabbinic Judaism and emerging Christianity. Thus, rather than seeing Luke-Acts as rooted in, and witnessing to, a situation in which Christianity had already become predominantly Gentile and had separated from Judaism, I view it as a document of separation-in-process. As one recent writer puts it, "The Lukan writings reflect and participate in the struggles and concerns of a community at the intersection between a past it tries to claim and a future it attempts to create."[5] In this extended process of communal definition and boundary setting, Luke's Pharisees become a trope for the shades of gray between two approaches to interpreting scripture and history that eventually gave birth to separate and distinct communities. It is worth emphasizing that my intention here is not primarily to recover and analyze the "actual" Pharisees, but to examine the narratives that present them and to inquire into the underlying historical and ideological background to which these narratives point.

The Pharisees in Luke's Narrative

Of all the Gospels, Luke's is the most careful to differentiate among various groups of Jews, and among these groups the Pharisees figure most prominently. It is interesting and important to note, as have most scholars of Luke-Acts, that Luke's portrayals of Pharisees vary greatly. David Gowler suggests that the Pharisees, in terms of their literary function in Luke-Acts, "are an intermediary group that bridges the gap between unbelieving Jews and believing Christians. . . . Any incoherence is a planned inconsistency that . . . serves to further the plot of the Gospel."[6] Though they are often depicted as two-dimensional type-characters, some individuals are painted quite vividly. If at times they appear as mere foils, individual Pharisees can also express substantive points of view that seem to be taken quite seriously.

Robert Brawley finds in Luke's Gospel less conflict surrounding the Pharisees than in parallel passages in Matthew and Mark; and in Acts, the Pharisees are viewed even more favorably.[7] Brawley argues that "Luke writes in an environment where the Pharisees hold a rather respectable position for both Luke and his readers. And this accounts for the positive way the Pharisees function in Luke-Acts."[8] John Darr, on the other hand, taking a cue from Luke Johnson, is at pains to show that Luke-Acts conveys an increasingly negative view of the Pharisees. He does not accept the oft-stated thesis that there is a distinct contrast between the treatment of the Pharisees in Luke's Gospel and in Acts, basing his argument on the cumulative effect of reading Luke-Acts in order, rather than slicing it into various pieces.[9] To be sure, the portrayal of Pharisees in Luke is, finally, a negative one. But against Darr, I would argue that the negativity conveyed through the Gospel serves to heighten the effect of the much more positive portrait in Acts.

Though Jack Sanders is convinced that Luke's overall portrait of "the Jews" is negative, he does show that Luke differentiates among Pharisees. In contrast to the universally negative picture of Pharisees offered in Mark and Matthew, Luke describes a number of Pharisees who are friendly to Jesus, inviting him to dinner (7:36; 11:37; 14:1), for example. As in the other Gospels, Luke keeps Pharisees completely out of the passion narrative, but only in Luke do Pharisees warn Jesus against going to Jerusalem because of danger from Herod (13:13). In Acts, Pharisees defend Paul and the apostles before the Sanhedrin and have nothing to do with the martyrdoms of Stephen (Acts 7–8) and James (Acts 12).[10]

According to Sanders, Luke emphasizes that Christianity ultimately became a Gentile religion, which was somehow in keeping with the divine plan. For Sanders, the term "Pharisees" in Luke-Acts really means Jewish Christians. "[W]hen the Lucan Jesus admonishes his followers (i.e., the church) to beware the pharisaic leaven of hypocrisy (Luke 12.1), he must have in mind the Christian Pharisees, not the non-Christian ones." The problem, he goes on, is that of Pharisees "within the church, not outside it."[12] While Sanders may have no problem with the idea of a "Christian Pharisee," Anthony Saldarini does, and criticizes Luke for historical inaccuracy:

Luke's idea that Paul could be a Pharisee and a Christian and that there were Christians who remained Pharisees is very unlikely, especially granted all the conflicts with Jewish authorities and teaching recounted in Acts and alluded to in Paul's letters. The Pharisees were a political interest group with a program for living Judaism and any interpretation of Christianity, no matter how Jewish, would have found itself in conflict with them. . . . Luke correctly perceives many things about the Pharisees, but he probably overemphasizes their positive relations with the early followers of Jesus.[13]

I tend to agree with Sanders here, against Saldarini, that Luke is likely referring to Jewish Christians who remained adamant about traditional criteria for admission, including circumcision. Luke is reflecting the continued closeness, the overlap that still existed between Jewish and Christian identities.

The existence of "Christian Pharisees" may be read, then, as pointing to a state of flux in the gradually emerging communal identities. Sanders and Saldarini, indeed most students of Luke-Acts,[14] operate with the explicit or implicit understanding that by the time of Luke's writing, Judaism and Christianity were recognizably separate religions: if you are a Pharisee, then you are a Jew, not a Christian; if you are a Christian of Jewish origin who wishes to remain faithful to Mosaic law, then the term "Pharisee" should not be used to describe you because it would be confusing. But this is perhaps to draw the lines too rigidly—Luke's construction of the Pharisees presses against such clear delineations.

The Lines Are Not Fixed

If we suppose that the lines were not fixed, that the "parting of the ways" had not fully come to pass by the time of Luke's writing, then it seems quite natural, and more accurate, to imagine that there could be something like "Christian Pharisees" (among whom Paul is the best known, though he is opposed to the view that Sanders ascribes to "Christian Pharisees"). As John Carroll points out, "Much depends on the scholar's decision to locate Luke inside or outside a Jewish milieu."[15] Sanders takes the traditional view that Luke is writing for a primarily Gentile church. Marilyn Salmon disagrees with Sanders over just this issue, arguing that Sanders's conclusion holds up only if one accepts his beginning assumption that Luke writes from a position outside the Jewish community.

Salmon offers evidence that Luke is writing as a Jewish insider, making an "intramural" argument: he makes distinctions between Jews and even between Pharisees; he is very concerned with Torah observance; his preoccupation with "mission to the Gentiles" implies a Jewish perspective; and he uses the term *hairesis* (Acts 15:5; 24:5; 28:22) in reference to both Pharisees and Christians, suggesting that both are constituent groups within Judaism.[16] On such a reading, Luke's condemnation of "the Jews" loses some of its sting: "It would have been obvious to him and to his audience which Jews he meant. They knew which Jews were guilty. We put too great a burden on our narrator to expect him to clarify for outsiders what is obvious to insiders."[17] Salmon's argument is intriguing, but she in turn places *too much* emphasis on the sense of "insiderness," which leads her to understate the ways in which Luke's narrative also points toward eventual separation between what will become rabbinic Judaism and Christianity.

Much current scholarship places the "parting of the ways" considerably later than has been commonly supposed. Reuven Kimelman, for example, argues that there is little evidence that the Birkat ha-Minim, a prayer thought to have been added to the daily synagogue service as a means of excluding Jewish Christians (and often pointed to as a sign of a formal and institutionalized separation between synagogue and church), was actually directed specifically at followers of Jesus.[18] Judith Lieu wonders about the very term *intramural*, when used to describe the New Testament polemics with Judaism:

It is only a metaphor [as is "parting of the ways"], but suppose there were no "muri," no walls. Once we "de-institutionalize" our understanding of Jewish communities, once we remove *the* synagogue, understood much as some Christians speak of the church, from the centre of our perception of their essential identity, with what are we left?[19]

Daniel Boyarin has suggested that the split between Judaism and Christianity was not complete until the fourth century, when Christianity became the official religion of the Roman Empire.[20] In this he follows Jacob Neusner, who writes, "Judaism and Christianity as they would live together in the West met for the first time in the fourth century."[21] To this contemporary discussion, I add my suggestion that the reference in Acts 15:5 to "some believers who belonged to the sect of the Pharisees"—though Sanders takes it as simply a reference to annoying Jewish Christians, and Saldarini dismisses it as a historical impossibility—may in fact reflect a more complex reality of communal lines that are still in flux.

Since the Pharisees so often appear in Christian texts as polemicized representatives of "Judaism," it is worth considering how close the caricature is to the likely reality. In much of the literature, the Pharisees are described as "strict" in their observance, or even "the strictest." Thus Luke has Paul describe the Pharisees in Acts 26:5 as "the strictest sect of our religion." The word that Paul uses, *akribestatein*, means "strict" or "exact," and with the definite article, "the strictest." Strict in comparison to what? Certainly Pharisees are drawn as being careful, even fastidious, in their concern for ritual observance, in comparison to the average Judean or Galilean peasant or artisan. On this much there is agreement in both the New Testament and rabbinic sources. But they were not "stricter" than the Essenes, who went so far as to separate themselves from the temple and the larger society.

From a sociological point of view, the Pharisees occupied an intermediate position within Judaism. They were not primarily associated with the temple and priesthood. They respected the Temple Cult, however, and demonstrated that respect by adopting certain aspects of temple purity in their non-temple ritual practice. They did not separate themselves altogether from the people, in the manner of the Essenes. In fact, they were the ones who enabled Jewish religious practice to continue after the destruction of the Temple in 70 CE. This is a critical point: in the post–70 CE situation, it can be seen more clearly that pharisaic approaches to Torah interpretation and observance made it possible for Jewish life to continue without the Temple. The Pharisees were "separatists" who did not separate themselves. As Neusner puts it, "The law alone set the Pharisees apart from the people among whom they lived."[22] And Neusner elaborates, "By keeping the rules of purity the fellow [the pharisaic *ḥaber*] separated from the common man." But by remaining within the towns and cities of the land, he preserved the possibility of teaching others by example.[23]

Though one must not depend too heavily on the historical accuracy of later rabbinic accounts of the Pharisees, there is some evidence that, of the various "schools" of the first century, the Pharisees, or at least some of them, were actually the most open to Gentile converts.[24] That is, some Pharisees may have mediated not only between Jews, but also between Jews and Gentiles. It seems reasonable to suggest, therefore, that the "strictness" of the Pharisees was not so much an instrument intended to exclude as it was an aspect of drawing boundaries and shaping a community in a fluid and changing situation. In other words, the careful ritual observance of the Pharisees could be viewed as a means of maintaining group identity in a period of political crisis and in a social situation that required extensive contact with a variety of Jews and Gentiles. In Luke's narrative the Pharisees seem to play this mediating role between Jews and Judaism on the one hand and nascent Christianity on the other.

Jesus in Conversation with Pharisees

Pharisees make their first appearance in the Third Gospel in a set of engagements with Jesus narrated in Luke 5:17—6:11. The discussion here will be limited to abbreviated considerations of a few illustrative passages. In this section there are four (some count five) separate incidents. The first is the healing of the paralytic lowered in through the roof (5:17-26). The issue here is whether Jesus, or God only, has the power to forgive sins. The second incident is a feast (5:27-39), at which "the Pharisees and their scribes were complaining to his disciples" for eating with tax collectors and sinners. This discussion also includes the question of fasting.

The third and fourth episodes in the group occur on the Sabbath and raise issues of Sabbath *halacha* (legal interpretation), specifically reaping and healing. In 6:1-5, Jesus' disciples are plucking ears of grain on the Sabbath, and some[25] Pharisees question this behavior. As is often the case in Luke, they do not question Jesus directly, but rather his disciples. Nevertheless, Jesus responds, engaging them in a brief discussion of an important issue of Sabbath observance. Jesus cites as a precedent the incident in 1 Sam 21:1-6, of David taking the bread of the Presence from the priests of Nob. As a legal precedent, this is a strange choice, since it could easily have been refuted by pointing out the disastrous consequences following in 1 Samuel 22, namely, the death of eighty-five priests at the hands of Saul's henchman, Doeg. Furthermore, the Samuel passage does not have anything to do with Sabbath law, so the main connection between the two episodes is taking food in a way that violates a Torah rule. Jesus gets the last word in this exchange, as usual, and by now the reader is clearly expected to understand that to mean that he wins the argument, though it is an argument this is left strikingly incomplete to the ear of a Jewish reader.

The fourth incident (6:6-11), the climax of the series, recounts Jesus' healing a man's withered right hand on the Sabbath in a synagogue in a way that heightens the feeling of confrontation. This time the narrator reveals the thoughts of the Pharisees who are present: they were watching Jesus "so that they might find an accusation against him" (6:7). The actual case is one of a chronic, nonlethal condition, but this is not discussed. Instead, Jesus challenges the Pharisees with a question that quite overstates the situation: "I ask you, is it lawful to do good or to do harm on the sabbath, to save life or to destroy it?" (6:9). But it would be known to all present that saving life on the Sabbath is a positive obligation, and destroying it is prohibited. Without waiting for a response, however, Jesus heals the man's withered hand. No argument accompanies this episode, even though the question of healing on the Sabbath is a complicated one.

If Brawley is correct that the Pharisees in Luke's Gospel serve in part to legitimate Jesus, their geographical spread may also signify the breadth of their influence. The section (5:17) begins with what is most likely an exaggeration: Is it really possible that "Pharisees and teachers of the law . . . had come from *every* village of Galilee and Judea and from Jerusalem" (italics added)? In the narrative, however, this hyperbole serves to call attention to the importance that Pharisees attached to Jesus' teaching—Jesus' reputation is getting around. The Pharisees in these narratives serve not only as prop, but also as foil. The overall direction, and increasing intensity, certainly leaves Luke's "ideal reader" with the impression that Jesus can and does get the better of the Pharisees every time.

Darr reads the cumulative effect of these passages as leading the reader inexorably toward a completely negative view of the Pharisees. Gowler, while admitting that their "hardness of heart is becoming painfully clear," nevertheless sees this portrayal as protecting the Pharisees from total negativity:

> Jesus—knowing their thoughts—offers the challenge. Other religious leaders, however, will later offer direct and sometimes mocking affronts to Jesus (e.g., Luke 20:1-8, 21-40). This narrative technique allows the Pharisees to remain as opponents, but not to be seen in as negative terms as the other religious leaders.[26]

Not only Jesus but also the omniscient narrator knows the inner feelings of his interlocutors: "They were filled with fury" (6:11). It has been noted by various commentators that despite their fury, Luke's Pharisees here only discuss "what they might do to Jesus," not "how to destroy him" (Matt 12:14; Mark 3:6).

Darr points out the unusual use of the verb *pareteirounto* in 6:7—the scribes and Pharisees watched, observed, scrutinized him. Darr views this word as a tag the narrator attaches to the Pharisees to highlight their "penchant for observing."[27] This is further emphasized in 17:20-21:

> Once Jesus was asked by the Pharisees when the kingdom of God was coming, and he answered, "The kingdom of God is not coming with things that can be observed; nor will they say, 'Look, here it is!' or 'There it is!' For in fact, the kingdom of God is among [or within] you."

The kingdom of God does not come through "observation." Darr emphasizes the ironic use of this term in connection with the Pharisees: "They have proven to be the great scrutinizers of Jesus and everything connected with his ministry. . . . The Pharisees are living proof that one can observe carefully and yet fail to perceive."[28] The word is even more heavily laden than Darr realizes. Like the English term "observe," the Greek can carry the meaning of both "look at" and "keep," as in "to observe the law." It appears this way in the Septuagint (= Hebrew *shamar*) more often without the prefix *para-*. In Tobit 14:9, for example, the word *teireison*, from the same Greek root, appears in the phrase "*keep the law and the commandments.*"[29] Luke's use of this verb surely carries the double meaning of "does not come by observable signs" and "does not come through observance of the law"—a wordplay that strikes this reader as a characteristically rabbinic way of teasing meaning from scriptural language.

The Pharisees are portrayed by Luke as engaged with Jesus as a fellow interpreter—dissenting, no doubt, on some major points, but nevertheless within the same universe of discourse, including interpretation of scripture and *halacha*. Luke's Pharisees also refrain from directly criticizing Jesus, questioning the actions of the disciples instead. The last appearance of Pharisees in Luke is in 19:39, just before Jesus enters Jerusalem, when they appeal to him to rebuke his disciples. Here they address Jesus directly and with respect (or irony?) as "Teacher" (though they separate themselves from the crowd that is acclaiming him "king") and make one final appeal to him to take his wayward disciples in hand.

Pharisees in Acts: Gamaliel

In the two incidents early in the book of Acts in which the disciples are arrested (4:1-4 and 5:17-18), the arresting authorities are identified as the high priest, the captain of the temple, and the Sadducees. The Pharisees are noticeable by their absence. The first time a Pharisee appears in Acts is in the person of Gamaliel, in 5:34. The quite positive portrait of the moderate Gamaliel sets the tone for most of the pharisaic appearances in Acts. In addition to the Pharisees who are believers (15:5), Paul is a Pharisee, and other Pharisees seem to recognize him as such (23:6; 26:5). "Some" of the Pharisees "find nothing wrong" with Paul (23:9). Indeed, the attitudes expressed by the Pharisees in Acts seem so different from the oppositional relationships in Luke (and in the other

Gospels even more so) that some have questioned whether the same authorial hand is really responsible for both.[30]

Gamaliel's speech to the council (Acts 5:34-39) appears to be either an eloquent expression of religious tolerance or a wise example of realpolitik. Gamaliel is "respected by all the people" (v. 34). Most commentators take this description seriously, as establishing Gamaliel's credentials, which, to the extent that he is seen as friendly toward the apostles, helps to establish their credentials as well.[31] It is almost certainly to be read as a positive view of Gamaliel, as is his being "respected by all the people," which is reminiscent of the description applied to the apostles a few verses earlier (5:13).[32] Further, Gamaliel's use of the phrase "I tell you" (5:38), the only time it appears in Acts, reminds the reader of the authority with which Jesus spoke in the Gospel (e.g., Luke 7:9; 15:7; 19:40).[33]

The Gamaliel of Acts is known in Jewish tradition as Rabban Gamliel Ha-Zaken ("the elder"). The honorific Rabban ("our master") may have been added later.[34] He is included among the brief "eulogies" in Mishnah Sotah 9.15: "When Rabban Gamaliel the Elder died, the glory of the Law ceased and purity and abstinence died."[35] Tradition knows him as a grandson of Hillel, but Neusner entertains doubts about that. In fact, "Gamaliel-traditions leave the man in a rather shadowy, vague state."[36] Still, there is enough evidence to conclude that "Gamaliel was both a Temple-council member, as Acts alleges, and leader within the Pharisaic sect, as the rabbinic traditions hold."[37]

Gamaliel's grandson, bearing the same name, became Nasi ("president") at Jabneh around 80 CE and apparently continued in office for the next thirty years or so. Thus the second Gamaliel was the leading rabbinic authority at the likely time of the composition of Luke-Acts. A question that might be worth pursuing is whether the appearance of Gamaliel in Acts is partly a nod in the direction of Luke's contemporary. If so, it would be additional evidence that Luke-Acts is reflecting a situation of emerging but not yet distinct boundaries.

Paul the Pharisee

Of course, the major pharisaic figure of Acts is Paul himself. In Paul's own letters he refers to himself as a Pharisee only once: "as to the law, a Pharisee" (Phil 3:5). The author of Acts makes a great deal more of Paul's pharisaic background. Alan Segal views Paul as a "convert" and refers to him as an "ex-Pharisee."[38] But neither Paul's letters nor Luke refers to him that way. In four of Paul's speeches in Acts he makes reference to his pharisaic identity, twice explicitly. His emphatic claim of pharisaic identity may, of course, serve rhetorical purposes—to show Jews that he is a fellow Jew with good credentials, and also to heighten the effect of the 180-degree turn in his convictions. Can he maintain both his pharisaic credentials and his loyalty to the risen Christ? He seems to think so.

In the first of the four speeches (Acts 22), addressing the Jerusalem crowd in Hebrew, Luke's Paul is specific about his background:

> "I am a Jew, born in Tarsus in Cilicia, but brought up in this city at the feet of Gamaliel, educated strictly according to our ancestral law, being zealous for God, just as all of you are today. I persecuted this Way up to the point of death by binding both men and women and putting them in prison, as the high priest and the whole council of elders can testify about me." (Acts 22:3-5a)

He does not use the term *Pharisee*, but implies it by referring to his teacher, Gamaliel. He also describes his education as "according to the strict manner of the law of our fathers"—and Luke's readers have already come to identify the term "strict" with Pharisaism. The crowd listens at first but eventually finds him worthy of death. The implication is that this opinion is based on his claims that he is being sent (by God) "far away to the Gentiles" (22:21). If, as we suggested earlier, there were at least some elements of the pharisaic party that favored some sort of "mission" or openness to Gentile conversion, this confrontation dramatizes this division in Jewish opinion. Paul, representing the "outreach" tendency within Pharisaism (now taken to another level), is going to specialize in "the Gentiles." Other Jews may well have seen such a program as betrayal—though why it would make Paul deserving of death is utterly unclear.

In his appearance before the council (Acts 23), Paul immediately gets in trouble by responding sharply to the illegitimate procedures of the high priest, Ananias. He recovers by exploiting the division between Pharisees and Sadducees, stressing belief in resurrection as the theological tenet he shares with his fellow Pharisees. This leads to "a great clamor," and "certain scribes of the Pharisees' group" openly declare that they find "nothing wrong with this man" (23:9). In the third speech of this series, Paul again makes reference to the pharisaic tenet of resurrection, climaxing his speech with the dramatic statement, "It is about the resurrection of the dead that I am on trial before you today" (24:21b).

In chapter 26, Paul once again stresses his pharisaic credentials and asserts that the Pharisees are the "strictest" sect:

> "All the Jews know my way of life from my youth, a life spent from the beginning among my own people and in Jerusalem. They have known for a long time, if they are willing to testify, that I have belonged to the strictest sect of our religion and lived as a Pharisee. And now I stand here on trial on account of my hope in the promise made by God to our ancestors. . . ." (Acts 26:4-6)

He also refers to resurrection: "Why is it thought incredible by any of you that God raises the dead?" (26:8).

The identity markers of Pharisaism receive different emphases in the different speeches. In the speech to the crowd (ch. 22) and in the speech before Festus and Agrippa (ch. 26), "strictness" is mentioned. In the speech to the council (ch. 23), Paul refers to himself as a Pharisee, sees no need to explain to this group that Pharisees are "strict," and stresses belief in resurrection. In the shorter speech to the council in Caesarea (ch. 24), he mentions resurrection once again. In the climactic speech of the series (ch. 26), he is explicit about all three markers: "Pharisee," "strict," and "resurrection."

As in the case of any historical narrative from antiquity, we must assume that the speeches are reconstructed by the author, if not wholly invented. While they may accurately reflect essential elements of Paul's self-understanding, the main point is that they here serve Luke's purposes. These purposes seem to be twofold: to show that both the rank and file as well as many leaders among the Jews are increasingly deaf, indeed hostile, to Paul's message, and at the same time to muster as many recommendations as possible on the side of Paul's Jewish legitimacy: he speaks Hebrew and was a student of Gamaliel, a strict Pharisee, and "kosher" (or at least kosher enough) in the eyes of at least some "scribes of the Pharisees," King Agrippa, and Roman officials (Acts 26:32).

Thus Paul's pharisaic credentials serve to heighten his legitimacy (as well as the drama of his turnaround). They also underline the possibility that a Pharisee from birth, trained in the strictest understanding and practice of Judaism, can become an enthusiastic follower of Jesus, a believer in his resurrection, and still remain a Pharisee. Thus, while other pharisaic voices in Acts may help to legitimate Paul, it is Paul more than any other figure who serves to legitimate the Jewish authenticity of this newly emerging Way.

Identity and Boundaries

A passage like Acts 21:20-21 may be read as reflecting Jewish fear about dissolving communal boundaries in the Diaspora, as well as Jewish-Christian anxiety about their own Jewish identity. In this passage, the Jewish-Christian leadership in Jerusalem greets Paul with an expression of anxiety concerning the reports of Paul's activities:

> "You see, brother, how many thousands of believers there are among the Jews, and they are all zealous for the law. They have been told about you that you teach all the Jews living among the Gentiles to forsake Moses, and that you tell them not to circumcise their children or observe the customs."

There are at least two aspects of Jewish observance that appear to be important here to the Jewish-Christian leadership in Jerusalem: the importance of ritual observance for Jews and their concern for the way they appear to other Jews (i.e., that they remain acceptable to fellow Jews by continuing to be observant of traditional Torah practices).

Ritual practice, it is suggested here, is at least as important an ingredient as theological belief in their own self-understanding as Jews. Or in any case, it is understood that it is observance that maintains their credibility with fellow Jews, despite what might be perceived as their quirky adherence to Jesus of Nazareth. This is not to suggest that ritual observance was *only* a boundary marker. It surely had its own internal logic as a faithful development of Torah as practice. But from a sociological point of view, it can *also* be seen as an effective and useful means of maintaining group identity against the many pressures of what today might be called assimilation.

Although the Pharisees may receive more positive treatment in Acts than in Luke's (or any other) Gospel, they must also be considered in the wider context of the portrayal of the Jewish people, of whom they are a part. The references to Pharisees in Acts place them in a largely positive light. However, these more positive portrayals depend for their impact on the mostly negative tone of all of the Gospel accounts, as well as the turning away of "the Jews" over the course of Acts. That is, the positive valence of Pharisees in Acts is achieved mainly by virtue of the contrast with the generally negative Gospel accounts of Pharisees and the increasingly negative portrayal of the Jewish people in Acts.[39]

The several references to Pharisees in Acts, despite some ambivalence, present them as a bridge entity in a fluid situation. Within Luke's narrative world, the Pharisees serve as a marker of contestation between emerging communities. For Luke, the Pharisees are a primary link to the teachings of Judaism, with particular stress on the belief in resurrection.[40] They often serve to legitimate Christian teachers and teachings. They also serve, especially in Luke, as a foil to Jesus' teachings. Luke-Acts, certainly more than any other New Testament work, presents a complex and ambivalent view of the Pharisees. In Luke, they are cast negatively as opponents of Jesus. Nevertheless, they are engaged in ongoing conversation with him, and Jesus and the Pharisees recognize each other as teachers whose authority carries weight and is to be taken seriously. Even if the overall narrative of the Gospel leads the reader to take a negative view of the Pharisees, their portrayal is more benign than in the other Gospels.

The shift in characterization that seems so striking in Acts is a further indication that Luke takes a complex view of who the Pharisees are and what they represent. As we have discussed, there is evidence that suggests that the lines were not yet clearly drawn between Jews and

Christians. If that is the case, then the Pharisees in Luke's narrative are presented with complexity because the situation in which Luke-Acts was written was complex. In the context of Luke's overall narrative, the Pharisees—who often seem so focused on maintaining communal boundaries—come to function as (and are reduced to) a metaphor or literary trope for the boundaries that were yet to be clarified, as two separate communities emerged out of the scriptural traditions and history of Israel. Luke's narrative is a major contribution to the drawing of the lines, and as such it also offers evidence that the boundaries were still in flux.

No matter how much a nuanced reading may seem to improve the overall image of Pharisees in Luke-Acts, a large problem remains. The general picture is still one of opposition, bordering on the lethal. Lectionary readings in churches do not point up fine distinctions. Many Christian preachers will emphasize the idea that the "Pharisees" represent hypocrisy in general, not something characteristic of Judaism alone. As one Presbyterian friend of mine said, "We were taught in church that whenever the text says 'Pharisee,' read 'Presbyterian.'" This helps defuse the anti-Jewish sting of the Gospels. However, it creates another problem, namely, that it tends to erase the Jewish context of Christianity, thereby severing Christianity from its roots.

Reading Together

When Jews and Christians read scripture together, there is the possibility of new voices rising to the surface or of old voices being heard in new ways. The words placed in the mouth of the Pharisee Gamaliel in the fifth chapter of Acts— "but if it is of God, you will not be able to overthrow them" (5:39)—connect on a deep level to the evolving relationship of Judaism and Christianity. The text is a verse from Christian scripture, but the line is attributed to a Jewish teacher, indeed the leading Pharisee of his generation. It is presented as a Jewish teaching concerning nascent Christianity, at this stage still one of a number of competing Judaisms. Gamaliel is portrayed here as the voice of reason and moderation, speaking to Jews who seek to punish the followers of Jesus: "Let them alone." This advice is based on historical reflection—we have seen such things before—and leads to a theological reflection: "If it is of God, you will not be able to overthrow them—in that case you may even be found fighting against God!"

The verse can be heard in at least two voices: the voice of a pharisaic Jewish teacher and the voice of Christian scripture. Speaking to fellow Jews, Gamaliel allows that there may be room for this different understanding of messianic history. In any case, it is not for us to put a stop to it, for God may have other plans. As a verse within Christian scripture, it speaks, however, primarily to Christians. The mutually confirming possibility that Gamaliel places before Christians, if they are open to it, is that of the continuing vitality of Judaism.[41] After two thousand years, if one accepts the biblical view that God works in and through history, the continuing existence and creative development of post-Temple Judaism is a sign: there is room in the divine plan for multiple religious traditions able to stand the test of time.

Thus a scriptural verse that reverberates in two voices, Jewish and Christian, suggests that an other may be *ek Theou*—from God, of God, destined to endure as a separate way—separate, but not completely so. From the tangled roots of Judaism and Christianity in the first century, through the often violent history of nineteen centuries twisted by claims of exclusive truth, emerges a new-old understanding mirroring back the need for dialectical embrace.

PART 4

Looking to the Present
and the Future

Can We Hope? Can Hope Be Divided?

WALTER BRUEGGEMANN

I was led to frame my chapter by a convergence of three impingements:

1. Michael Lerner, editor at *Tikkun*, wrote to ask if I would write a piece on hope. *Tikkun* is, of course, preoccupied with the Israeli-Palestinian conflict, where it is clear that the missing ingredient on all sides is enough hope to think beyond present arrangements.

2. Yoko Ono Lennon, on August 30, 2004, had a full-page ad in the *New York Times* with only two large words—very large words—"Imagine Peace." The juxtaposition of *peace* and *imagine* is a recognition that peace will not come by thinking "inside the box," but only by pushing beyond presently available reality to a newness that is given at the edge of the human spirit.

3. The 9/11 Commission concluded, along with a general critique of bureaucratic dysfunction, that the primary "intelligence" failure is a "failure of imagination." The Commission, of course, was constituted by "hard men," so that the imagination that is missing in their purview was an imagination of power and control; nonetheless, their judgment reflects an awareness that technical management of power resources cannot by itself secure a livable future.

These three moments together suggest to me the theme of hope. Given that, I have made a decision that a reflection on the way in which Jews and Christians have between themselves contested texts—given Jewish particularity and recurring Christian hegemony—is not very interesting or very helpful. I have decided then to reflect rather upon the ways in which Jews and Christians share a common inheritance of hope, albeit with elements of contestation, a common inheritance that makes its way in and against a dominant culture that is, by design and conviction, a venue for hopelessness and despair. Thus my topic is based on two convictions. First, that Jews and Christians constitute together, in common grounding, communities of hope. Second, that that shared inheritance of hope is all the more noticeable, more spectacular, and more urgent when set down in a societal context of despair. I do not want to gloss over defining distinctions and long-standing tensions between Jews and Christians, but I think that these distinctions and tensions, while theologically rooted, are massively exaggerated and problematized by a sociopolitical history of control and abuse that ought not to be defining for our future interaction.

Thus I take my lead from Hebrews 11:1: "Now faith is the assurance of things hoped for, the conviction of things not seen." This, as you know, is a Christian text; but it is a Christian text that is preoccupied with the history of ancient Israel and in fact makes only a passing Christological claim. The hopers who constitute this recited history are people in Israel who could imagine beyond present circumstance to "things not seen." I submit that it is a present task of Jews and Christians together to focus on "things not seen" but promised, in a context that is mired in and mesmerized by present power arrangements. It goes without saying, of course, that such unseen things are not otherworldly, but pertain precisely to the gifts and tasks in our midst.

I.

I begin by asking about the common inheritances of hope shared by Jews and Christians by identifying four necessary components for the practice of hope:

1. Hope requires *a Source and Agent of newness* who is, in inscrutable ways, generative, who is not imprisoned in old habits or present-tense commitments. That, of course, is a theological statement about the character of God that Jews and Christians commonly confess. Thus I begin with the affirmation that hope is theologically grounded, which of course stacks the cards at the outset. But the alternative to such an agency that stands outside present arrangements is to find ground for hope within present life arrangements themselves, a strategy that

inescapably produces the absolutizing of some power arrangement that soon or late becomes idolatrous and self-destructive. The exodus narrative is a clear assertion of hope introduced into the slave community from outside the Pharaonic system of abuse and exploitation. In Christian tradition, Calvin's great hymn makes a Moses-like affirmation, "My hope is in none other, save in thee alone."

2. Hope requires *a community of faith and action* that is open to newness that is given as a gift. Hope is indeed a communal activity, for none can fully hope alone. The intention of holy agency is to form communities of obedient action that rely upon and respond to divine intention. The formation and maintenance of such a community are always problematic because the many narratives of despair are, on the face of it, more impressive and more reassuring than the narratives of hope. Thus the community of faith and action formed around Moses struggled for fidelity and sought immediately to return to Egypt for guaranteed food (Num 14:6); and when cut free from Egypt, that community promptly made for itself images that would witness against the free generativity of YHWH (Exod 32:4). It is not different, moreover, in Jesus' formation of a community of disciples who are characteristically fearful, obtuse, and unresponsive. Thus the community of faithful obedience is always in jeopardy; in its jeopardy, however, it manages over time to make enough of a response to divine generativity to make its way in the world.

3. Hope requires *a text* that mediates between *holy generativity* and *communal obedience.* Jews and Christians share such a text that is grounded in oracular assurances and that provides an account of narrative possibility that continues to be available amid the vagaries of lived reality. This mediating text that is a primal connection between holy generativity and communal obedience is perforce an odd text, or in the words of Karl Barth, always "strange and new." Over time, there are many strategies to try to make what is strange manageable and to make what is new commonplace; such strategies, however, cannot, in the long run, succeed, because of the character of the text itself and because of the Character who occupies the text. That is why, on the one hand, there are endless quarrels about the text and why, on the other hand, the protagonists agree in a rough way that the text is revelatory, offering glimpses of that which remains hidden from us.

4. As the text mediates between holy generativity and communal obedience, hope requires *a community of interpretation* that is emancipated, emancipatory, generative, and daring in its interpretation. Both the Jewish and Christian communities of interpretation have had such an interpretive energy to move between contemporary circumstance and ancient text with hermeneutical agility, as Gerhard von Rad has seen so well in the tradition of Deuteronomy. These communities at the same time, however, have found ways to resist the generative force of interpretation, whether by fundamentalist reductionism or by critical explanation, for both reductionism and explanation inescapably curb the dangerous subversive force of a text that witnesses to hidden holy mystery.

Thus my beginning point about hope as a ground for *imaginative reconciliation* of the world is to focus on what Jews and Christians share of the *mystery of God*, the *derivative mystery of community*, the *revelatory power of a text*, and a *culture of interpretation*. Old violences between these communities, of course almost completely from the Christian side, have tended to obscure that which is common between us.

II.

Jews and Christians are *practitioners of hope* amid a culture of despair. While despair is no doubt a recurring human condition, here I want to consider the particular shape of despair in dominant Western society to which these two communities of hope are able to respond in transformative ways. I will identify five components of contemporary despair:

1. *The maintenance of a "national security state"* creates an environment that is inimical to dissent and that believes that all questions can be solved by power and control. Such an environment leads to a sense of self-sufficiency that relies on the capacity to control the global economy, and consequently to a readiness to engage in violence and an equal readiness to collude in the violence of others, all in the self-justifying name of security.

2. The silencing of dissent in the interest of security requires *a closed ideology* that depends upon a cooperative, accommodating religion for legitimacy. The closed ideology that is offered in the name of the holy through policies of exploitative violence is incapable of self-criticism,

incapable of moral reflection, and incapable of entertaining any alternative to present power arrangements. The only project that remains is to ensure that present power arrangements are sustained and made even more absolute, and this in the name of the holy.

3. One tool for such self-securing that is legitimated by a closed ideology in the name of the holy is *uncriticized technology* that would seem to deliver a capacity for limitless power and control. The practical cost of such technology in terms of the human infrastructure is characteristically unrecognized and kept invisible, so that huge investments in technologies of control are made to seem both normal and moral, as well as inescapable.

4. The convergence of ideology and technology produces *a shameless kind of certitude* that closes off the future and shrivels the human spirit. It is clear, nonetheless, that such shameless certitude is only a veneer that conceals depths of anxiety that feed back into a quest for greater certitude. It is evident that because the human spirit finally must have something other than such a "shutdown," no amount of technology-cum-ideology can satisfy such longing. Thus the system of security makes us even more insecure.

5. The surface antidote to such anxiety that cannot be denied is that we do our best to remain *smitten by commodities*, for commodities not only keep the economy growing in ways that fund the technology, but soothe the human spirit into "happiness." The consequence, of course, is that as the security system leaves us *insecure*, so the happiness system leaves us *unhappy*. My sense is that the primary commitments of our culture to *security, ideology, technology, certitude, and commodity* constitute a system of hopelessness. But it was ever thus, from Pharaoh to Nebuchadnezzar to Caesar and on until now. Dominant culture—even with its myth of progress—is characteristically a culture of despair. It becomes so because it regards itself as ultimate and can countenance no suggestion of its own penultimacy. It becomes so because it banishes the power of the holy and cannot recognize its own profanation. It becomes so because it lives by control and can entertain no openness to gift. And so despair yields a culture of death . . . and violence . . . and brutality that is mostly unnoticed by the shoppers, attended only by an occasional poet.

It is in that matrix that Jews have forever been Jews. It is in that matrix that Christians have been placed, certainly since the book of Acts; the faithful are called before the authorities to give an alternative account of reality, an alternative consisting in imaginative leaps beyond the given, imaginative leaps that at best are gifts of God's own Spirit.

III.

The question that concerns Jews and Christians is "Can we hope?" Just as I worked on the question, I was pointed by my colleague George Stroup to some pages of Karl Barth in section III.2, "Ending Time," of *Church Dogmatics.* In that closely, intensely argued chapter, Barth makes three points that provide an answer to our question of hope in a despairing culture of death:

1. Death is a defining reality of human life that constitutes divine judgment before which all are afraid:

> The inevitability of death means that this threat overshadows and dominates our whole life. It cannot be gainsaid or defied. It might well be, indeed it is necessarily the case, that the ultimate truth about man, which dominates every prior truth, is that he stands under this threat which is not to be gainsaid or defied. Less than this we cannot say. Death, as it meets us, can be understood only as a sign of God's judgment. For when it meets us, as it undoubtedly does, it meets us as sinful and guilty men with whom God cannot finally do anything but whom He can only regret having made. For man has failed as His creature. He has not used the previous freedom in which he was privileged to exist before God. He has squandered it away in the most incredible manner. He can hope for nothing better than to be hewn down and cast into the fire. . . . There has never been a man who was not afraid of death. It is possible to stifle this fear. But in so doing, we only show that we have it none the less. Man lives in fear for his life. But this fear in all its forms, even that of Stoic resignation, is basically the fear of death which we cannot talk ourselves out of.[1]

It takes no imagination at all to see that the elements of a despairing culture cited above, most especially the national security state with all its accoutrements, are evidence of the force of death.

2. The reality of God presides over and transcends that threat of death:

> It is not merely death but God Himself who awaits us. Basically and properly it is not that enemy but God who is to be feared. In death we are not to fear death itself but God. . . . But the God who awaits us in death and as the Lord of death is the gracious God. He is the God who is for man. Other gods who are not gracious and not for man are idols. . . . Death is our frontier. But our God is the frontier even of our death. For He does not perish with us. He does not die or decay. As our God He is always the same. Even in death He is still our Helper and Deliverer.[2]

3. The assurance of God's rule beyond the threat of death is known fully in the Old Testament, to which the New Testament and the witness of Jesus add concreteness, but not anything not already known:

> The God of whom we do not say too much when we view our lives wholly and utterly in the light of His existence as our Helper and Deliverer, and therefore wholly and utterly on the other side of death, and conversely the God of whom we do not say too little when we seek and find our own being out of and above death wholly and utterly and exclusively in Him, is the God of the New Testament revelation and perception. But this God is the same as that of the Old Testament. Hence there is no need to retract or correct anything we have said. But as the same God, as the Lord of death and our gracious God, and therefore as the infinitely saving but exclusive frontier beyond death, He is revealed and perceptible to us according to the New Testament in such a way that all inquiry concerning Him necessarily carries a positive answer, and the positive answer which we grasp in Him necessarily leads us to genuine inquiry concerning Him.

We learn nothing materially new when we formally enter New Testament ground. We are again concerned with our God as the limit of our death: with the One who is the Lord of death and therefore alone is to be feared in death; with our gracious God and consolation, our Helper and Deliverer in the midst of death, so that in hope in Him death is already behind and under us. . . . The material unity of the Old and New Testament revelation and perception is clear and convincing at this point. God is always the One concerning whom we must ask exclusively when it is a matter of our preservation from death and victory over it. It is the fact that this exclusiveness is now made concrete that the suggestion concerning Him becomes meaningful and relevant.[3]

Barth, of course, has more to say about the full disclosure of God as the God of life in the event of Jesus Christ. For our purposes, however, it is enough to see that even Barth, given his Christological accent, affirms that Christians stand alongside Jews. Or better, Christians stand after Jews and are instructed by them; or perhaps better, both Judaism and Christianity stand after ancient Israel in its practice of hope. We Christians give different nuance to that hope because of the claim of Jesus Christ, and Barth, of course, is unambiguous on this claim:

For it summons us to gather around Jesus Christ, to believe in Him alone and resolutely to refuse all other offers. Without Him we should not only be under the sign of God's judgment in death. We should be under the judgment itself and irretrievably lost. In Him alone God is our gracious God. If our sin and guilt were not laid upon Him, they would still rest upon us, and it could be no real consolation to us to meet our God in our death. In Him alone is God our Helper and Deliverer. For in His death alone our deliverance from sin and guilt and therefore our liberation from death is accomplished. In Him alone death has not merely been endured but overcome. In Him alone it is really for us a defeated foe. In Him alone we may and must seriously reckon with the fact that God is the boundary of the death which bounds us. In Him alone that menacing no man's land is stripped of its menace, and invading chaos repulsed. In Him alone rests our hope, namely, that we may expect everything from God even in and beyond our death when we shall be no more. If we cannot fix our hopes too high when they are set on Him, we cannot be too reserved or cautious or critical in respect of all expectations which are not directed to Him and Him alone. It cannot and should not be too small a thing for us that He and He only is our hope, our future, our victory, our resurrection and our life. Nor should we regret that we have to gather around Him, concentrate wholly upon Him, wholly and utterly believe on Him as God's positive answer to us, allow God's Word of help and deliverance to be spoken to us wholly and exclusively in His person, in His death and resurrection.[4]

I will comment more on that; but for now, it is this third point of Barth that I accent, that is, that we hope together in the God who opposes death. For that reason, all derivative seductions of despair—the ones I have identified as *security, ideology, technology, certitude,* and *commodity*— are fruits of the realm of death against which we hope, hope from the God of life, hope toward the neighbor.

IV.

Barth avers, "We learn nothing materially new when we formally enter New Testament ground."[5] From this awareness, our theme invites Christians to inquire again, without triumphal smugness, to see how we have learned hope—against the kingdom of death—from Jews who are before us and alongside us. The evidence from Judaism as a ground for hope after the manner of ancient Israel is rich and complex, and we Christians are able to be practitioners of that same hope as children of the same God. Here I mention four aspects of that practice of hope before considering some texts with more specificity:

1. One might begin at many points on the counterpractice of hope, and I will return to Genesis later. But for now perhaps the classic text on hope is in the enigmatic formulation of Exod 3:14 that is translated something like, "I will be who I will be," or "I will cause to be that which will be." The enigmatic quality of the statement in YHWH's mouth

is to be reckoned as crucial, for the God of hope is profoundly elusive. This is an elusiveness that resists precise, idolatrous formulation. The God who speaks to Moses is the God of the ancestors who long ago made promises. But now the presence is an abiding presence. Buber finally judges:

> This promise is given unconditional validity in the first part of the statement: "I shall be present," not merely, as previously and subsequently, "with you, with your mouth," but absolutely, "I shall be present." Placed as the phrase is between two utterances of so concrete a kind that clearly means: I am and remain present. ... This is followed in the second part by: "That I shall be present," or "As which I shall be present." In this way the sentence is reminiscent of the later statement of the God to Moses: "I shall be merciful to him to whom I shall be merciful." But in it the future character is more strongly stressed. YHWH indeed states that he will always be present, but at any given moment as the one as whom he then, in that given moment, will be present. He who promises his steady presence, his steady assistance, refuses to restrict himself to definite forms of manifestation.[6]

What begins with the burning bush culminates later in Israel and in the church as "Emmanuel." Samuel Terrien agrees with Buber about presence, but notes its enigmatic, free quality:

> The God of biblical faith, even in the midst of a theophany, is at once *Deus revelatus atque absconditus*. He is known as unknown. The semantics of the phrase "I shall be whoever I shall be" prepares the syntactically similar saying of the third Sinai theophany, "I shall grace whomever I shall grace and I shall be merciful with whomever I shall be merciful" (Exod. 33:19). . . . He wanted religious certainty. He wished to see with his own power of perception. He intended to comprehend. Yahweh's disclosure of his name was both an answer and the denial of a request. Such an ambivalence was to remain "forever" (vs.15*b*) the mark of the Hebraic theology of presence.[7]

What counts the most, of course, is that the name of the promise-maker who speaks here is disclosed amid Pharaonic slavery. The disclosure is a counter to Pharaonic presence that was as oppressive as it was palpable in the slave community. The declaration of YHWH's presence has an emancipatory intention, providing a community that is on the move to a better future (see Heb 11:15-16).

2. The divine disclosure sets in motion a community on the way. Indeed, the purpose of the divine self-disclosure is to be on the way to a new place and to a new history. The word that counters YHWH's word is a generative, emancipatory word that moves the community along *from slavery to well-being,* and eventually *from exile back to the land.* To be sure, there is each time a rearguard action of despair; the "National Security State" of Pharaoh and then of Nebuchadnezzar has a deep grip upon Israel's imagination. Thus in Exodus 16, just after the departure from Egypt, some want to return to oppressive security. And in Babylon, some shrink from departure from the Babylonian Empire, being sure that YHWH's hand is too short (Isa 50:2) and that Israel's way is hid from the Lord (Isa 40:27). Such timid collusion, of course, will not prevail in the community of hope, for the God of hope comes to occupy the life of the hopers.

3. The God of hope did indeed accompany the hopers. The signs of that accompaniment were *fire* and *cloud* and *name* and *glory* and *ark.* If, however, we think of *praxis,* we may imagine that the presence was in singing, singing that eventually became text, and thus the God of textual presence. Singing as *praxis* is the way hopers regularly defy Pharaonic power, even when frightened and anxious. And so we may notice that the promise as *song-become-text* was on the lips of Miriam and the others with tambourines: "And Miriam sang to them: 'Sing to the LORD, for he has triumphed gloriously; horse and rider he has thrown into the sea'" (Exod 15:21). They sang in defiance and in fear, but surely against fear.

It must not have been different, moreover, in the second departure, the one from Babylon, for that poet understands the entry to the future via song-become-text:

For you shall go out in joy,
and be led back in peace;

149

the mountains and the hills before you
  shall burst into song,
    and all the trees of the field shall clap their hands. (Isa 55:12)

The hopers sing a defiant echo of Miriam, defiance in sixth-century Babylon, and then in Selma and in Pretoria and wherever hope defies the national security system and other manifestations of the kingdom of death.

4. The singers generated songs. The songs became text. And the text was to be read and reread, heard and reheard, interpreted and reinterpreted. It is a community of equilibrium that can confine texts to one meaning. But a community of hope has texts that always "mean" afresh; hopers engaged inescapably in the juggling act of hope that defiantly moves between acquiescence to present arrangements and risk that opens through many layers of interpretation, imagination, polyvalence. Such layered interpretation refuses closure, for the closure of the text would only bespeak the closure of the empire and, before that, the closure of the brickyard. James C. Scott has chronicled surreptitious defiance on the part of peasants in Malaysia and in other cultures that are attuned to the defiance of hope.[8] Hope is always such an act of defiance. In these communities of hope, it is done through reiterated text that traces the presence and power of the One who is sung.

V.

The texts of hope make YHWH palpably present in a way that saturates the imagination of Judaism and Christianity, and that empowers against the kingdom of death.

1. At the outset of this matrix of hope is *the initial promise to Abraham and Sarah*:

Now the LORD said to Abram, "Go from your country and your kindred and your father's house to the land that I will show you. I will make of you a great nation, and I will bless you, and make your name great, so that you will be a blessing." (Gen 12:1-2)

As long ago as Albrecht Alt and subsequently Gerhard von Rad and Jürgen Moltmann, this initiatory utterance of promise has been seen as the ground of biblical hope.[9] In Gen 12:3, moreover, that articulation of hope looks through and beyond the Abraham community to the nations: "I will bless those who bless you, and the one who curses you I will curse; and in you all the families of the earth shall be blessed." This text, with its reference to the nations, surely looks back to the great promise of Gen 9:8-17:

> "I will remember my covenant that is between me and you and every living creature of all flesh; and the waters shall never again become a flood to destroy all flesh. When the bow is in the clouds, I will see it and remember the everlasting covenant between God and every living creature of all flesh that is on the earth." (Gen 9:15-16)

2. The initial ground of hope in Gen 12:1-3 is strangely matched late in the Hebrew Bible by that text that has long occupied Christians, namely, the text concerning the one "coming with the clouds of heaven":

> As I watched in the night visions,
>> I saw one like a human being
>>> coming with the clouds of heaven.
>> And he came to the Ancient One
>>> and was presented before him.
>> To him was given dominion
>>> and glory and kingship,
>> that all peoples, nations, and languages
>>> should serve him.
>> His dominion is an everlasting dominion
>>> that shall not pass away,
>> and his kingship is one
>>> that shall never be destroyed. (Dan 7:13-14)

This text and others like it, of course, opened faith for both Judaism and Christianity, to apocalyptic that is perhaps the extreme mode of hope, an extremity now so grossly misconstrued among us. The opening toward cosmic vision later in the Old Testament kept the community from excessive focus upon itself as the aim of hope.

3. But between Gen 12:1-3, which focuses on the community of Israel, and Daniel 7, which is cosmic in scope, I focus upon *the great exilic prophetic promises* that imagined and waited for a newness from YHWH that would override the defilement of deportation and make a worldly newness available to the people of God. The outcome of such prophetic promise is, in the first instance, Judaism, an outcome not fully commensurate with the lyric anticipation of the poets; but then, Jews and Christians together live with visible outcomes that are, for the most part, short of expectant rhetoric.

Judaism and Christianity share texts of promise that are, to be sure, contested between them about the goal and outcome of such promises. As case studies in contestation, I will consider three texts, one from each of the three major prophets:

1. In the tradition of Isaiah, the promise in exile is dramatically and authoritatively voiced in Isa 43:16-21:

> Thus says the LORD,
>> who makes a way in the sea,
>> a path in the mighty waters,
> who brings out chariot and horse,
>> army and warrior;
> they lie down, they cannot rise,
>> they are extinguished, quenched like a wick:
> Do not remember the former things,
>> or consider the things of old.
> I am about to do a new thing;
>> now it springs forth, do you not perceive it?
> I will make a way in the wilderness
>> and rivers in the desert.
> The wild animals will honor me,
>> the jackals and the ostriches;
> for I give water in the wilderness,
>> rivers in the desert,
> to give drink to my chosen people,

the people whom I formed for myself
so that they might declare my praise.

Taken as best as we are able on historical-critical grounds, the text anticipates a return from exile for deported Jews. The imagery appeals to the remembered exodus and then imagines that this restoration to Jerusalem is so wondrous and so glorious that it displaces the remembered exodus in the faith of the community. The imagery is of a general restoration, including a restoration of creation. The purpose of new "rivers in the desert," however, is clearly for the sake of "my chosen people, the people whom I formed for myself." This anticipated restoration, of course, took the form of returned exiles who caused a newly formulated Judaism in Babylon to be resituated in Jerusalem, eventually under the leadership of Ezra.

Christians of a historical-critical variety have not interpreted the promise of Isa 43:16-21 differently and have seen in it the emergence of Judaism. But of course Christian interpretation is not satisfied with such a reading; it must, as it is able, always draw the text close to Jesus. When this text is drawn toward the Christian gospel, it is, of course, the work of Christ and the community that he has founded that constitute the "new thing." So the New Testament specialized in the word new—new wineskins, new covenant, new commandment. Christian interpretation does not bother to assess the "plain meaning" of Isaiah's utterance, because it historically has had no interest in such a newness, but reads promptly and programmatically beyond that to the newness of Jesus. Indeed, Walter Moberly has made the argument, with reference to Genesis and Exodus, that in the Old Testament itself the text regularly moves from an old meaning to a *new*. Consequently, the displacement of sixth-century newness by first-century Christological newness is consistent with the hermeneutical maneuvers already evident in the Old Testament itself. Except, of course, that this potential supersessionism from Judaism to Christianity has been historically *a power move* as well as *an interpretive move*, so that the transformation and transposition of memory are not merely reinterpretation but characteristically a powerful preemption.

2. The same move is surely the case in the more familiar text from Jer 31:31-34:

The days are surely coming, says the Lord, when I will make a new covenant with the house of Israel and the house of Judah. It will not be like the covenant that I made with their ancestors when I took them by the hand to bring them out of the land of Egypt—a covenant that they broke, though I was their husband, says the Lord. But this is the covenant that I will make with the house of Israel after those days, says the Lord: I will put my law within them, and I will write it on their hearts; and I will be their God, and they shall be my people. No longer shall they teach one another, or say to each other, "Know the Lord," for they shall all know me, from the least of them to the greatest, says the Lord; for I will forgive their iniquity, and remember their sin no more.

That text, in the book of Jeremiah, characteristically understands that the exile is a consequence of the covenant "which they broke." That is, exile is God's punishment upon recalcitrant Israel.

The hope for the new covenant, of course, is that it is grounded in unconditional divine forgiveness, permitting a reengagement with YHWH (see Jer 33:8 as well). That is, the future of Judaism as YHWH's covenant people is grounded in divine grace and forgiveness. In that way, the oracle anticipates full reassertion of covenant with Torah provisions but without lingering over merited covenant punishment.

This text, as it is quoted in Heb 8:8-12, is utilized in one of the most remarkable supersessionist texts in the New Testament. The text of Jeremiah is quoted in full; then a verdict is given over that old covenant now displaced: "In speaking of 'a new covenant,' he has made the first one obsolete. And what is obsolete and growing old will soon disappear" (Heb 8:13). The text dismisses Judaism as old and obsolete and soon to disappear. This, of course, is a theological and not a historical judgment, but that makes the statement no less disastrous. We can see here, as clearly as anywhere, that not only does Christian interpretation sometimes preempt texts from Judaism, but it does so in an aggressively exclusionary way that dismisses the legitimacy of Jewish claim and Jewish community.

3. In Ezek 47:1-12, the Priestly tradition anticipates a new future that is grounded in a restored temple so that the river of life that had

flowed from the Garden of Eden (Gen 2:10-14) now flows from beneath the threshold of the temple. Jerusalem has now replaced Eden as the generative rootage for the source of life. The rebuilt temple, of course, is in the service of a restored Judaism, so that the holy place of YHWH and the holy place of Jews are expected to be the source of life for all of creation.

The usage of this text in Christian formulation of Rev 21:22 is closely reminiscent of Ezekiel. Thus there is an anticipation of a new holy city, a new Jerusalem (Rev 21:2). As in Ezekiel, the "water of life" flows from the throne of God: "Then the angel showed me the river of the water of life, bright as crystal, flowing from the throne of God and of the Lamb through the middle of the street of the city" (Rev 22:1-2a). But instead of the temple that is absent in this vision, the reference is to "the throne of God," which, of course, can be the temple in Jerusalem. The distinguishing feature of the rhetoric, however, concerns "the Lamb." As a result, the vision now pertains to Jesus, the one crucified as "the slain Lamb," but the Lamb that rules in power. Thus the temple in Jewish tradition is transposed in Christian discourse to be not a place, but a person, the Christ who rules with God.

There is nothing terribly surprising or exceptional in the interpretative moves made in these three texts in Christian interpretation. In each case, the historical-critical judgment surely coheres in the main with Jewish hope that is invested in restored Judaism, Judaism as the *new thing*, the *new covenant*, and the *new temple*. In each case, of course, the text is drawn, in Christian teaching, toward Jesus, who is *the new thing*, the giver of *the new covenant*, and *the presence of God* in crucified form. Nothing of this is exceptional, and it is commonly taken for granted among us.

This capacity for the transposition of the text is congruent with the nature of the text itself, for these are indeed figurative texts that do not have precise meanings but are verbal acts of hope that perforce must be open-ended. Because the texts are acts of hope and not prediction or predetermination, there is an openness to more than one meaning. The risky point of such contestation is not that the texts in Christian purview have a different meaning from their meaning in Judaism, but that the different meaning in Christian form is taken as exclusionary so that the text can mean this and only this, "this" being the Christian claim that perforce excludes Jewish reading.

Thus the matter to note in textual contestation is not that the texts have a second, different meaning for the second belated community, but that the new meaning is characteristically claimed as the *only* meaning, a claim that all too often has been supported by political leverage. This contestation about text between Christians and Jews takes place with recognition that texts have variable meanings and no single meaning is adequate to the text. Judaism has been characteristically open to polyvalence in the text. The problem is that Christian interpretation has not, for the most part, allowed for polyvalence, but has insisted on single meanings, of course single meanings that serve Christian hegemony and that regard Jewish reading as inadequate and now superseded.

Thus hope is possible in these twinned communities. But when that hope, rooted in text, is reduced to an intolerant confessional position, then hope is shot through with ideology and is no longer hope that hopes in God. Such exclusionary exposition characteristically produces partisan and self-serving interpretation. Of course, such exclusionary practice is not necessarily willful self-serving. It is rather a confessional zeal that by intention and by default eliminates the "other" as a valid interpreter. There is no doubt that supersessionist interpretation has functioned to eliminate the "other" of Judaism. My point is that alternative readings per se do not require this; that requirement arises rather from the exclusionary presupposition that texts have only one meaning and only one legitimate interpretation. Such an exclusionary presupposition is rooted in a failure to understand the nature of the text and a further failure to appreciate the nature of Jewish interpretation. Thus I answer my first question, "Can we hope?" by answering, "Yes, Judaism and Christianity are communities that hope"; but the exclusionary dismissal of the "other" runs the ready risk that hope devolves into ideology.

The church over the centuries has found many ways to practice exclusionary interpretation that imagines its appropriation of texts as the only possible reading:

1. *Sectarianism* seeks to exclude reading by the "other" within the community of faith under a tight exclusionary discipline.

2. *Hegemony* seeks to comprehend all other readings, even those outside the community of faith in the larger culture.

3. So-called *canonical reading*, if pressed to its logical extremity, turns out to be hegemonic and regards all other readings as illegitimate or at least as preliminary readings.

4. In a very different way, *historical-critical reading* has served to foster an exclusionary reading from a modernist perspective, with an implied if not stated dismissal of readings that reflect confessional perspective, either Jewish or Christian.

In sum, the Western church, perhaps especially Protestant traditions, has been an institution of closure that has practiced a certain form of hope, but a form of hope that has been tightly bound in preemptive modes.

Thus I would answer, yes, we can hope, even in an environment of the national security state. But that leads to my second question, "Can hope be divided?" I understand the hope of these confessing communities, Jewish and Christian, to be expectation of "a better country . . . a city [prepared] for them" (Heb 11:16); or put differently, the promised coming of the rule of the creator-redeemer God in the earth as it is already established in heaven. That, of course, is why we pray for the coming of the kingdom on earth. Or as David Novak concludes his telling book, *Jewish-Christian Dialogue: A Jewish Justification*:

> Beginning with creation and nurtured by our respective revelations, Jews and Christians can and do hope for the future. From creation and revelation comes our faith that God has not and will not abandon us or the world, that the promised redemption is surely yet to come.[10]

That is our hope. And yes, Jews and Christians have the necessary gifts and prerequisites for such hope in the God whom we jointly confess, hope for the world that is jointly entrusted to us along with all humanity.

But then, as I reflected on the purpose of this conference and our long history of abuse and alienation, I wondered if that hope could be parceled out as we have done it. My judgment is that when hope is divided among our communities of interpretation, it is likely that our hope is lodged with an idol who cannot keep promises; it follows that hope in the promises of the true God can be practiced only as we hope together, and that in spite of all our differentiations.

1. Jews and Christians may hope together, and that given our different defining communities. For Jews the promises are rooted in Abraham but shaped by Sinai; for Christians hope is given a trace of fulfillment in Jesus of Nazareth. These specificities place Christians and Jews very differently about a shared hope and cause us to read texts differently, such texts as "new things" in Isaiah 43, as "new covenant" in Jeremiah 31, and as "rivers of life" in Ezekiel 47. None of that is to be minimized. But because what Novak calls "the all mysterious end" is larger, more sweeping, more glorious, and more hidden than any of us in our distinct communities can yet know, we may hope beyond the confines of our own confessional passions.

2. When I ponder this title, "Can Hope Be Divided?" I have in mind precisely Jewish-Christian practices of hope. But then came the incredible religious polarizing of the churches in the United States with the 2004 presidential election. In that context I take this question back toward the church and ask again, "Can hope be divided?" The issue of "already and not yet" is an immensely acute one among Christians just now. Between Christians and Jews it is also acute, for Christians are wont to overstate the "already" in Jesus Christ, whereas Jews wait for Messiah who has not yet come. But of course both Christians and Jews who stand together in the "not yet" could not do so without an "already." The "already" of Christians is explicit in Jesus of Nazareth; but Jews are also able to hope because of the "already" of Sinai and the "already" of the promises already kept to Jews and to the world.

But now concerning "already and not yet," I ask about the church. The current accent on "dispensationalism" and the coming rapture and the Left Behind series—a movement that is particularly committed to the security of the state of Israel—are all about "not yet." Conversely, so-called mainline churches that tend to have weak eschatology focus on the "already" of Jesus Christ, not so much in the form of the "realized eschatology" of C. H. Dodd, but in an easy confession that the big matters have been settled in the Christ event.

It is clear, however, is it not, that the settlement of the tension of "already/not yet"—either by a futuristic hope that despairs of present life or an "already" that expects to be barely interrupted—is a betrayal, in one direction or the other, of the in-betweenness of the life of faith that lives by a revelation and that awaits a full disclosure? The political fallout of such division of hope among us Christians is in its own way as disastrous as the way in which Jews and Christians have divided hope.

3. Reflecting on "already and not yet," there is then a third way in which we have divided hope, namely, "red and blue" (borrowing from contemporary descriptions of the U.S. political landscape). *Red hope* is, in current discussion, privatized and individualized without any sense of the public. And *blue hope*, in much of its articulation, is public and social, but without attentiveness to the personal conviction concerning the God of all promises that is so palpable, for example, in the psalms of lament and in the songs of thanksgiving.

On all three of these issues, hope requires a repentance of our divisions of hope:

- *Jews and Christians* hope for the reign of God that maintains a special but modest place for chosenness, but the rule of God is surely beyond hope for Israel or hope for the church. Perhaps the most stunning text for hope beyond these divisions is the oracle in Isa 19:24-25, wherein in time to come God will have many chosen peoples:

    > On that day Israel will be the third with Egypt and Assyria, a blessing in the midst of the earth, whom the LORD of hosts has blessed, saying, "Blessed be Egypt my people, and Assyria the work of my hands, and Israel my heritage."

    In the days to come, there will be many chosen peoples, each named by one of YHWH's pet names for the beloved.

- Christians maintain the *"already and not yet"* without collapse in another direction; this tension is nicely articulated in Paul's familiar summation of the Eucharistic tradition. On the one hand, "in remembrance"; on the other hand, "you proclaim the Lord's death until he comes" (1 Cor 11:25-26).

- *Red and blue Christians* together recognize that there is no way that hope in faith can be only private or only public. The promises are to the community and to each member of the community for whom a particular blessing is given.

VI.

Christians then have a common vocation with Jews to hope; indeed, Christians can hope only with Jews:

1. Christian rootage for the future hope is inescapably related to the Friday-Saturday-Sunday triduum. That dramatic narrative has been given sacramental force in the Eucharistic formulation:

Christ has died;
Christ has risen;
Christ will come again.

The third element in this formulation looks beyond Easter to the complete victory for God's new life in the world. It is, however, the case that the large completeness of the drama does not leave Friday behind. Clear to the end hope continues to keep the memory and reality of failure, deficit, and emptiness at the center of awareness.

2. What is missed in the Eucharistic formula, however, that barely made it into the creed is the long stretch of Saturday where the world is mostly lodged. There is no better exegesis for the world's Saturday than that of Allen Lewis in his book *Between Cross and Resurrection*, which offers a reflection on Auschwitz, Hiroshima, Chernobyl, plus the ending of his own life.[11] And George Steiner, in his characteristic eloquence, speaks of the "immensity of waiting" that is "the long day's journey of the Saturday."[12] An immense pause over Saturday will save the church from triumphalism that rings false amid the barbarism of the world all around in which we ourselves are so deeply implicated. Such a pause, moreover, may curb the shrill triumphalist voice of Christian supersessionism in the presence of Jews.

3. Hope that moves beyond a claim of privilege requires an emptying of an exclusionary posture that is linked to absolutist readings. Because Jews have lived characteristically on turf other than their own, Christians may be instructed by Jews about textual readings that are not absolute and about faith claims that are not exclusionary. And, of course, Jews and Christians together may be alerted to the emptiness of hope mixed with power when we see that some forms of Israeli Zionism now practice the same absolutist claims that have been the hallmark of so much Christian hegemony. Hope that is possessed and administered in such a way is not hope but "sight." It is known among us, moreover, that we shall never enter the future by sight, but only by faith.

4. Psalm 73 is a narrative articulation that I believe provides a clear account of the *seduction of hopelessness*. After a conventional affirmation that God is good to Israel and to the pure in heart (v. 1), the psalmist tells of the seduction of *a life of commodity* that can be learned from the self-sufficient and replicated (vv. 2-14). Only at the last instant in some kind of liturgical moment (v. 17), the psalmist pulls back from that seduction and comes to realize that *communion with God* is the only real hope for life:

> Whom have I in heaven but you?
> And there is nothing on earth that I desire other than you.
> My flesh and my heart may fail,
> but God is the strength of my heart and my portion forever.
> (Ps 73:25-26)

In the end, it is nearness to God that counts, and nothing matters beyond that. Thus:

1. *Can we hope?* Only if we have interpretive practices that are open beyond our habitual exclusionary commitments.
2. *Can hope be divided?* Hope in God cannot be divided,

- not divided between Jews and Christians,
- not divided between "already and not yet,"
- not divided between "red and blue."

When hope is divided, it is a practice of hope that appeals to an idol who cannot deliver. The alternative to such idolatrous practice is trust of the future to the God who remakes creation for good, only not on our terms,

- not on Jewish or Christian terms,
- not on our treasured "already" or our passionate "not yet," and
- not "red or blue," but in many colors in the sky that remind God of the postflood covenant with all flesh, many colors beyond our particular shade of preference.

In terms of contestation, we will give the penultimate word to Karl Barth as it is mediated through the exposition of Eberhard Busch:

> In Barth's thinking there were two additional prerequisites for being able to talk to each other in the church of Christ, and these two are inextricably linked. First, such a dialogue between Christians, even if it has the form of an argument with each other, occurs in the brackets of the assumption that both are in the church of Christ. This gives the discussion its true seriousness but also marks the clear boundaries of the argument. Barth once said that the person we should drop completely could "only be an arch-heretic who is totally lost to the invisible church as well." But he adds, "We do not have the ability to ascertain such lost arch-heresy, we do not have this ability even in the case of Christians who are perhaps under strong suspicion." Barth concludes that this is true of two theologians with whom he especially took issue: "For me, Schleiermacher also belongs (in the community of the saints) and Bultmann does too; there is no question about that." This approach has some immediate specific consequences. As a Christian I can criticize other Christians only if I am also in solidarity with them. Furthermore, when I criticize others I can distance myself from them not on a tone of harsh indignation but only in a tone of sad dismay at a threat that had somehow turned into a temptation for me as well. And finally, believing that Israel's shepherd does not slumber or sleep even in the

church, I have to keep myself open to the possibility not only that the "favorite voices" I like to hear testify to the truth of God in the church, but "that we need . . . totally unexpected voices even though these voices may at first be quite unwelcome."

The other prerequisite for talking to each other and having an argument with each other is this: Even when I boldly stand up for my understanding of the truth, I can do so only by paying attention to the boundary that is drawn by the fact that God's truth and my understanding of it are always two completely different things. At the very moment I forget this border, it will shift, and the border between my understanding of God's truth and other Christians' understanding of it will become absolute. At that very moment the other person and I no longer stand before our common judge, rather I become the judge of the other.[13]

What Barth and Busch say about Christians in dialogue of course applies to Jews and Christians in dialogue. Dialogue occurs on the assumption that both communities are chosen communities beloved of God and sent in missions of obedience and hope. The call to repent, to move beyond our chosenness, is a call common to our two communities; in this company it is important to accent that it has been the Christian community that has been tempted to an exclusionary posture that works against the largeness of hope rooted in the promise of God that is always well beyond our own inclination.

The Bible Is Active in Politics Today

A CHRISTIAN RESPONSE TO *CONTESTING TEXTS*

SUSAN BROOKS THISTLETHWAITE

JESUS SUPPORTS CANDIDATE
FOR GOVERNOR IN FLORIDA

The Rev. O'Neal Dozier said, in introducing the Republican candidate for governor, Charles Crist, that he had had a dream in which "The Lord Jesus spoke to me and he said 'There's something I want you to know. Charlie Crist will be the next governor of the state of Florida. . . .' I introduce to you, as the Lord Jesus has said, the next governor of the state of Florida, Charlie Crist."

—*Sun-Sentinel* of South Florida, May 22, 2006

The words *silly* and *stupid* come to mind when one is confronted with newspaper reports such as the one above. But for such an event, you also have to include "actually happened" and "increasingly common." Steven Weitzman, in chapter 5 of this volume, notes that the events of September 11, 2001, have had cultural effects that are "still reverberating" especially in the field of biblical studies: "9/11 imposes a new interpretive responsibility on critical biblical scholarship" (pp. 79–80). Not only 9/11, but Karl Rove and his ilk, trading on and fanning the flames of the culture of fear created by the attacks of 9/11, are part of these reverberations. This culture of fear has been successfully marketed to the Christian community, and it is in the Christian community that we must struggle to resist its effects. We cannot ignore that these are the religious *and* cultural effects of our time.

If we were to make a list of the problems we face, a critical one is the profound distortion of the landscape in which biblical interpretation is done today. Religion, and, in this new "wedge" marketing of politics, Christianity especially, is dangerously and superficially mixed with politics today. This grossly complicates the work of interpreting the Bible with and to Christians, as well as interpretation in interfaith contexts.

Walter Brueggemann, in chapter 9 in this volume, points out the judgment of the 9/11 Commission that along with general bureaucratic dysfunction, "the primary 'intelligence' failure was a 'failure of imagination.'" Brueggemann suggests that "failure of imagination" defines our dominant ethos today in the United States. And since biblical interpretation is a work of the imagination, this does give a sense of the difficulties one faces in trying to do this kind of work today. *On the other hand, it also tells you that the kind of biblical interpretation offered in this volume may be part of the work of "healing the world" (Isaiah 58) so sorely needed today.*

Brueggemann has a prescription for the healing of the world—he prescribes hope. Unfortunately, he argues, the political forces named above have divided hope. We have created "red hope" and "blue hope." "*Red hope* is, in current discussion, privatized and individualized without any sense of the public. And *blue hope*, in much of its articulation, is public and social, but without attentiveness to the personal conviction concerning the God of all promises that is so palpable, for example, in the psalms of lament and in the songs of thanksgiving" (p. 159).

Who Would Jesus Bomb?

During the buildup to the attack on Iraq, I challenged the wisdom of using Christianity to justify preemptive war. I did this on radio, on TV, and in the pages of newspapers such as the *Chicago Tribune* and the *Dallas Morning News*. The *Dallas Morning News* actually invited me to debate the question of whether Jesus was for or against the war. I argued that Jesus was against the war, given that those were the only two options. I have been very tempted simply to ask those who argue that preemptive war is the Christian response needed today, "Who would Jesus bomb?"

I can therefore relate to those who have started to call themselves "Red Letter Christians." If you have not heard of this movement, it is a recent Christian evangelical movement designed to cut through partisan politics by sticking to the "actual words of Jesus." "Red Letter" refers to those editions of the New Testament that use red letters to indicate the words considered to be actually spoken by Jesus.

This movement has been promoted and given leadership by Anthony "Tony" Campolo and the Rev. Jim Wallis. Campolo founded the Evangelical Association for the Promotion of Education (EAPE) that works with at-risk youth in the United Staes and Canada. Wallis is the well-known founder and editor of *Sojourners* magazine and has gained great visibility with the publication of his book *God's Politics*.[1] Campolo and Wallis are two fine individuals, and the "Red Letter" Christian movement is helping many people, including especially young people, who have become disaffected from the church because it preaches one thing and does another, as well as the hungry, the homeless, the sick, and prisoners, just as Jesus did.

In the context of this volume, however, and the larger issue of the relationship of Christianity to the Hebrew Bible, Red Letter Christianity is an interesting trend. Wallis in fact credits a "secular Jewish country music songwriter" with suggesting the term "Red Letter Christian." When Wallis was interviewed by this songwriter in Nashville, he told the interviewer that he and some others were starting a new movement and did not have a name for it yet. "I've got an idea for you," the songwriter said. "I think you should call yourselves 'The Red Letter Christians,' for the red parts of the Bible that highlight the words of Jesus. I love the red letter stuff."[2]

The trouble with the Red Letter Christian approach, of course, is that it could be incipient Marcionism. Marcionism is a dualist belief that arose in Christian circles around the middle of the second century CE. Marcionites taught that Christianity was distinct from, and in opposition to, Judaism. Marcionism was declared a heresy. David Novak, in chapter 2 in this volume, discusses Jewish-Christian disputation through the ages and notes that "even Rabbi Joseph Albo, a famous fifteenth-century Spanish Jewish disputant against Christianity, conceded that Christians live under a divinely given law (*dat elohit*), thus concluding that Jews are mistaken when some of us say Christianity has totally rejected God's Torah. (From the Christian side, only a

Marcionite would say this; and let it be remembered that Marcionism was the first heresy denounced by the early church)" (p. 38).

Now Marcion would scarcely recognize Red Letter Christians as agreeing with him; their attachment to Jesus would have been anathema since Marcion treated Jesus as distinct from Christ. But Marcionism has come to mean the privileging of the Christian scriptures and the disprivileging of the Hebrew Bible in the interpretation of Christianity. From the time of Irenaeus, it has been clear that Christians run a huge theological risk if they cut themselves off from their heritage in Judaism.

Both Campolo and Wallis concede that the Red Letter Christian approach to Christian faith is a reaction to the politics of faith in our time. "Because being evangelical is usually synonymous with being Republican in the popular mind, and calling ourselves 'progressive' might be taken as a value judgment by those who do share our views, we decided not to call ourselves 'progressive evangelicals.' We came up with a new name: Red-Letter Christians."[3] The words of Jesus are to be taken as the new political guide:

> In those red letters, He calls us away from the consumerist values that dominate contemporary American consciousness. He calls us to be merciful, which has strong implications for how we think about capital punishment. When Jesus tells us to love our enemies, he probably means we shouldn't kill them. Most important, if we take Jesus seriously, we will realize that meeting the needs of the poor is a primary responsibility for His followers.[4]

Using All the Letters in the Bible: The Contesting Texts Conference and Volume

Campolo and Wallis and those who are joining this movement are not just blowing rhetoric around in their commitment to living by the words of Jesus. Their work with the poor and the outcast is tangible and a much-needed corrective to the right-wing political captivity of Christianity. Even so, I think that down the road Red Letter Christians may find they are running a big theological risk in so overemphasizing the words of Jesus that the connection of those words to their roots in the work of the prophets and the relationship of the Hebrew people to the God of Exodus (to name only a few possible lacunae) will be neglected. They set a high bar, however, for the test of the work with the Bible today—and that I am interpreting as "Does it serve the healing of the world, or not?"

After several years of serving on an ad hoc committee of the United States Institute of Peace called "Abrahamic Dialogue," I can say without hesitation that one of the greatest barriers to the healing of the world and the wounds of religiously motivated violence among these three great religions, Judaism, Islam, and Christianity, is that of supersessionism. Supersessionism is the traditional view that the Christian church has superseded Israel, that Christianity "supersedes" or even "replaces" Judaism. (Today, supersessionism can also be taken to include the view that Islam has superseded both Judaism and Christianity.) I think our Abrahamic Dialogue group as a whole would agree that a direct challenge to supersessionism is very important for the world today.

In a volume on Jewish-Christian dialogue, it is appropriate that it be the Christians who raise and address this important question of supersessionism. Ralph Klein, in chapter 3, on the one hand, states flatly that he will continue to use the term "Old Testament" for the Jewish scriptures instead of more recent terms such as Hebrew Bible, the First Testament, or the Prime Testament, since "I see no diminution of the value of this testament by calling it 'old'" (p. 191–92, n. 2). On the other hand, he takes a very controversial topic such as "promise and fulfillment," one of the usual stepping-stones to supersessionism, and offers that (a) Christians significantly reinterpreted Israel's messianic hope and that (b) many of the promises and prophecies of the New Testament "still cry out for fulfillment" (p. 62). This undermines to some degree the usual use of "promise and fulfillment" in supersessionist theologies, but it does not directly challenge the premise.

In chapter 9, Walter Brueggemann goes further in letting go of supersessionist premises in an explicit way. Citing Karl Barth, Brueggemann points out, "For our purposes, however, it is enough to see that even Barth, given his Christological accent, affirms that Christians stand alongside Jews. Or better, Christians stand after Jews and are instructed by them; or perhaps better, both Judaism and Christianity stand after

ancient Israel in its practice of hope" (p. 144). Judaism as teacher and
Christianity as student or Judaism and Christianity both as students of
ancient Israel—both of these images take seriously the corrosive heritage of supersessionism and offer a possible way forward that honors the
history of both religions.

   Another topic that arises often in this volume is the question, "Why
do we do Jewish-Christian dialogue?" David Novak simply assumes that
there is one goal: discovering commonalities. Referring to the "Jewish
Statement on Christians and Christianity" first published in the *New
York Times* in September 2000, of which Novak was one of the four
authors, Novak writes:

> *Dabru Emet* speaks of biblical authority as 'God's revealed word'
> for both Judaism *and* Christianity. To avoid mention of biblical
> authority when speaking of Christianity is to defame Christianity
> as being antinomian, even if only by omission.[5] Surely, Jewish and
> Christian commonality, which the dialogue is meant to uncover,
> should not be located in a common antinomianism. (p. 38)

   This is an interesting, even provocative statement in a chapter that
itself is very challenging. "Antinomian" is simply assumed by the author
to be a very negative term; indeed, to describe any Christian as antinomian is, according to Novak, to "defame" them. Yet Quakers, for example,
are explicitly antinomian, and they are widely regarded as among the
most admirable of Christians for their consistent ethical commitments.
This raises the question of whether the goal of Jewish-Christian dialogue is always to be the discovery of commonality, or whether at least a
goal can and should legitimately be the discovery of difference. Novak's
chapter, with its very helpful discussion of how to find a way forward in
a "dispute for the sake of heaven," models how dialogue can try to find
common ground but is especially helpful in pointing out that *common
ground, when tested, may not be all that common.*

   In the twenty-odd years during which I have been teaching at Chicago Theological Seminary (CTS) with our excellent concentration in
Jewish-Christian studies, I have learned that it is in Jewish-Christian
dialogue that we can learn to expect the unexpected, to see the unfamiliar

in the familiar, to encounter the stranger, and that this has deepened my understanding of the Bible.

On the one hand, it has been our way within the progressive churches to reach out to those of other faiths to increase understanding and find common ground. This is typically the way we have approached our Ph.D. program in Jewish-Christian studies at CTS. Many who enroll with us are looking for the common ground, often in ethics, where we can resist those who use religious difference as a way to engage in enemy stereotyping. If there ever was a time when we should not abandon such strategies of continuity with other faiths, notably the faiths of Judaism, Islam, and Christianity, now is that time.

But what happens if we pay attention not just to the commonalities, but to the differences between one faith and another? This volume and the conference from which it emerges, after all, have been called *Contesting Texts*. The root word *contest* means "competition" and even "fight." This is, interestingly, part of the Jewish commentary tradition. The tradition of the rabbis has been to study scripture from a multiplicity of perspectives and consciously cultivate the otherness of the text to mine its depths: the irruption, the unexpected, the countertext. In his wonderful book *Facing the Abusing God: A Theology of Protest*, David Blumenthal combines the rabbinical tradition of arguing with the text from multiple perspectives with the post-Holocaust sense of irruption of the impossible into the possible.[6] The rabbinical tradition of commentary, especially after the Holocaust, allows a space for protest, for argument with the text and with God. As a way of looking at the scripture, the Jewish tradition of argument offers a multiplicity of perspectives to startle you and allow for the in-breaking of the strange. "I was a stranger and you welcomed me . . . into your mind" (cf. Matt 25:35; author's paraphrase).

I found that all of the chapters by Jewish commentators in this volume provoked me and offered me a wide range of perspectives, a range of perspectives many of which I now think I disagree with. But now I'm *thinking about it*.

I'm thinking about whether the Pharisees are really such polar opposites to Jesus of Nazareth (Laurence L. Edwards, chapter 8) as I have always thought, or have I set them up as the "other" (Barbara Bowe, chapter 6) in order to engage in a very Christian-congratulatory project of enemy stereotyping? I'm thinking about biblical authority and governance (David Novak) and whether my own cherished antinomian views are part of the reason the United Church of Christ cannot more effectively articulate its witness in the world through sound and lively biblical interpretation. On the other hand, I am a child of the 1960s, and "Question authority" hasn't just been a button or bumper sticker for me, but a way of engaging in social justice ministry that challenges militaristic, patriarchal established authorities, both religious and civil. I don't know that I'll completely give up antinomianism, but after reading this volume, I'm *thinking about it.*

Conclusion

As the Bible has become a more active player in politics, *thinking about it* has been one of the first casualties. The work of a volume such as this one is to invite the reader to *think about it* from many different perspectives and engage in contesting these texts for the sake of greater understanding among these two great religions and their adherents. Will this volume contribute to the healing of the world? I don't know that for sure, but I *think* so.

Contesting Texts

AN AFTERWORD

DAVID FOX SANDMEL

Contemporary Jewish-Christian relations have been forged by three interrelated phenomena: the Shoah (Holocaust) and its moral and theological implications, the legacy of Jewish-Christian dialogue, and the contributions of the historical-critical study of religion to our understanding of sacred scriptures and their interpretations. The Contesting Texts conference, represented by the essays in this volume, amply demonstrates the interplay of these phenomena.

The Shoah profoundly affected not only Jews and its other victims, but also Christianity. Irving Greenberg has argued that it is a "revelatory" event for Christians as well as for Jews,[1] and the emergence of what has come to be known as post-Holocaust Christian theology attests to its significance in Christian thought. *Dabru Emet* states, "Nazism was not a Christian phenomenon." At the same time, however, the role of traditional Christian teaching about Jews and Judaism in creating the cultural climate in which Nazism could take hold and the participation of so many who considered themselves Christians in carrying out the Final Solution were a terrible shock to the world. The Shoah challenged Christians to confront the history of anti-Judaism and to seek ways of understanding both the New Testament and what it means to be a Christian that are not dependent upon the denigration of Jews and Judaism. Both national and international adjudicatory bodies and individual theologians began wrestling with implications of the Shoah, a process that continues today, the evidence of which can be seen in lengthy bibliographies of Jewish-Christian relations and what now constitutes a significant corpus of official statements and positions from a wide variety of church bodies.[2]

The Shoah also provided the impetus for the development of Jewish-Christian dialogue (what David Novak refers to in his essay as "*the dialogue*") as both Jews and Christians sought to establish new ways of relating to each other and to each other's traditions. This dialogue has engendered not merely better understanding of, and increased respect for, the other but also a transformation of self-understanding among both Jews and Christians that has changed the nature of the relationship between them. The new relationship is evident in the titles given to works in this area, such as Mary Boys's *Has God Only One Blessing? Judaism as a Source of Christian Self-Understanding*,[3] or *Jews and Christians: Rivals or Partners for the Kingdom of God? In Search of an Alternative for the Theology of Substitution*, edited by Didier Pollefeyt.[4] In many communities around North America and Great Britain, there are well-established dialogues, some of which have been in existence for thirty years or more.

The legacy and significance of this dialogue are apparent in two recent "major events" in the world of Jewish-Christian relations. One was the release of Mel Gibson's movie *The Passion of the Christ* in 2004. Jewish and some Christian scholars and leaders warned that the film's depiction of the role of the Jews in the crucifixion of Jesus might provoke a resurgence of anti-Semitism. Although the film does contain many scenes and images that communicate Jewish guilt for the death of Jesus, the association of Jews with evil and the devil, and the replacement of Israel by the church as God's covenantal partner, these messages were not picked up by most Christian viewers who focused almost entirely on the suffering of Christ. It is tempting to suggest that the negative images of Jews in the film did not register because they are no longer part of the cultural language of the majority of the audience. It is even more tempting to attribute this change, at least in part, to the work of Jewish-Christian dialogue through the years, though whether and to what extent the dialogue has in fact changed society cannot be determined. It is also worth noting that in many communities, Jews and Christians with a history of engaging each other in dialogue came together to watch and to discuss this movie and were able to draw upon past experience to explore and to have substantive conversations about their starkly different reactions.

The second "major event" was the outrage in the Jewish community in reaction to a number of "overtures" (resolutions) adopted by the Presbyterian Church (USA) at its 2004 General Assembly regarding Israel, Christian Zionism, and evangelism. Over the subsequent two years, in an attempt to understand what had provoked the reaction and to repair the rift, dialogue between members of PC(USA) and the Jewish community from the highest national organizational level to the local synagogue and church mushroomed. At its 2006 General Assembly, PC(USA) adopted a new overture specifically regarding its approach to the conflict between Israel and the Palestinians that began by acknowledging the "hurt and misunderstanding among many members of the Jewish community and within our Presbyterian communion" that the 2004 decisions had provoked. Once again, the role of dialogue in the process that led to this outcome is impossible to ascertain. A number of factors were involved, among them the complicated inner dynamics of the church itself and the changing situation in the Middle East, including the Israeli withdrawal from Gaza and the election of a Hamas government. Nonetheless, both Jews and Presbyterians agree that a lack of dialogue in recent years exacerbated the misunderstanding,[5] while the reinvigoration of dialogue the crisis provoked has demonstrated its importance to both communities.

In the case of both *The Passion of the Christ* and Presbyterian overtures, the personal and institutional relationships between Jews and Christians that the dialogue movement has nurtured over two generations provided a context and a vocabulary in which the communities could address each other honestly about deeply held beliefs and convictions.

In his contribution to this volume, Walter Brueggemann correctly gestures toward the critical role historical-critical scholarship has played in the process (p. 142). At the same time, however, critical scholarship has played an essential role in the process of discovery and reconciliation between Jews and Christians. The methods, terminology, and insights of modern biblical scholarship and history have provided Jews and Christians with a common language and common frame of reference for discussing scripture and the people and events described in it. This has made possible a shift from the arena of debate and polemic, in which each side relies on its own interpretive tradition to reject the truth claims of the other and promote its own, to a mode of discourse that presupposes the complex interplay of historical, intellectual, and literary forces that have shaped both traditions, including the ways that each has reacted to and influenced the other.

One example of how critical scholarship has influenced Jewish-Christian dialogue can be seen in the growing appreciation among both Jews and Christians of the "Jewishness" of Jesus. Today, the fact that Jesus was Jewish has become axiomatic, so much so that we tend to forget that for much of history the church taught that Jesus was opposed to, rather than part of, the Judaism of his day, an attitude that was prevalent not only in church teaching but also in scholarship of the nineteenth and twentieth centuries as well. There have even been Christian scholars (admittedly a small minority) who denied altogether that Jesus was Jewish.[6] Jews have always accepted that Jesus was a Jew, but rabbinic tradition constructed its own image of Jesus as a rebellious disciple of the rabbis and as an "enticer" (cf. Deuteronomy 13) who brought calamity upon the Jewish people, even if, as some, including Moses Maimonides, argued, Christianity (and Islam) had resulted in the spreading knowledge of God to a broad Gentile audience.

The evolution of critical scholarship on Second Temple Judaism, New Testament and Christian origins, and rabbinic Judaism has shown both Jews and Christians that Jesus can be understood only within the context of the Jewish world in which he lived. This has made possible a new appreciation of the figure of Jesus for Jews and of the Judaism of Jesus' day for Christians. Recent scholarship has even challenged the once firmly held notion of a definitive "parting of the ways" between Judaism and Christianity, replacing it with a construct in which the boundary between Judaism and Christianity developed over a long period of time in different geographic and social locations.[7] Laurence L. Edwards's essay in this volume consciously places itself within this newer discourse.

As noted above, the dialogue relies, to a great extent, on the results of scholarship. At the same time, scholarship is indebted to the principles of dialogue as a way of testing its own validity, to see if attitudes that reflect a religious bias are influencing the scholarship. If, as Thomas Aquinas insisted in the Middle Ages, philosophy is the handmaiden of theology, perhaps today we might say that scholarship and dialogue have a symbiotic relationship: each depends on and nurtures the other.

If the scripturally-based, theological debate was typified by denying what the other held most sacred, today's dialogue is predicated on affirming the historical and theological commonalities as the foundation of the relationship as a prerequisite for embarking on explorations of the differences. Jews and Christians will continue to disagree about the theological significance of Jesus, but agreement about Jesus' Jewishness provides a point of entry for Christians to learn about the Jewish roots of Christianity and for Jews to learn about the diversity of Judaism in the formative period that culminated in the emergence of rabbinic Judaism. For those who are engaged in *"the* dialogue," this perspective on the origins of both traditions provides a model of the relationship between Judaism and Christianity that is not merely of historical interest but instructive for today as well.

Barbara Bowe's essay in this book, "The New Testament, Religious Identity, and the Other," is illustrative of the influence of the Shoah, Jewish-Christian dialogue, and critical scholarship. Although she does not reference the Shoah directly, she does mention the genocide in Rwanda, a tragedy that has rightly been described as a "holocaust." She also relies on the work of the Jewish philosopher Emanuel Levinas, whose writings were deeply affected by his experiences during World War II. Bowe cites Levinas in her informative discussion of the philosophical understandings of the "other" and the options that are presented to us for our understanding of the others we encounter both in the text and today. Finally, Bowe's chapter is informed by current New Testament scholarship that makes it possible for contemporary readers of the New Testament to see these scriptures as descriptive of the historical circumstance in which they were produced, but not necessarily prescriptive of the way that Jews and Christians related to each other in antiquity or how they must relate today. According to Bowe, "It becomes imperative, therefore, to distinguish ever so carefully between the *encoded* adversaries with their ascribed traits in the narrative world of the text and their real-life counterparts in the real world behind [and I would add: in front of] the text" (p. 100).

In a similar manner, Ralph Klein applies the methods of biblical scholarship to the subject of "promise and fulfillment" in both the Old Testament/Tanakh and the New Testament *"in order to clarify the limits and legitimacy of the New Testament claims"* [emphasis added], a clarification that Klein believes is "important for Jewish-Christian understanding" (p. 47). Readings of promise and fulfillment, as Klein points out, have been used by Christian theologians such as Rudolf Bultmann to deny the legitimacy of Jewish faith in the continued validity of the Jewish covenant (p. 47). Klein suggests an alternative—that both Christians and Jews see promise and fulfillment in their reading of their sacred scriptures and sacred histories, allowing these to serve as "important talking points between Jews and Christians" (p. 63).

A final example is the essay by Steven Weitzman, which begins with reference to September 11, 2001, as a point of departure for an examination and exposition of the "Bible's dark side, its sanction of violence" (p. 80). Although he distinguishes between Jewish martyrdom in antiquity and "contemporary suicide bombings or attacks like that of Baruch Goldstein" (p. 81), he applies the methods of critical scholarship, specifically a careful reading of Josephus, to point out the possibility of a critique of martyrdom anchored in biblical exegesis. He concludes that the "failure to recognize the interpretive possibilities is a measure not of the text's moral limits but of the poverty of one's own literary and ethical imagination" (p. 89).

Jews and Christians have contested through and over their sacred texts for centuries. In some cases the "contest" is located within the texts themselves. Often it has been the way the texts have been read and interpreted that has produced prejudice and misunderstanding. The Contesting Texts conference and volume demonstrate that in the aftermath of the Shoah, Jews and Christians who have benefited from the achievements of the dialogue and who utilize the tools of critical scholarship can expose and explore the contests of the past as well as create from them a bridge of understanding.

APPENDIX

Dabru Emet

Dabru Emet

A JEWISH STATEMENT
ON CHRISTIANS AND CHRISTIANITY

In recent years, there has been a dramatic and unprecedented shift in Jewish and Christian relations. Throughout the nearly two millennia of Jewish exile, Christians have tended to characterize Judaism as a failed religion or, at best, a religion that prepared the way for, and is completed in, Christianity. In the decades since the Holocaust, however, Christianity has changed dramatically. An increasing number of official Church bodies, both Roman Catholic and Protestant, have made public statements of their remorse about Christian mistreatment of Jews and Judaism. These statements have declared, furthermore, that Christian teaching and preaching can and must be reformed so that they acknowledge God's enduring covenant with the Jewish people and celebrate the contribution of Judaism to world civilization and to Christian faith itself.

We believe these changes merit a thoughtful Jewish response. Speaking only for ourselves—an interdenominational group of Jewish scholars—we believe it is time for Jews to learn about the efforts of Christians to honor Judaism. We believe it is time for Jews to reflect on what

Judaism may now say about Christianity. As a first step, we offer eight brief statements about how Jews and Christians may relate to one another.

Jews and Christians worship the same God. Before the rise of Christianity, Jews were the only worshippers of the God of Israel. But Christians also worship the God of Abraham, Isaac, and Jacob; creator of heaven and earth. While Christian worship is not a viable religious choice for Jews, as Jewish theologians we rejoice that, through Christianity, hundreds of millions of people have entered into relationship with the God of Israel.

Jews and Christians seek authority from the same book—the Bible (what Jews call "Tanakh" and Christians call the "Old Testament"). Turning to it for religious orientation, spiritual enrichment, and communal education, we each take away similar lessons: God created and sustains the universe; God established a covenant with the people Israel; God's revealed word guides Israel to a life of righteousness; and God will ultimately redeem Israel and the whole world. Yet, Jews and Christians interpret the Bible differently on many points. Such differences must always be respected.

Christians can respect the claim of the Jewish people upon the land of Israel. The most important event for Jews since the Holocaust has been the reestablishment of a Jewish state in the Promised Land. As members of a biblically based religion, Christians appreciate that Israel was promised—and given—to Jews as the physical center of the covenant between them and God. Many Christians support the State of Israel for reasons far more profound than mere politics. As Jews, we applaud this support. We also recognize that Jewish tradition mandates justice for all non-Jews who reside in a Jewish state.

Jews and Christians accept the moral principles of Torah. Central to the moral principles of Torah is the inalienable sanctity and dignity of every human being. All of us were created in the image of God. This shared moral emphasis can be the basis of an improved relationship between our two communities. It can also be the basis of a powerful witness to all humanity for improving the lives of our fellow human beings and for standing against the immoralities and idolatries that harm and degrade us. Such witness is especially needed after the unprecedented horrors of the past century.

Nazism was not a Christian phenomenon. Without the long history of Christian anti-Judaism and Christian violence against Jews, Nazi ideology could not have taken hold nor could it have been carried out. Too many Christians participated in, or were sympathetic to, Nazi atrocities against Jews. Other Christians did not protest sufficiently against these atrocities. But Nazism itself was not an inevitable outcome of Christianity. If the Nazi extermination of the Jews had been fully successful, it would have turned its murderous rage more directly to Christians. We recognize with gratitude those Christians who risked or sacrificed their lives to save Jews during the Nazi regime. With that in mind, we encourage the continuation of recent efforts in Christian theology to repudiate unequivocally contempt of Judaism and the Jewish people. We applaud those Christians who reject this teaching of contempt, and we do not blame them for the sins committed by their ancestors.

The humanly irreconcilable difference between Jews and Christians will not be settled until God redeems the entire world as promised in Scripture. Christians know and serve God through Jesus Christ and the Christian tradition. Jews know and serve God through Torah and the Jewish tradition. That difference will not be settled by one community insisting that it has interpreted Scripture more accurately than the other; nor by exercising political power over the other. Jews can respect Christians' faithfulness to their revelation just as we expect Christians to respect our faithfulness to our revelation. Neither Jew nor Christian should be pressed into affirming the teaching of the other community.

A new relationship between Jews and Christians will not weaken Jewish practice. An improved relationship will not accelerate the cultural and religious assimilation that Jews rightly fear. It will not change traditional Jewish forms of worship, nor increase intermarriage between Jews and non-Jews, nor persuade more Jews to convert to Christianity, nor create a false blending of Judaism and Christianity. We respect Christianity as a faith that originated within Judaism and that still has significant contacts with it. We do not see it as an extension of Judaism. Only if we cherish our own traditions can we pursue this relationship with integrity.

Jews and Christians must work together for justice and peace. Jews and Christians, each in their own way, recognize the unredeemed state of the world as reflected in the persistence of persecution, poverty, and human degradation and misery. Although justice and peace are finally God's, our joint efforts, together with those of other faith communities, will help bring the kingdom of God for which we hope and long. Separately and together, we must work to bring justice and peace to our world. In this enterprise, we are guided by the vision of the prophets of Israel:

> It shall come to pass in the end of days that the mountain of the LORD's house shall be established at the top of the mountains and be exalted above the hills, and the nations shall flow unto it . . . and many peoples shall go and say, "Come ye and let us go up to the mountain of the LORD to the house of the God of Jacob and He will teach us of His ways and we will walk in His paths" (Isa 2:2-3).

Notes

Chapter 1
Dabru Emet, Jewish-Christian Dialogue, and the Bible

1. See for instance, David Novak, *Jewish-Christian Dialogue: A Jewish Justification* (New York: Oxford University Press, 1989); John Pawlikowski, *Christ in the Light of the Christian-Jewish Dialogue* (Eugene, Ore.: Wipf & Stock, 2001); idem., "The Search for a New Paradigm for the Christian-Jewish Relationship: A Response to Michael Signer," in *Reinterpreting Revelation and Tradition: Jews and Christians in Conversation*, ed. John Pawlikowski and Hayim Goren Perelmuter (Franklin, Wis.: Sheed & Ward, 2000), 25–48.

2. Consider, for example, the manner in which Jacob Milgrom draws on the history of Jewish interpretation of biblical texts in his three-volume commentary on Leviticus, or the way Brevard Childs utilizes the Christian tradition in his study of Exodus. See Jacob Milgrom, *Leviticus: A New Translation with Introduction and Commentary*, Anchor Bible 3, 3a, 3b (New York: Doubleday, 1991, 2000, 2001); and Brevard Childs, *The Book of Exodus: A Critical Theological Commentary*, Old Testament Library (Philadelphia: Westminster, 1974).

3. Jürgen Moltmann, *God for a Secular Society: The Public Relevance of Theology* (Minneapolis: Fortress Press, 1999), 234–35.

4. Ibid., 228.

5. The authors of *Dabru Emet* are Tikva Frymer-Kensky, Professor of Hebrew Bible and the History of Judaism, Divinity School, University of Chicago; Peter Ochs, Professor of Modern Judaic Studies,

University of Virginia; Michael Signer, Professor in the Department
of Theology, Senior Fellow of the Medieval Institute, and Director
of the Notre Dame Holocaust Project, University of Notre Dame;
and David Novak, Professor of Jewish Studies, Religion, and Philosophy and Director of the Jewish Studies Program, University of
Toronto. Novak also served as the overall editor of the document.

6. Although the number of signers of *Dabru Emet* suggests broad support for the document, the statement is not without its critics. See,
for example, David Berger's paper, "*Dabru Emet*: Some Reservations
about a Jewish Statement on Christians and Christianity," delivered
October 28, 2002, at the inaugural meeting of the Council of the
Centers on Jewish-Christian Relations (CCJR) in Baltimore, Md.
See also Victoria Barnett, "Provocative Reconciliation: Reflections
on the New Jewish Statement on Christianity," *Christian Century*
(September 27–October 24, 2000). Both articles are available at
www.jcrelations.net.

7. The full text of *Dabru Emet* is printed at the end of this volume and
is also available at www.jcrelations.net. See also the companion volume to the document, *Christianity in Jewish Terms*, ed. Tikva Frymer-
Kensky, David Novak, Peter Ochs, David Fox Sandmel, and Michael
A. Signer (Boulder, Colo.: Westview, 2000).

8. Essentially all major Christian denominations in North America
and Europe have issued such statements of remorse and repentance.
Most of these can be accessed at www.jcrelations.net.

9. "A Sacred Obligation" is available at www.jcrelations.net. It is also
printed in the document's companion volume, *Seeing Judaism Anew:
Christianity's Sacred Obligation*, ed. Mary C. Boys (Lanham, Md.: Rowman & Littlefield, 2005).

10. Supersessionism is the belief that the divine covenants with the Jewish people have been terminated and transferred to Christians, who
are the "true" Israel.

11. On the limitations of the kinds of scholarly advances sketched in
this paragraph for Jewish-Christian relations, see Sara J. Tanzer's
essay in this volume, "The Problematic Portrayal of 'the Jews' and
Judaism in the Gospel of John: Implications for Jewish-Christian
Relations."

12. See, for instance, the Pontifical Biblical Commission's statement "The Jewish People and Their Sacred Scriptures in the Christian Bible." The document is available at www.jcrelations.net.

13. For an important discussion and analysis of this earliest, "inner-biblical," interpretation, see Michael A. Fishbane, *Biblical Interpretation in Ancient Israel* (Oxford: Clarendon, 1984).

14. *Tanakh* is an acronym for the three traditional sections of the Hebrew Bible: *Torah* (Law), *Nevi'im* (Prophets) and *Ketuvim* (Writings). An excellent English translation of the Tanakh is *Tanakh: The Holy Scriptures, the New JPS Translation according to the Traditional Hebrew Text* (Philadelphia: Jewish Publication Society, 1988). *The Jewish Study Bible*, ed. A. Berlin, Marc Zvi Brettler, and M. Fishbane (New York and Oxford: Oxford University Press, 2004), contains the NJPS text and includes study notes by Jewish scholars that allude especially to the history of Jewish biblical interpretation. For a convenient introduction to the Tanakh and other classical Jewish religious books, see Barry W. Holz, ed., *Back to the Sources: Reading the Classical Jewish Texts* (New York: Touchstone, 1984).

15. *Rashi* is an acronym for Rabbi Shlomo ben Itzhak (1040–1105), the famous medieval rabbi from France.

16. *The HarperCollins Study Bible: New Revised Standard Version, with the Apocryphal/Deuterocanonical Books*, ed. Wayne A. Meeks (New York: HarperCollins, 1993), conveniently includes a number of charts that list the biblical books that are canonical for Jews and different Christian traditions.

17. On this issue and related matters, see, for example, Jon D. Levenson, *The Hebrew Bible, the Old Testament and Historical Criticism: Jews and Christians in Biblical Studies* (Louisville: Westminster John Knox, 1993).

18. The term *halacha* (or *halakha*) refers to the body of law in Judaism, largely derived from scripture, which seeks to regulate all aspects of Jewish life. The adjective *halachic* here thus refers to those parts of scripture that are of a legal nature.

19. In the Tanakh, along with the writing prophets, or books that bear the name of a particular prophet (for example, Amos or Isaiah), the Prophets or *Nevi'im* include the books of Joshua, Judges, 1–2

Samuel, and 1–2 Kings, the so-called Former Prophets. These texts narrate the activities of a variety of prophets (for example, Elijah, Elisha, Nathan). Christians, however, do not regularly regard these books as prophetic.

20. The classic text is Julius Wellhausen's *Prolegomena zur Geschichte Israels* (1883). This text has been translated and reprinted several times. See, for example, *Prolegomena to the History of Israel* (Atlanta: Scholars, 1994).

21. The Romantic Movement originated in Europe in the late eighteenth century and, in the words of the *American Heritage Dictionary*, was characterized by a "heightened interest in nature, emphasis on the individual's expression of emotion and imagination," and "rebellion against established social rules and conventions."

22. See especially the foundational work of Kaufmann: Yehezkel Kaufmann, *The Religion of Israel, from Its Beginnings to the Babylonian Exile* (Chicago: University of Chicago Press, 1960).

23. David Rosen, "Religion, Identity and Peace in the Middle East" (Templeton Lecture, September 2005). This article is available at www.jcrelations.net.

24. Edward Kessler has likewise considered the account of Isaac's binding in relation to Jewish-Christian relations. See his *Bound by the Bible: Jews, Christians, and the Sacrifice of Isaac* (Cambridge: Cambridge University Press, 2005); "Bound by the Bible: Jews, Christians, and the Binding of Isaac," in *Two Faiths, One Covenant? Jewish and Christian Identity in the Presence of the Other*, ed. Eugene B. Korn and John T. Pawlikowski (Lanham, Md.: Rowman & Littlefield, 2005), 11–28.

25. Further resources and bibliography that document the range of opinions regarding Jewish-Christian relations and liberation theology are available at www.jcrelations.net.

26. This statement is not offered here as a theological declaration that seeks to equate Jesus of Nazareth with the God of Israel. Rather it is intended to sketch the dynamics of how analogies are sometimes drawn in Christian liberation theologies. Christians, of course, have made and do make claims regarding the divinity of Jesus. Jews, of course, reject these claims.

27. Levenson, *The Hebrew Bible*, 156–57. See also Levenson's exchange

with Christian liberation theologian George Pixley in *Jews, Christians, and the Theology of the Hebrew Scriptures*, ed. Alice Ogden Bellis and Joel S. Kaminsky (Atlanta: Society of Biblical Literature, 2000), 215–46.

28. See, for instance, Naim Ateek, *Holy Land, Hollow Jubilee: God, Justice, and the Palestinians* (London: Melisende, 1999); idem., *Justice and Only Justice: A Palestinian Theology of Liberation* (Maryknoll, N.Y.: Orbis, 1989).

29. See, for example, the conflict between Presbyterian and Jewish groups following the adoption of certain resolutions by the Presbyterian Church (USA) in 2004, to which David Fox Sandmel alludes in his contribution to this volume, "*Contesting Texts*: An Afterword."

Chapter 2
Jews, Christians, and Biblical Authority

1. Menachem Marc Kellner, *Dogma in Medieval Jewish Thought: From Maimonides to Abravanel*, Littman Library of Jewish Civilization (Oxford: Oxford University Press, 2004 [1986]).

2. Notwithstanding being a Holocaust survivor, though, Isaac does not harbor prejudice against Christians per se.

3. *Christianity in Jewish Terms*, ed. Tikva Frymer-Kensky, David Novak, Peter Ochs, David Fox Sandmel, and Michael A. Signer (Boulder, Colo.: Westview, 2000).

Chapter 3
Promise and Fulfillment

1. I wish to thank my Jewish colleague and friend Professor Isaac Kalimi for discussing this essay with me and suggesting a number of ways for its improvement.

2. The term "Old Testament" goes back to Melito of Sardis in the second century CE. Jews call these books "Tanakh," an acronym formed by the first letters of the Hebrew words for the three divisions in their canon: Torah (Pentateuch), Prophets, and Writings. For Jews, the Tanakh is itself the Bible, while in Christianity the same books (albeit in a different order) are one of two canonical testaments. The "Old Testament" today is sometimes called the Hebrew Bible, the

First Testament, the Prime Testament, and the like. Since I see no diminution of the value of this testament by calling it "old," I will retain the traditional terminology in this essay. While there are some differences between the Protestant, Orthodox, and Roman Catholic canons of the Old Testament, these differences are not germane to the present discussion.

3. Italics added. See also Gen 13:15-17; 15:5, 7, 18-21; 17:2-8; 22:17-18; 24:60; 26:2-4; 28:3-4, 13-15.

4. As a result, the Lord considered Abram righteous. The text can also be construed to mean that Abram considered the Lord's renewed promise as evidence of divine righteousness. In my judgment, righteousness in the Bible usually means the fulfillment of the demands inherent in a relationship. So Abram in believing the promise meets the requirement of the divine-human relationship, and the Lord in keeping the promise of descendants also fulfills the demands of the divine-human relationship.

5. According to Exod 12:40-41, the Israelites lived in Egypt for 430 years.

6. Gen 23:19; 25:9; 49:31; 50:13.

7. These additional words express the force of the Hebrew imperfect verb form.

8. The New Testament writers accepted traditional designations of authorship (Moses, Isaiah, etc.) and read the Bible synchronically. My training in historical criticism means that I usually read the Bible diachronically, recognizing various layers in the texts, often stemming from different writers.

9. Within the canon itself, Malachi promises the return of the prophet Elijah before the day of the Lord (Mal 4:5).

10. See also John 7:40, 52; Acts 7:37.

11. Note the play on words between "raising" someone as prophet and raising Jesus from the dead.

12. In Deut 15:11, the text grants that there will always indeed be needy people and therefore urges readers to open their hands in generosity toward the poor. This may be another occasion when a secondary hand adds a corrective addition.

13. Jeremiah invoked this principle against the false prophet Hananiah,

who prophesied that within two years the temple vessels captured by Nebuchadnezzar would be returned and Jeconiah (Jehoiachin) would be restored to the throne. Jeremiah appealed to the tradition of his predecessors, who customarily announced judgment and said that a prophet who announced good times would be proven true only when this happened. Jeremiah did not wait for this eventuality, however, and returned a few days later and renounced Hananiah as a person whom the Lord had not sent. Jeremiah said that Hananiah was under a divine death sentence, and he did indeed die within a year, proving the word of Jeremiah true (Jer 28:1-17).

14. Walther Zimmerli, *Ezekiel 2*, ed. Paul D. Hanson and Leonard Jay Greenspoon, trans. James D. Martin (Philadelphia: Fortress Press, 1983), 120–21.

15. The postexilic territory called Yehud was about as big geographically as the city of Chicago, with a total population possibly of less than twenty thousand.

16. The New Testament citations of this passage misconstrue the Hebrew poetry. Second Isaiah did not speak of a voice crying in the wilderness, but rather a voice cried out with a message in poetic parallelism: "In the wilderness prepare the way of the LORD, / make straight in the desert the superhighway of our God" (Isa 40:3).

17. See also Isa 26:19 (the dead are raised); 29:18 (the deaf hear); 42:7, 18 (the blind and deaf see and hear); 61:1 (good news to the oppressed and brokenhearted).

18. If by messianic hope we mean the expectation of a new or eschatological king who is a descendant of David, there is no messianic promise in the Pentateuch. The same could be said for a number of other Old Testament books. Second Isaiah democratizes the promise made to David by reapplying it to all members of the community (Isa 55:3). There were expectations of other eschatological figures in the Old Testament that are often merged with the messianic hope in Christian thinking. We have already discussed the expectation of a prophet like Moses in Deuteronomy, and the coming Son of Humanity is mentioned in Daniel 7. The servant figure in Second Isaiah (cf. Wisdom of Solomon 2 and 5) played a prominent role in early Christian attempts to understand the significance

of the death of Jesus, but the servant is *not* a messianic figure in the biblical text itself.

19. The inconsistency of the message in 2 Samuel 7 is often resolved by analyzing the text diachronically and assigning the verses of the chapter to several different authors.

20. For recent studies of this issue, see *Israel's Messiah in the Bible and the Dead Sea Scrolls*, ed. Richard S. Hess and M. Daniel Carroll (Grand Rapids: Baker, 2003); and *King and Messiah in Israel and the Ancient Near East*, ed. John Day, Journal for the Study of the Old Testament Supplement 270 (Sheffield: Academic Press, 1999).

21. An apparent exception is Ps 45:6: "Your throne, O God, endures forever and ever." The addressee in the psalm to this point is the king in Jerusalem. The psalm deals with the king's marriage.

22. Cf. the similar Jewish Publication Society translation: "The Mighty God is planning grace; the Eternal Father, a peaceable ruler."

23. Isa 9:1-2 is cited as fulfilled in Matt 4:15-16, where Matthew sees the Galilean ministry as a fulfillment of the word of Isaiah.

24. Ezekiel shared this doubt about the legitimacy of Zedekiah since he dates his oracles not to the reign of Zedekiah, but to the reign of his predecessor, Jehoiachin.

25. The Revised Common Lectionary selects this secondary text as the Old Testament lesson for the First Sunday in Advent in Year C.

26. New names for Jerusalem are also cited in the last verse in Ezekiel ("The name of the city from that time on shall be, The Lord Is There") and in Third Isaiah, 62:4, where Zion/Jerusalem is renamed Hephzibah ("My delight is in her").

27. Other messianic passages can be found in Micah, Ezekiel, Haggai, and perhaps Zechariah. A restoration of the Davidic line is also included in Amos 9:11-15. In this short paper, we make no pretense of referring to every possible messianic promise. In intertestamental times the notion of the messiah was very prominent. See Psalms of Solomon 17, 2 Esdras 11–12, Testament of Judah 24, and Testament of Dan 5:10-13. The latter two texts *in their present form* are Christian, but they were originally Jewish texts.

28. It is usually noted in the Dead Sea Scrolls that two messiahs, one of Aaron and one of David/Israel, were expected by those who wrote

the scrolls. For the messianic expectations at Qumran, see James VanderKam and Peter Flint, *The Meaning of the Dead Sea Scrolls* (San Francisco: HarperSanFrancisco, 2002), 265–73.

29. Cf. already Exod 4:22, 23, for the Lord designating Israel as "my son."

30. Italics added. Rudolf Bultmann, "Prophecy and Fulfillment," in *Essays on Old Testament Hermeneutics*, ed. Claus Westermann (Richmond: John Knox Press, 1963), 73–75. Antonius H. J. Gunneweg stated that the definition of the relationship between the Old and New Testaments is the most difficult historical and theological question faced by Christians. See Isaac Kalimi, "Die Bibel und die klassisch-jüdische Bibelauslegung. Eine interpretations- und religionsge-schichtliche Studie," *Zeitschrift für die Alttestamentliche Wissenschaft* 114 (2002): 594.

Chapter 4
Apocalyptic Violence and Politics

1. Nicholas D. Kristof, "Jesus and Jihad," *New York Times*, July 17, 2004; see also David Kirkpatrick, "Wrath and Mercy: The Return of the Warrior Jesus," *New York Times*, April 4, 2004.

2. Stephen Moyise, "Does the Lion Lie Down with the Lamb?" in *Studies in the Book of Revelation* (Edinburgh and New York: T. & T. Clark, 2001), 181–94.

3. Karen Armstrong, "The Freelance Monotheism of Karen Armstrong," interview by Krista Tippett, *Speaking of Faith*, Minnesota Public Radio, originally aired March 18, 2004. See http://speakingoffaith.publicradio.org/.

4. Elisabeth Schüssler Fiorenza, *Revelation: Vision of a Just World* (Minneapolis: Fortress Press, 1991), 58.

5. Loren L. Johns, "The Lamb in the Rhetorical Program of the Apocalypse of John," *Society of Biblical Literature 1998 Seminar Papers* (Atlanta: Scholars Press, 1998), 775–77; Loren L. Johns, *The Lamb Christology of the Apocalypse of John* (Tübingen: Mohr Siebeck, 2003). Similarly, David Aune argues that "the Messiah is never symbolized as a lamb in Judaism" and that Revelation's lamb is an original creation of the author. See Aune, *Revelation 1–5*, World Biblical Commentary 52a (Dallas: Word, 1997), 353.

6. Tim LaHaye and Jerry Jenkins, *Soul Harvest: The World Takes Sides* (Wheaton, Ill.: Tyndale, 1998), 414.

7. Scholars divide on whether the blood that stains Jesus' garments in Rev 19:13 is his own blood or that of his enemies. Jürgen Roloff argues, for example, that "the blood is not the actual blood of Jesus which he poured out for sinners, but rather the blood of God's enemies: 'Their juice [lifeblood] spattered my garments, and stained all my robes' (Isa 63:3)" (*Revelation*, A Continental Commentary [Minneapolis: Fortress Press, 1993], 218). Similarly, Frederick Murphy, in *Fallen Is Babylon: The Revelation to John* (Harrisburg, Pa.: Trinity Press International, 1998), 389. But for the counterargument see, for example, Pablo Richard, *Apocalypse: A People's Commentary on the Book of Revelation* (Maryknoll: Orbis, 1998), 147; Steven Friesen, *Imperial Cults and the Apocalypse of John: Reading Revelation in the Ruins* (Oxford: Oxford University Press, 2001), 190.

8. John Howard Yoder, *The Politics of Jesus* (Grand Rapids: Eerdmans, 1972), especially ch. 12, "The War of the Lamb"; Lee Griffith, *The War on Terrorism and the Terror of God* (Grand Rapids: Eerdmans, 2002).

9. Griffith, *War on Terrorism and the Terror of God*, 205. For nonviolence in Revelation, see also Nelson Kraybill, *Imperial Cult and Commerce in John's Apocalypse*, Journal for the Study of the New Testament: Supplement Series 132 (Sheffield: Sheffield Academic Press, 1996); Walter Wink, *Engaging the Powers: Discernment and Resistance in a World of Domination* (Minneapolis: Fortress Press, 1992); Friesen, *Imperial Cults and the Apocalypse of John*.

10. Richard, *Apocalypse: A People's Commentary on the Book of Revelation*, 33, 74.

11. Ward Ewing, *The Power of the Lamb: Revelation's Theology of Liberation for You* (Cambridge, Mass.: Cowley, 1990), 199.

12. Hal Lindsey, *The Late Great Planet Earth* (Grand Rapids: Zondervan, 1970), 173–74.

13. David Barr, "Towards an Ethical Reading of the Apocalypse: Reflections on John's Use of Power, Violence, and Misogyny," *Society of Biblical Literature 1997 Seminar Papers* (Atlanta: Scholars Press, 1997), 362.

14. Ibid., 361.
15. Ibid., 373.

Chapter 5
Unbinding Isaac

1. John Collins, "The Zeal of Phinehas: The Bible and the Legitimation of Violence," *Journal of Biblical Literature* 122 (2003): 3–21.

2. Yvette Sherwood, "Binding and Unbinding: Divided Responses of Judaism, Christianity, and Islam to the 'Sacrifice' of Abraham's Beloved Son," *Journal of the American Academy of Religion* 72 (2004): 821–61.

3. See Marc Brettler, "Is There Martyrdom in the Hebrew Bible?" in *Sacrificing the Self: Perspectives on Martyrdom*, ed. Margaret Cormack (Oxford: University Press, 2002), 3–22.

4. See Shalom Spiegel, *The Last Trial: On the Legends and Lore of the Command to Abraham to Offer Isaac as a Sacrifice* (New York: Schocken, 1969); Jon Levenson, *The Death and Resurrection of the Beloved Son* (New Haven: Yale University Press, 1993), 187–92; James Kugel, *The Bible as It Was* (Cambridge: Harvard University Press, 1997), 174–75.

5. See Florentino Garcia Martinez, "The Sacrifice of Isaac in 4Q225," in *The Sacrifice of Isaac: The Aqedah (Genesis 22) and Its Interpretations*, ed. Edward Noort and E. J. C. Tigchelaar (Leiden: Brill, 2002), 44–57.

6. Louis Finkelstein, ed., *Sifre on Deuteronomy* (New York: Jewish Theological Seminary of America, 1969), 58.

7. Jan Willem Van Henten, "Noble Death in Josephus: A Survey" (paper presented at the annual meeting of the Society of Biblical Literature, Denver, Colorado, 2001). See also Raymond Newell, "The Suicide Accounts in Josephus: A Form Critical Study," in *SBL 1982 Seminar Papers* (Chico, Calif., 1982), 351–69; idem, "The Forms and Historical Value of Josephus' Suicide Accounts," in *Josephus, the Bible and History*, ed. Louis Feldman and Gohei Hata (Detroit: Wayne State University Press, 1989), 278–94.

8. For these and other negative elements in the Masada story, frequently obscured in translation, see David Ladouceur, "Josephus

and Masada," in *Josephus, Judaism and Christianity*, ed. Louis Feldman and Gohei Hata (Detroit: Wayne State University Press, 1987), 95–113. Citations of Josephus are according to the Loeb edition of his writings.

9. Steven Weitzman, *Surviving Sacrilege: Cultural Persistence in Jewish Antiquity* (Cambridge, Mass.: Harvard University Press, 2005).

10. Donald McGuire, *Acts of Silence: Civil War, Tyranny, and Suicide in the Flavian Epics* (Hildsheim: Olms-Weidman, 1997), 185–229.

11. For the centrality of the theme of dying for the law in Josephus's paraphrase of 1 Maccabees, see Isaiah Gafni, "Josephus and *1 Maccabees*," in *Josephus, the Bible and History*, 116–31.

12. For a more detailed contrast of Philo and Josephus's accounts, see Daniel Schwartz, "Josephus and Philo on Pontius Pilate," in *Josephus Flavius: Historian of Eretz Israel in the Hellenistic-Roman Period*, ed. Uriel Rappaport (Jerusalem: Yad Izhak Ben Zvi, 1982), 217–36 (in Hebrew).

13. See Michael Fishbane, *The Kiss of God: Spiritual and Mystical Death in Judaism* (Seattle: University of Washington Press, 1994), 87–124; Lawrence Fine, "Contemplative Death in Jewish Mystical Tradition," in Cormack, *Sacrificing the Self*, 92–106.

14. For this and other efforts in early Islam to render other religious activities the equivalent of martyrdom, see Keith Lewinstein, "The Revaluation of Martyrdom in Early Islam," in Cormack, *Sacrificing the Self*, 78–91, esp. 82–83.

Chapter 6
The New Testament, Religious Identity, and the Other

1. Edward Farley, *Good and Evil: Interpreting a Human Condition* (Minneapolis: Fortress Press, 1990), 28. Important studies of otherness include, for example, Michael Theunissen, *The Other: Studies in the Social Ontology of Husserl, Heidegger, Sartre and Buber*, trans. C. Macann (Cambridge, Mass.: MIT Press, 1984); T. J. Owens, *Phenomenology and Intersubjectivity: Contemporary Interpretations of the Interpersonal Situation* (The Hague, Nethlerlands: Nijhoff, 1970); Robert R. Williams, *Recognition: Fichte and Hegel on the Other* (Albany: State University of New York Press, 1992); *Theology and the Interhuman: Essays in Honor*

of Edward Farley, ed. Robert R. Williams (Valley Forge, Pa.: Trinity Press International, 1995).

2. Farley, *God and Evil*, 35.

3. Ibid., 37.

4. Ibid., 39.

5. Quoted in Terry Veling, "Levinas and the Other Side of Theology," February 12, 2005, see www.jcrelations.net/en/index.php?id=794.

6. Farley, *Good and Evil*, 41.

7. On this parable read from a social science perspective, see the very perceptive essay by Philip F. Esler, "Jesus and the Reduction of Intergroup Conflict," in *The Social Setting of Jesus and the Gospels*, ed. Wolfgang Stegemann, Bruce J. Malina, and Gerd Theissen (Minneapolis: Fortress Press, 2002), 185–205.

8. Farley, *Good and Evil*, 45.

9. John H. Elliott, "The Jewish Messianic Movement: From Faction to Sect," in *Modelling Early Christianity: Social-Scientific Studies of the New Testament in Its Context*, ed. Philip F. Esler (New York: Routledge, 1995), 78.

10. Elliott, "Jewish Messianic Movement," 79.

11. These eight indicators are drawn from Elliott's analysis in "Jewish Messianic Movement," 79–80.

12. Elliott, "Jewish Messianic Movement," 90.

13. John G. Gager, *Kingdom and Community: The Social World of Early Christianity* (Englewood Cliffs, N.J.: Prentice-Hall, 1975), 79–88.

14. Quoted in ibid., 83.

15. See, for example, especially Sean Freyne, "Vilifying the Other and Defining the Self: Matthew's and John's Anti-Jewish Polemic in Focus," in *"To See Ourselves as Others See Us": Christians, Jews, "Others" in Late Antiquity*, ed. Jacob Neusner and Ernest Frerichs, Scholars Press Studies in the Humanities (Chico, Calif.: Scholars Press, 1985), 117–43, and the other articles in this collection; Adela Yarbro Collins, "Vilification and Self-Definition in the Book of Revelation," *Harvard Theological Review* 79 (1986): 308–20; Andre du Toit, "Vilification as a Pragmatic Device in Early Christian Epistolography," *Biblica* 75 (1994): 403–12; Luke T. Johnson, "The New Testament's Anti-Jewish Slander and the Conventions of Ancient

Polemic," *Journal of Biblical Literature* 108, no. 3 (1989): 419–41; Harry O. Maier, "*1 Clement* and the Rhetoric of *Hybris*," *Studia Patristica* 31 (1997), 136–42.

16. Robert J. Schreiter, *Reconciliation: Mission and Ministry in a Changing Social Order* (Maryknoll, N.Y.: Orbis, 1992).

17. I summarize here Schreiter's list in *Reconciliation*, 52–53.

18 Peter L. Berger and Thomas Luckmann, *The Social Construction of Reality: A Treatise in the Sociology of Knowledge* (Garden City, N.Y.: Doubleday, 1966), 114.

19. Ibid., 114.

20. For this listing I am indebted to du Toit, "Vilification," 405–10. He notes that classical rhetoric also admitted the use of ridicule as a lighter form of vilification (see Quintilian, *Institutio oratoria* 6.3.37) and gives as the best example Paul in Gal 5:12—"Would that the knife would slip!" The warnings about impending judgment, as Sean Freyne ("Vilifying the Other," 134–35) has shown, are characteristic of apocalyptic rhetoric enlisted to "establish its exclusive claims on the Jewish inheritance that its opponents also claim."

21. Johnson, "Anti-Jewish Slander," 434–41.

22. Du Toit, "Vilification," 411.

23. Emmanuel Levinas, *Ethics and Infinity: Conversations with Philippe Nemo* (Pittsburgh: Duquesne University Press, 1985), 87.

Chapter 7
The Problematic Protrayal of "the Jews" and Judaism in the Gospel of John

1. Kaufmann Kohler, "New Testament," in *The Jewish Encyclopedia: A Descriptive Record of the History, Religion, Literature, and Customs of the Jewish People from the Earliest Times to the Present Day*, vol. 9, ed. Cyrus Adler and Isidore Singer et al. (New York and London: Funk & Wagnalls, 1901–1912), 251. Kohler wrote that "this teaching of love is combined with the most intense hatred of the kinsmen of Jesus."

2. From this perspective, a fitting bumper sticker for the Gospel of John would be "Judgment Happens."

3. Although the Gospel of John is especially known for the way that it portrays judgment as something that the individual (or commu-

nity) brings down upon him- or herself because of the way one has responded to the presence of the Son of Man in the world, there are also hints of a future judgment in this Gospel—there is even a reference to a judgment on the "last day" (12:48).

4. It occurs at least seventy-one times in John. Apart from the Acts of the Apostles with eighty occurrences, John refers to "the Jews" about ten times more than any other New Testament text. The more typical New Testament references to Pharisees, scribes, and Sadducees suggest sects of Jews more distant from our own time, whereas "the Jews" brings to mind a people and religion present today, and this is at the heart of the problem.

5. For an excellent essay that explores the problematics of treating the Bible with a "special hermeneutics" because of its authoritative status, see Mary Ann Tolbert, "A New Teaching with Authority: A Reevaluation of the Authority of the Bible," in *Teaching the Bible: The Discourses and Politics of Biblical Pedagogy*, ed. Fernando F. Segovia and Mary Ann Tolbert (Maryknoll, N.Y.: Orbis, 1998), 168–89.

6. This looks very much like the custom of *Shiva*, which means "seven" and refers to the seven days immediately following the burial, during which members of the Jewish community visit the mourners to console and support them.

7. This language is utilized in John also to show the greatness of the signs/works that Jesus does (John 1:51 and 5:20), the superiority of Jesus' testimony over John the Baptist's (5:36), the greatness of Jesus' love (15:13), and various other aspects of the relationships between the disciples, Jesus, and the Father.

8. The centrality of the Temple Cult can be seen in pharisaic and later in rabbinic Judaism in the way that these Jewish leaders adapt temple practices for ritual carried on in the Jewish household and also in their hope for a restored Temple in the Messianic era.

9. This text also manages to make two accusations against the Jews: that they are responsible for Jesus' death (vv. 17-19) and that they have caused the destruction of the Temple (v. 19).

10. Only in 9:22 is this threat specified ("His parents said this because they were afraid of the Jews; for the Jews had already agreed that anyone who confessed Jesus to be the Messiah would be put out

of the synagogue"); otherwise we are not told why people fear the Jews.

11. Although the alignment of the Jews with the negative pole of the dualism is found throughout the Gospel, reading chapter 8 will give the reader a quick sense of how the Jews are evaluated from the dualistic perspective of the Gospel and why that is significant.

12. This is also part of the dualism of the Gospel: the Jews' father is the devil; Jesus' father is God. Those who believe become children of God.

13. Actually, there is an ironic play around the issue of who really has "power" in this scene. Neither the Jews nor Pilate has power over Jesus. (Compare Jesus to Pilate in 19:11: "You would have no power over me unless it had been given you from above; therefore the one who handed me over to you is guilty of a greater sin.")

14. There are a number of references to indicate this: 19:14—"the day of Preparation for the Passover; and it was about noon" (the time at which Passover lambs were being slaughtered; cf. Exod 12:6); 19:29—"a branch of hyssop" (a bunch of hyssop is used in Exod 12:22 to spread the blood of the Passover lamb on the lintels of the Hebrews' homes); 19:33, 36—none of Jesus' bones are broken to fulfill scripture, while the legs of others crucified with him are (Exod 12:46 and Num 9:12 both preserve a command that the people are not to break a bone of the Passover lamb).

15. In fact, it seems to me that by aligning the Jews with the world and the devil and as the opposite pole from Jesus and God, the Gospel attempts to reach its true missionary target audience: fence straddlers (people like Nicodemus, the parents of the man born blind, and Joseph of Arimathea), possibly secret Christian Jews who wanted to retain their communal identity as Jews while showing a beginning belief in Jesus, and possibly also followers of John the Baptist. It attempts to reach this target audience by pinning them between the dualistic poles of the Gospel and forcefully exhorting them to align themselves with those who believe, Jesus, God, and the Johannine community and to separate themselves from the Jews, the world, and the devil. See also my essay "Salvation Is *for* the Jews: Secret Christian Jews in the Gospel of John," in *The Future of Early*

Christianity: Essays in Honor of Helmut Koester, ed. Birger A. Pearson (Minneapolis: Fortress Press, 1991), 285–300.

16. John H. Elliott, "The Jewish Messianic Movement: From Faction to Sect," in *Modelling Early Christianity: Social-Scientific Studies of the New Testament in Its Context*, ed. Philip F. Esler (New York: Routledge, 1995), 78–80.

17. Barbara Bowe, in chapter 6 in this volume, cites Andre du Toit ("Vilification as a Pragmatic Device in Early Christian Epistolary," *Biblica* 75 [1994]: 403–12).

18. Adele Reinhartz (*Befriending the Beloved Disciple: A Jewish Reading of the Gospel of John* [New York and London: Continuum, 2001]), in an innovative blend of literary analysis, ethical criticism, and social location reading, models four reading strategies with the Gospel: reading compliantly, reading resistantly, reading sympathetically, and reading with engagement. She defines the second of these, the resistant reading (*Befriending*, 81), as reading "from the point of view of the Other as defined by the text." In this chapter, Reinhartz offers an alternative, sympathetic Jewish context for understanding the language attributed to "the Jews" in the Gospel. Although it doesn't reconstruct any negative polemic that may have been a part of the Jewish side of things, it does help to make sense of the Gospel by imagining what the argument may have looked like from the perspective of the "other."

19. I have looked most closely at scholarship focused on the term *hoi Ioudaioi* ("the Jews") and its use in the Gospel, though the issue as it pertains to interfaith relationships should be more broadly construed, considering, for example, the exclusivistic theology/Christology of the Gospel, the dualistic polarities, and the inward focus of the Gospel on a community of believers.

20. D. Moody Smith, "Judaism and the Gospel of John," in *Jews and Christians: Exploring the Past, Present and Future*, ed. James H. Charlesworth (New York: Crossroad, 1990), 76–99.

21. Urban C. von Wahlde, "The Gospel of John and the Presentation of Jews and Judaism," in *Within Context: Essays on Jews and Judaism in the New Testament*, ed. David P. Efroymson et al. (Collegeville, Minn.: Liturgical, 1993), 67–84.

22. Martinus de Jonge, "The Conflict between Jesus and the Jews and the Radical Christology of the Fourth Gospel," *Perspectives in Religious Studies* 20 (1993): 343.

23. Compare, for example, Eldon J. Epp, "Anti-Semitism and the Popularity of the Fourth Gospel in Christianity," *CCAR Journal* 22 (1975): 35–57; and N. A. Beck, *Mature Christianity* (Selinsgrove, Pa.: Susquehanna University Press, 1985), 248–74.

24. Janis E. Leibig, "John and 'the Jews': Theological Anti-Semitism in the Fourth Gospel," *Journal of Ecumenical Studies* 20 (1983): 209–34.

25. Urban C. von Wahlde, "The Johannine 'Jews': A Critical Survey," *New Testament Studies* 28 (1982): 33–60. In this article, a previous one ("The Terms for Religious Authorities in the Fourth Gospel: A Key to Literary Strata?" *Journal of Biblical Literature* 98 [1979]: 231–53), and then in his later book about source critical analysis of the earliest signs Gospel (*The Earliest Version of John's Gospel: Recovering the Gospel of Signs* [Wilmington, Del.: Michael Glazier, 1988]), he points out numerous differences between the earlier and later editions of the Gospel, including, for example, that the religious authorities in the signs Gospel are referred to as Pharisees, chief priests, and rulers and that in the signs Gospel the authorities fear the reaction of the people, whereas in the second edition the people fear "the Jews" (presumed to be the religious authorities).

26. Von Wahlde, "The Johannine 'Jews,'" 33.

27. R. Alan Culpepper, "The Gospel of John as a Threat to Jewish-Christian Relations," in *Overcoming Fear between Jews and Christians*, ed. James H. Charlesworth et al. (New York: Crossroad, 1992), 27.

28. Robert Fortna, "Theological Use of Locale in the Fourth Gospel," *ATR* Supplementary Series 3 (March 1974), 58–94; Malcolm Lowe, "Who Were the ʾIOYΔAIOI?" *Novum Testamentum* XVIII/2 (1976): 101–30.

29. Lowe, "Who Were the ʾIOYΔAIOI," 130.

30. John Ashton offers an excellent evaluation and critique of Lowe's proposal in "The Identity and Function of the ʾIOYΔAIOI in the Fourth Gospel" *Novum Testamentum* 27, no. 1 (1985): 40–75.

31. Rudolf Bultmann, *The Gospel of John* (Oxford: Basil Blackwell, 1971), 86ff.

32. R. Alan Culpepper, *Anatomy of the Fourth Gospel* (Philadelphia: Fortress Press, 1983), 129.

33. There are too many worthy historical-critical studies to cite here. One, which includes a methodological twist and is pragmatically aimed at engaging a broader readership in the issue, is Robert Kysar's "Anti-Semitism and the Gospel of John," in *Anti-Semitism and Early Christianity*, ed. Craig A. Evans and Donald A. Hagner (Minneapolis: Augsburg Fortress, 1993), 113–27. Kysar suggests that one first utilize reader-response criticism as a way to ask how the hearer/reader experiences what the Gospel has to say about Jews and Judaism. Then he suggests that one follow this up with historical-critical analysis to understand the Johannine community and the issues it faces, to deepen the understanding of who "the Jews" are in this Gospel, and to contextualize the rhetoric. Finally, Kysar concludes by assessing how this process makes us look at the anti-Jewish tone of the Gospel.

34. J. L. Martyn, *History and Theology in the Fourth Gospel*, rev. ed. (Nashville: Abingdon, 1979). Raymond E. Brown developed a similar proposal in his commentary, *The Gospel according to John*, Anchor Bible 29 and 29a (Garden City, N.Y.: Doubleday, 1966). This sort of proposal about expulsion from the synagogue was made even earlier by K. L. Carroll, "The Fourth Gospel and the Exclusion of Christians from the Synagogue," *Bulletin of the John Rylands University Library* 40 (1957): 19–32; and J. Parkes, *The Conflict of the Church and the Synagogue: A Study in the Origins of Antisemitism* (New York: World, 1961), 83.

35. Martyn, *History and Theology*, 61–62.

36. Reuven Kimmelman, "*Birkat Ha-Minim* and the Lack of Evidence for an Anti-Christian Jewish Prayer in Late Antiquity," in *Jewish and Christian Self-Definition*, vol. 1, *The Shaping of Christianity in the Second and Third Centuries*, ed. E. P. Sanders (Philadelphia: Fortress Press, 1981), 226–44; and S. T. Katz, "Issues in the Separation of Judaism and Christianity after 70 CE," *Journal of Biblical Literature* 103 (1984): 43–76.

37. Luke T. Johnson, "The New Testament's Anti-Jewish Slander and the Conventions of Ancient Polemic," *Journal of Biblical Literature* 108 (1989): 419–41.

38. Ibid., 441.

39. Ibid.

40. Beck, *Mature Christianity*, 248–74.

41. Ibid., 255.

42. Ibid., 261.

43. "Good news" is the most problematic for me from a practical stance. I find that students and preachers who are preparing to teach or preach from the text are driven to find the "good news" in a text and avoid focusing on the potential "bad news" in a text. For those texts with invective aimed at the Jews or Judaism, this means that the "bad news" is read as scripture, but not dealt with, making it potentially more damaging.

44. I have one overidealized scenario that I use with my students as an exercise to begin this work: You are members of a church that has shared a building with a synagogue for several years. A lot of good things have come out of this: many joint educational opportunities, some planned attendance of each other's services with the chance to ask questions afterwards, designing and carrying out social action projects together, and so much more. As a result, the communities have really gotten to know, understand, and respect each other in ways that are somewhat unique. More recently, the two communities have planned a series of interfaith dialogues built on this trust and understanding, and as a part of this have agreed to tackle the more difficult sacred texts that are often problematic for Jewish and Christian relationships. The Jewish community has already presented its difficult texts. Now it is your church's turn, and you are the church members (and members of this dialogue group) who are to plan for this dialogue. You have decided to focus on the Gospel of John. Your task is twofold: (1) with honesty and integrity to lift up for discussion the challenges that this Gospel presents for Jewish/Christian relationships and to promote a constructive discussion around how to deal with these challenges; and (2) to present to the Jewish community why/how this Gospel is nevertheless essential for your community's self-understanding. What texts (if you were to choose just a few) would you pick to help you do these two things? Make a plan for your dialogue that will help you meet your two goals.

Chapter 8
Luke's Pharisees

1. Joseph B. Tyson, *Luke, Judaism, and the Scholars: Critical Approaches to Luke-Acts* (Columbia: University of South Carolina Press, 1999), 1. Tyson's study analyzes the attitudes of a number of modern New Testament scholars and reveals some evolution in ideological tendencies.

2. John A. Darr, *On Character Building: The Reader and the Rhetoric of Characterization in Luke-Acts* (Louisville: Westminster John Knox, 1992), 23.

3. John T. Carroll, "Luke-Acts," in *The New Testament Today*, ed. Mark Allan Powell (Louisville: Westminster John Knox, 1999), 63. In the same paragraph Carroll very briefly summarizes some representative positions. A longer and more helpful summary is offered by Daryl D. Schmidt, "Anti-Judaism and the Gospel of Luke," in *Anti-Judaism and the Gospels*, ed. William R. Farmer (Harrisburg, Pa.: Trinity Press International, 1999), 66–76. Many of the scholars involved in the discussion are conveniently found in *The Jewish People in Luke-Acts: Eight Critical Perspectives*, ed. Joseph B. Tyson (Minneapolis: Augsburg, 1988).

4. This is one of many metaphors that has been invoked to describe the separation of Christianity from Judaism, or the "coemergence" of two post-Temple communities rooted in the scriptures of Israel.

5. David W. Pao, *Acts and the Isaianic New Exodus*, Biblical Studies Library (Grand Rapids: Baker, 2002; previously published by Mohr Siebeck, 2000), 71.

6. David Gowler, *Host, Guest, Enemy, and Friend: Portraits of the Pharisees in Luke-Acts*, Emory Studies in Early Christianity (New York: Peter Lang, 1991), 307–8.

7. Robert Brawley, *Luke-Acts and the Jews: Conflict, Apology, and Conciliation*, Society of Biblical Literature Monograph Series 33 (Atlanta: Scholars Press, 1987).

8. Ibid., 92.

9. Darr, *On Character Building*. See also his essay "Irenic or Ironic? Another Look at Gamaliel," in *Literary Studies in Luke-Acts: Essays in Honor of Joseph B. Tyson*, ed. Richard P. Thompson and Thomas E. Phillips (Macon, Ga.: Mercer University Press, 1998).

10. Jack T. Sanders, *The Jews in Luke-Acts* (Philadelphia: Fortress Press, 1987), 85–87. He seems to forget momentarily the presence of Saul, the self-identified Pharisee (see Acts 23:6; 26:5; Phil. 3:5) at the death of Stephen (Acts 8:1).

11. Ibid., 129.

12. Ibid., 111.

13. Anthony J. Saldarini, *Pharisees, Scribes, and Sadducees: A Sociological Approach* (Wilmington, Del.: Michael Glazier, 1988), 186.

14. So too Philip Esler, *Community and Gospel in Luke-Acts: The Social and Political Motivations of Lucan Theology* (Cambridge: Cambridge University Press, 1987), esp. 53–58.

15. Carroll, "Luke-Acts," in Powell, *The New Testament Today*, 63.

16. *Haireisis* in its earlier meaning of "sect" or "party" rather than its later meaning of "heresy." Marilyn Salmon, "Insider or Outsider? Luke's Relationship with Judaism," in Tyson, *The Jewish People in Luke-Acts*, 79–80.

17. Salmon, "Insider or Outsider?" 82.

18. Reuven Kimelman, "*Birkat Ha-Minim* and the Lack of Evidence for an Anti-Christian Jewish Prayer in Late Antiquity" in *Jewish and Christian Self-Definition*, vol. 2, *Aspects of Judaism in the Greco-Roman Period*, ed. E. P. Sanders (London: SCM, 1981), 226–44. Esler, however, is convinced that there already was a split, which the Birkat ha-Minim merely reinforced. See Esler, *Community and Gospel in Luke-Acts*, 55. See also Steven T. Katz, "Issues in the Separation of Judaism and Christianity after 70 CE: A Reconsideration," *Journal of Biblical Literature* 103, no. 1 (1984): 43–76, esp. 48–53.

19. Judith M. Lieu, "'The Parting of the Ways': Theological Construct or Historical Reality?" *Journal for the Study of the New Testament* 56 (1994): 116; reprinted in Judith M. Lieu, *Neither Jew nor Greek? Constructing Early Christianity* (London: T. & T. Clark, 2002), chap. 2.

20. Lecture at Catholic Theological Union, Chicago, January 26, 2000. This is more fully developed in Daniel Boyarin, *Dying for God: Martyrdom and the Making of Christianity and Judaism*, Figurae (Stanford: Stanford University Press, 1999); and Daniel Boyarin, *Border Lines: The Partition of Judaeo-Christianity* (Philadelphia: University of Pennsylvania Press, 2004).

21. Jacob Neusner, *Judaism and Christianity in the Age of Constantine* (Chicago: University of Chicago Press, 1987), ix.

22. Jacob Neusner, *From Politics to Piety: The Emergence of Pharisaic Judaism* (Englewood Cliffs, N.J.: Prentice-Hall, 1973), 89.

23. Jacob Neusner, *A Life of Yohanan ben Zakkai, ca. 1–80 CE*, 2nd ed. (Leiden: Brill, 1962), 23.

24. A well-known talmudic passage (BT Shabbat 30b–31a) portrays the Pharisee Hillel (perhaps not incidentally, he was, according to tradition, the father or grandfather of Gamaliel) as going out of his way to welcome Gentile converts to Judaism, though his colleague Shammai seems not to have been as eager. There is also Matthew's reference to Pharisees who will cross the sea to win a single convert (Matt 23:15).

25. Luke's use of "some," in contrast to Mark 2:24 and Matt 12:2, is often pointed to as lessening the accusatory tone of the narrative (though Gowler, *Host, Guest, Enemy, and Friend*, 207n66, suggests that it may be merely aesthetic).

26. Gowler, *Host, Guest, Enemy, and Friend*, 214–15.

27. Darr, *On Character Building*, 98.

28. Ibid., 112–13.

29. The prefix probably intensifies the meaning. See also Ps 130:3 (129:3 Septuagint).

30. This is one piece of evidence for the argument that Luke and Acts are separate works, as discussed by Mikeal C. Parsons and Richard I. Pervo, *Rethinking the Unity of Luke and Acts* (Minneapolis: Fortress Press, 1993), 39–40: "In Luke the Pharisees are willing to entertain and listen to Jesus on occasion, but receive harsh criticism for their attitudes and practices. In Acts, however, they are often supportive of the movement."

31. Much attention has been directed to the grammar of Gamaliel's advice in vv. 38-39. The clause that describes the possibility that the work of the apostles is "from men" is constructed with *eán* + subjunctive, whereas the clause describing the possibility that it is "of God" is constructed with *ei* + indicative. Some have therefore construed Gamaliel's statement as actually giving greater credence to the latter, making him into a quasi-Christian or at least a fellow traveler.

Brawley refutes the idea that this would have been Gamaliel's own opinion (which would in any case likely have been stated in Aramaic rather than Greek). Instead, it is further evidence of Luke's authorial hand: Luke's opinion, not Gamaliel's, gives greater credence to the apostles' work being *ek Theou*, from God.

32. Although Darr, "Irenic or Ironic? Another Look at Gamaliel," 134–35, sees here yet another "ironic twist," since "the people" have already been shown to be quite fickle.

33. Gowler, *Host, Guest, Enemy, and Friend*, 276–78.

34. Jacob Neusner, *The Rabbinic Traditions about the Pharisees before 70*, pt. 1, *The Masters*, Dove Studies in Bible, Language, and History (Leiden: Brill, 1971), 341.

35. Herbert Danby, trans., *The Mishnah* (London: Oxford University Press, 1933), 306. The Hebrew for "abstinence" is *perishut*, related to the term "Pharisee."

36. Neusner, *The Rabbinic Traditions*, pt. 1, 375.

37. Ibid., 376.

38. Alan F. Segal, *Paul the Convert: The Apostolate and Apostasy of Saul the Pharisee* (New Haven: Yale University Press, 1990).

39. Jews barely appear as such in Luke's Gospel, but in Acts the references to Jews move quickly from a description of "devout" men (2:5), to many more passages describing Jews plotting against Paul (9:23; 21:27-32; 22:22-23; 23:12; 25:7). Peter states that "the Jews" killed Jesus (2:23; 10:39), a charge repeated by Stephen (7:52) and further emphasized by Paul (13:28). Paul, facing opposition from "the Jews," curses them and declares that he will go to the Gentiles (18:6). Finally, there is the declaration that salvation has been sent to the Gentiles, apparently instead of the Jews (28:28, although this interpretation has been debated).

40. This point of apparent similarity should not be oversimplified. Jack Sanders cautions us about "Luke's fairly unconvincing apologetic that the Christian belief in the resurrection (of Jesus) is in reality the familiar Pharisaic belief in the (coming) resurrection." See "The Jewish People in Luke-Acts," in Tyson, *The Jewish People in Luke-Acts*, 57.

41. I recently came across a Christian reading of this passage pointing

in a direction similar to the interpretation offered here. See the Foreword by Edward A. Synan to F. E. Talmage, ed., *Disputation and Dialogue: Readings in the Jewish-Christian Encounter* (New York: KTAV Publishing House and Anti-Defamation League of B'nai Brith, 1975), xi–xiv.

Chapter 9
Can We Hope? Can Hope Be Divided?

1. Karl Barth, *Church Dogmatics: The Doctrine of Creation*, vol. 3, pt. 2, ed. Thomas F. Torrance and Geoffrey W. Bromily (Edinburgh: T. & T. Clark, 1961), 597–98.
2. Ibid., 608, 609, 611.
3. Ibid., 613, 615.
4. Ibid., 615.
5. Ibid., 613.
6. Martin Buber, *Moses: The Revelation and the Covenant* (Atlantic Highlands: Humanities Press International, 1988), 52.
7. Samuel Terrien, *The Elusive Presence: Toward a New Biblical Theology* (New York: Harper & Row, 1978), 119.
8. James C. Scott, *Weapons of the Weak: Everyday Forms of Peasant Resistance* (New Haven: Yale University Press, 1985); idem, *Domination and the Arts of Resistance: Hidden Transcripts* (New Haven: Yale University Press, 1990).
9. Albrecht Alt, *Essays in Old Testament History and Religion* (Oxford: Blackwell, 1966), 1–77; Gerhard von Rad, *The Problem of the Hexateuch and Other Essays* (New York: McGraw-Hill, 1966), 1–78; and Jürgen Moltmann, *Theology of Hope: On the Ground and the Implications of a Christian Eschatology* (New York: Harper & Row, 1967).
10. David Novak, *Jewish-Christian Dialogue: A Jewish Justification* (Oxford: Oxford University Press, 1989), 156.
11. Alan E. Lewis, *Between Cross and Resurrection: A Theology of Holy Saturday* (Grand Rapids: Eerdmans, 2001); see Walter Brueggemann, "Reading from the Day 'In Between,'" in *A Shadow of Glory: Reading the New Testament after the Holocaust*, ed. Tod Linafelt (New York: Routledge, 2002), 105–16.

12. George Steiner, *Real Presences* (Chicago: University of Chicago Press, 1989), 232.
13. Eberhard Busch, *Karl Barth and the Pietists: The Young Karl Barth's Critique of Pietism and Its Response*, trans. Daniel W. Bloesch (Downers Grove, Ill.: InterVarsity, 2004), 289.

Chapter 10
The Bible Is Active in Politics Today

1. Jim Wallis, *God's Politics: Why the Right Gets It Wrong and the Left Doesn't Get It* (San Francisco: HarperSanFrancisco, 2005).
2. Jim Wallis, "Red Letter Christians," *Sojourners* (March 2006): 7.
3. Tony Campolo, "What's a 'Red-Letter Christian'?" www.beliefnet.com/story/185/story_18562.html.
4. Ibid.
5. Antinomianism (literally from the Greek "against" and "law") in theology is the idea that members of a religious group are under no particular obligation to obey the laws of ethics or morality as set down by religious authorities. It is the opposite of legalism.
6. David Blumenthal, *Facing the Abusing God: A Theology of Protest* (Louisville: Westminster John Knox, 1993).

Chapter 11
Contesting Texts

1. Greenberg explores this notion in some detail in *For the Sake of Heaven and Earth: The New Encounter between Judaism and Christianity* (Philadelphia: Jewish Publication Society of America, 2004).
2. Representative sample documents can be found online at http://www.bc.edu/research/cjl/cjrelations/resources/documents/. An extensive bibliography is available at http://www.jcrelations.net/en/?area=Bibliographies.
3. Mary Boys, *Has God Only One Blessing? Judaism as a Source of Christian Self-Understanding* (Mahwah, N.J.: Paulist, 2000).
4. Didier Pollefeyt, ed., *Jews and Christians: Rivals or Partners for the Kingdom of God? In Search of an Alternative for the Theology of Substitution*, Louvain Theological and Monographs 21 (Louvain: Peeters, 1997).

5. When Jewish-Christian dialogue began in the 1950s and 1960s, most of the Christian participants were from mainstream liberal Protestant denominations, such as the Presbyterians. Following the Six-Day War in 1967, many of these same churches exhibited pro-Palestinian and anti-Israel sentiments that alienated the Jewish community. Then in 1965, the Vatican promulgated *Nostra Aetate* as part of the Second Vatican Council; Roman Catholics became enthusiastic proponents of interfaith dialogue, and much of the energy that had gone into discussions with Protestants was focused on dialoguing with the Roman Catholic Church.

6. For example, Houston Stuart Chamberlain.

7. See, for example, Adam H. Becker and Annette Y. Reed, eds., *The Ways That Never Parted: Jews and Christians in Late Antiquity and the Early Middles Ages*, Texts and Studies in Ancient Judaism 95 (Tübingen: Mohr Siebeck, 2003).

Index of Scriptural References and Ancient Writings

Old Testament Pseudepigrapha

Index of Names and Subjects